WALKING
WITH
NOMADS

Also by Alice Morrison

Adventures in Morocco: From the Souks to the Sahara

ALICE MORRISON

WALKING WITH NOMADS

One woman's adventures
through a hidden world from the
Sahara to the Atlas Mountains

**SIMON &
SCHUSTER**

London · New York · Sydney · Toronto · New Delhi

First published in Great Britain by Simon & Schuster UK Ltd, 2022

Copyright © Alice Morrison, 2022

The right of Alice Morrison to be identified as the author
of this work has been asserted in accordance with the
Copyright, Designs and Patents Act, 1988.

1 3 5 7 9 10 8 6 4 2

Simon & Schuster UK Ltd
1st Floor
222 Gray's Inn Road
London WC1X 8HB

www.simonandschuster.co.uk
www.simonandschuster.com.au
www.simonandschuster.co.in

Simon & Schuster Australia, Sydney
Simon & Schuster India, New Delhi

The author and publishers have made all reasonable efforts
to contact copyright-holders for permission, and apologise
for any omissions or errors in the form of credits given.
Corrections may be made to future printings.

A CIP catalogue record for this book
is available from the British Library

Hardback ISBN: 978-1-3985-0342-7
eBook ISBN: 978-1-3985-0343-4

Typeset in Bembo by M Rules
Printed and bound by CPI Group (UK) Ltd, Croydon, CR0 4YY

*This book is dedicated to my constant and true
companions Brahim Ahalfi and Addi Bin Youssef.*

*And with grateful thanks to Jean-Pierre
Datcharry, our expedition organiser.*

CONTENTS

Quran, Chapter 88, Surat of the Overwhelming,
الغاشية

بِسْمِ اللّٰهِ الرَّحْمٰنِ الرَّحِيْمِ

اَفَلَا يَنْظُرُوْنَ اِلَى الْاِ بِلِ كَيْفَ خُلِقَتْ

وَاِلَى السَّمَاءِ كَيْفَ رُفِعَتْ

وَاِلَى الْجِبَالِ كَيْفَ نُصِبَتْ

وَاِلَى الْاَرْضِ كَيْفَ سُطِحَتْ

In the name of God, the Compassionate, the Merciful
Haven't they looked at the camel — how she is created?
And at the sky — how it is raised?
And at the mountains — how they are formed?
And at the earth — how it is spread out?

Acknowledgements

It takes a brave publisher to contract a travel book in the midst of a worldwide pandemic which has grounded us all and Ian Marshall and Simon & Schuster are just that. My heartfelt thanks for making that bold move and continuing to believe in me and the value of women exploring the world and telling their stories. Ian, you always make me feel supported and you make me laugh. Thank you.

A big thanks goes to my agent, Rachel Conway from Georgina Capel Associates, for her continuing and enthusiastic help and support. Thanks to Fran Jessop and Victoria Godden from Simon & Schuster for their hard work in editing and proofreading. Victoria – you've made me realise I need to do a punctuation refresher! Also thanks to Harriett Collins, who is publicity maven for the book.

Sponsors are a vital part of any exploration of this size and I would like to sincerely thank mine:

Craghoppers supported all three stages and also supplied me with their kit, which worked brilliantly – from cool desert shirts to warm bobbly hats. Thanks especially to the team in Manchester who worked so hard with me: Jim McNamara, Gill Russell and Sophi Lynch.

NTT DATA UK Diversity and Inclusion Team, headed by Kim Gray, also supported all three stages and have been stalwart cheerleaders. It is always a huge pleasure to share the journey with them.

Epic Travel were a major sponsor for the Draa Expedition and Charlie Shepherd drove for twenty-two hours to visit us, bringing chocolate treats and slotting right into the adventure.

My deepest thanks to the team, both on the journey and those at Dar Daif and Désert et Montagne Maroc, beginning with our amazing expedition organiser Jean-Pierre Datcharry, who always gave 110 per cent and whose passion, knowledge and experience made this so special. I hope we will always remain a brother and sister in the desert, JP.

شكراً جزيلاً

Shukran bizzaf and *tanmirt bahra* to: Brahim Ahalfi for everything – looking after me in every way and leading the expedition so successfully; Addi Bin Youssef for his unflinching hard work, his friendship and riddles; Brahim Boutkhoum for baking cakes in the wilderness and the best stories; Lhou Ounasser for his humble and generous spirit and his great tea; Ali Ahalfi for his easygoing nature and his huge store of information; Ychou for his light spirit and warmth; and Mohamed for his desire to explore.

Acknowledgements

Thank you to brilliant cameraman Abdellah Azizi. We always looked forward to his visits and he raised the mood of the whole team with his infectious laugh and kind heart. I enjoyed all our philosophical discussions together. Thanks also to Alicia Arce for joining us on the Draa and providing her filming expertise and companionship.

Finally, thank you to Carla Petzold-Beck for sending me my journals, Mum and Dad for supporting me as I wrote in the back room and the Al Aziam family in Imlil for looking after Squeaky the Cat.

INTRODUCTION

'Adventurers have got to adventure,' says my mum, and she is right. If you sign your emails 'Alice Morrison, Adventurer', then you've really got to live up to that. It was with this thought ringing in my brain that I had started looking around for my next big challenge.

I'd been sedentary for too long. I wanted to get out there and explore. I was longing for the wild places and for a journey with purpose and meaning. Every day in Morocco is a mini adventure but I needed more than that. I feel most at peace and most truly myself when I am out there questing, moving over the earth's surface. Then, all the noise and distraction of the world fades and you can become truly human again. We are designed to walk. From our earliest times we hunted and gathered and migrated, and it is hard-wired into me – into all of us, I believe.

I'm also driven by a desire to explore and to see things for myself. I want to learn as much as I can about the world I live in and the people I live in it with. I want to understand what is happening far away from the headlines and far beneath the surface of the media, and the way I learn best is by seeing, listening, touching and feeling things.

By this time, I'd been living in Morocco for about four years and so decided to search for something that would build on that experience but still allow me to discover new things. I got out the map and started scoping.

The Draa River leapt out as an obvious possibility. It was a distinct geographic route which made sense. Following a river from source to sea is something we all understand. It was about the right length for walking, too, about 1,500km which would take around three months, and it passed through different types of terrain, from the mountains of Saghro, through the green of the oases, to the vast plains on the outskirts of the Sahara.

I had been to very few places along the route so it would all be fresh to me. I also thought it would give me an opportunity to investigate how the damming of the river in the north impacted the southern regions and to look at the wider issue of climate change.

When I started the journey, I didn't know that it would end up being a full crossing of Morocco (including the disputed region of the Western Sahara). Nor did I realise that I would be witnessing and documenting the changing lives of the nomadic peoples of the regions I walked through. And none of us could have foreseen that the last part of it would be undertaken during a worldwide pandemic. However, the most unexpected thing – barring Covid-19 – was the sheer amount of stuff there was to discover. History was waiting for us.

You need three things to be an adventurer: an optimistic nature, a short memory and a big dollop of good luck. Optimism may sometimes lead you into foolhardy exploits but it saves you from too much worry and allows you to believe that things will get better. A short memory means you forget how much this stuff hurts, which is a massive advantage, as if I remembered I would be tempted not to do it. And luck? Well, that is in the hands of the gods, but I do side with Napoleon when he (allegedly) said, 'Give me lucky generals,' although, in fairness, that didn't work out entirely well for him.

Having decided on the Draa, I needed to sort out the logistics, and this is where luck intervened. I was talking it all through with my friend Charlie from Epic Travel when he suggested I talk to Jean-Pierre (JP) Datcharry of Désert et Montagne Maroc. JP is originally French but is now a Moroccan citizen and has been guiding in Morocco for over forty years. He is the foremost expert on desert trekking in the country. *Good idea!* I thought and hopped into my trusty ancient Toyota Yaris for the eight-hour drive across the Atlas and the desert to Ouarzazate to meet him. JP has the face of a medieval saint: large, brilliant eyes, prominent cheekbones and an immaculate white beard. When I explained to him that I was hoping to trot across the Draa in April with one camel and a guide, those eyes widened, he staggered slightly and spluttered, '*C'est impossible!*', which wasn't quite the reaction I had hoped for. Tempests, heat, scorpion season, government permission, water transport . . . JP quickly opened my eyes to the reality. We sat down, got the maps out, opened a spreadsheet and a great partnership and friendship began.

It was nearly a year later when, with total confidence in JP's organisational skills and months of planning, I got to six weeks before the start with little to worry me. We had agreed the route and that I would be travelling with five camels and three guides and I had found excellent sponsors to support the expedition: Craghoppers, who also supplied all my clothes, NTT DATA UK Diversity and Inclusion Team, and Epic Travel.

Then, on 17 December 2018, the bodies of Louisa Vesterager Jespersen, a 24-year-old Danish woman, and Maren Ueland, a 28-year-old Norwegian woman, were found decapitated about 5km from my house in Imlil in the Atlas Mountains. They had been killed by terrorists from the Islamic State of Iraq and the Levant who had come into the mountains looking for innocent victims and had found the two girls camping alone. It was a dreadful crime and sent shockwaves through my home village but also the whole of Morocco.

There were knock-on consequences for the expedition. Security was stepped up right across the country and the authorities hesitated on their approval of our trip, taking a lot of persuasion to let us go.

The murders and subsequent security tightening had shaken me up. I feel very safe in Morocco and have lived alone very happily here and travelled all over the country on my own. However, the fact that this murder took place in a tiny village like Imlil, a place where I would have sworn to you that it could never happen, did make me pause. I was about to set off for three months into the wilderness and, what is more, I was going to be talking about it widely in the press and on social media. I was definitely putting my head above the parapet.

I had one long night of the soul, but then I decided to go with my years of experience in the country rather than the disruptive act of a group of extremists bent on destruction and terror. The only precautions I took were to remove the map of the prospective route from my website and social media and give up my plans to broadcast a live tracker so people could follow me in real time. I also reminded my parents where a copy of my will was.

So, here we are together now, on the eve of this expedition, full of hope and excitement (and a little trepidation), with no idea of what the future is going to bring. Join me on the journey. Walk with me, my companions and the camels. Walk with us through this book and explore the hidden world of the desert sands and the lives and lore of the nomads who live there. There are tremendously exciting days of discovery. There are days of trudging drudgery too. We will face unforeseen dangers and difficulties and as our caravan rolls slowly forward we will grow closer and closer together in the face of them. Escape with me and come and see a different place, a different world.

PS: Be warned – you will also learn an enormous amount about the sex lives of camels.

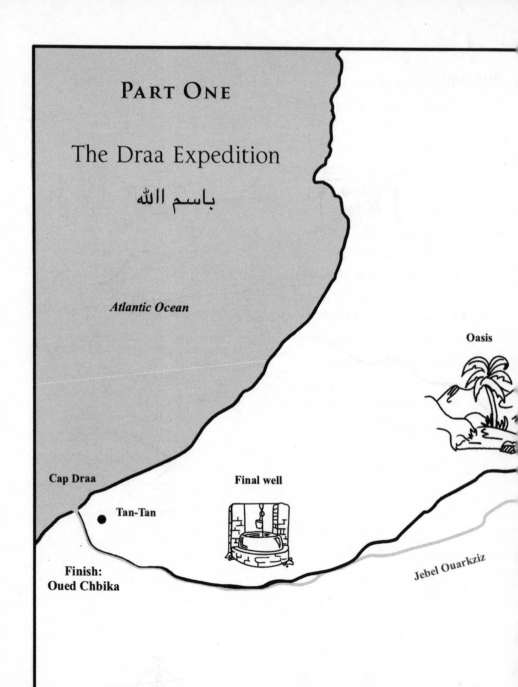

PART ONE

The Draa Expedition

باسم الله

Atlantic Ocean

Oasis

Cap Draa

Final well

Tan-Tan

Finish:
Oued Chbika

Jebel Ouarkziz

SAHAR

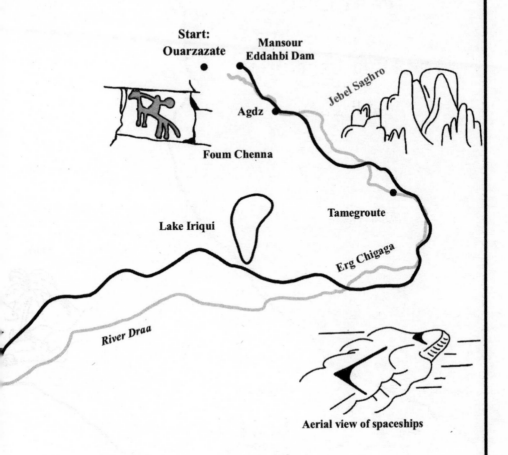

Marrakech

**Start:
Ouarzazate**

**Mansour
Eddahbi Dam**

Jebel Saghro

Agdz

Foum Chenna

Tamegroute

Lake Iriqui

Erg Chigaga

River Draa

Aerial view of spaceships

E S E R T

1

FEET ON THE ROAD

Mansour Eddahbi Dam – Agdz

'It's too hot for the camels.' Brahim turns to me, his brown eyes full of concern above the bright blue of the scarf wrapped around his head and over his mouth against the broiling sun. 'The weak one can't go any further.' I look round and sure enough, there is Struan in the process of couching on the dirt track, kneeling down with his front legs and then tucking his long back legs neatly under him. His caramel-coloured neck and back are darkened with sweat and his face clearly says, 'Enough is enough.' I totally empathise but also feel vaguely outraged at this failure in what I understand to be the fundamental operating system of the camel. 'Too hot for the camels? These are Saharan animals,' I say to Brahim; panting a bit as the heated air hits my throat, 'What about me? I am from Scotland. I'm built for rain; camels are actually designed for the desert.' Brahim gives me a long, measured look and his eyes crinkle at the sides, 'Zahra, your face is red just like a tomato. We'll unload Struan and leave him here till it cools, then I'll come back for him. *Anfitou*, let's go, we still have a way to walk till it's time to set up camp.'

But this is further down the road. Let's reel back to the beginning and the start of the expedition.

~

It's 9 January 2019 and, at last, we are off in a maelstrom of activity. The crew and the camels have gone on ahead to our official start point, a half day's walk from the banks of the Mansour Eddahbi dam. The rest of us pile into the pickup to take us and our supplies from Dar Daif in Ouarzazate to the rendezvous point. We are led by Jean-Pierre Datcharry (JP) of Désert et Montagne Maroc, who is my expedition organiser. He has over forty years of experience in the desert, speaks fluent Tashlaheet (Berber)* and is going to spend the first couple of days with us and then will pop back at various points when we get reprovisioned. With me are also my friend and director/camerawoman Alicia Arce, who will be filming the start, and Abdellah Azizi, a local cameraman who will also be with us intermittently. I'm fizzing with excitement and with nerves, launching into the unknown with strangers.

The pickup turns off the tarmac and onto the top of some flat cliffs overlooking the desert plain. It's big and barren. Two men come up to greet us. They are Brahim Boutkhoum (BB), who is my guide and chef, and Addi Bin Youssef, camelteer. We exchange polite and rather shy hellos and then all get straight to work unloading the supplies from the pickup.

Coming up from the plain, I see a lone figure leading the five camels, who have been grazing in the basin. It's Brahim Ahalfi, our expedition leader.

---

* My transliterations from Tashlaheet (also spelled Tachelhit) are as I hear them as there is no recognised system.

JP overtakes me, I can only see his eyes as his face is totally concealed by his scarf (*chech*), but they look kind. I stick out my hand to shake, always a judgement call, as not all men are keen to shake hands with a woman. 'Brahim? Peace be upon you. How are you? My name is Alice and this is my friend, Alicia. We start our journey together. May God grant us success.'

'Upon you be peace. We are honoured to meet you. Yes, if God wills it our journey will succeed.' He turns to each of us and looks us over carefully. 'I am going to give you Arabic names. Now you will stop being Alice and Alicia.' He smiles beneath his *chech* and says, pointing at me, 'You will be Zahra,' and to Alicia, 'you are Hanan.' Arabic works on a root system – every word is based on three letters and Hanan has the meaning of tenderness. Zahra means flower, and *zihr* – from the same root *z h r* – is the word for luck. It feels like a welcome and a baptism for a new beginning.

First impressions are so important and I want to make a good one. I want to be part of the team, not a client. I need to belong even though I am so different. So, feeling a bit foolish but determined to set the right intention from the very start, I grab my bags and head towards the nearest camel, Hamish as I would come to name him, and ask where I should put them. Brahim shows me how to put them in the big green woven panniers that sit on the camel's saddle and distributes the weight carefully. I am almost certain that my help is more of a hindrance at this stage, but the men know that I am trying and that is the most important thing. We finish loading and then the camels lurch up and off.

The pace is steady but brisk. Camels always look as though they're just cruising along slowly, but in fact they walk quite quickly if they're in good shape and it isn't too hot. When

I stop to take a picture, it is a trot to catch up. Alicia and Abdellah are filming and running gazelle-like (ish) up and down the slopes to get the best shots. 'They're doing the marathon,' says BB with a chuckle.

We arrive as the sun is sinking at the shores of the Mansour Eddahbi barrage, bathing it, appropriately, in gold – *eddahbi* means 'the Golden One' in Arabic. The dam services the city of Ouarzazate and its surroundings and has a capacity of 560 million cubic metres. It was completed in 1972 and is filled by rivers and streams flowing down from the Atlas Mountains, fuelled by rainfall and snow melt. Before it was built, the Draa flooded the upper and middle reaches regularly, but the dam now controls the river flow for the benefit of the huge oases that lie along its upper shores – the date basket of Morocco.

The camels couch and the men strip them quickly of their loads, dumping everything higgledy-piggledy on the ground. Seeing my surprised face, Brahim tells me, 'It's important to get everything off them as fast as possible. The loads are heavy and their backs are tired. They want to go and graze.' In fact, our campsites always looked as though a tornado had just passed through, with stuff all over the place, a definite cultural difference, although we could always find what we wanted in spite of the seeming chaos.

I help Brahim put up my tent – grateful that I don't have to do it on my own. JP hovers around it like an expectant father. He had actually designed it and had it made specially for the expedition, 'Look, Zahra, we call it Le Petit Fromage [LPF], because it looks just like a little cheese.' He holds up a wrapped triangle of Laughing Cow to compare the two and, sure enough, it's a doppelgänger. I bend down to pick up a largish rock to weigh down the edge but he stops me. 'No, no. Never pick up a rock with your hands.' He turns over the stone carefully with his foot and there in the centre of the pressed earth is a small hole with the end of a scorpion's tail poking up out of it. They nest under the rocks and can give you a nasty nip if you disturb them. You wouldn't die from a sting from one of these small ones but it would make you feel very sick and cause the area around the bite to swell up badly. I was glad of the warning.

Sitting on my folding camp chair that first evening, looking at the lake turning from gold to silver with a single fishing boat cutting a sliver through the calm, I hear the first words of the evening prayer.

'In the name of God, the Merciful, the Compassionate
Thanks be to God, the Lord of the worlds
The Merciful, the Compassionate ...'

The voice is clear and strong; musical and full of faith. It is Brahim, our expedition leader, and his prayers are to be the time markers throughout our days on the expedition. I somehow know that this is all going to be all right.

It was so cold that night that when we get up in the morning, the olive oil that the men dip their bread into for breakfast has frozen. But we are soon heated by the rising sun.

JP and Abdellah leave us that morning just after we cross a dried-mud plateau, fissured like a giant jigsaw puzzle. 'When it rains, Zahra, you can't cross this at all,' BB tells me. 'The mud will suck you in right up to your neck.' Before he leaves, JP tries to download forty years of desert experience into my brain with a list of random advice.

1. Always wear sunglasses; you have pale eyes, they will burn.
2. Collect firewood for camp, even if you are just going off for the bathroom, come back with something.

3. Care for your feet.
4. Put all your clothes and sleeping stuff in plastic bags in case it rains. (It didn't – we didn't see a drop for nearly three months.)
5. Make sure you keep all your electronics in the red bag which I made for you. Keep them separate from your other luggage.
6. Zip up Le Petit Fromage so that no scorpions or snakes enter, or even ticks.
7. Check your shoes for creatures before you put them on in the morning.
8. You are entitled to a small (kids' sandcastle-size) bucket of hot water to wash twice a day when the men get the same to perform the *wudu* (ritual washing before prayers) if there is water. If there isn't, they perform *wudu* with stones.
9. Put some bleach in the water for rinsing glasses. (The men weren't keen on this one.)
10. Take your GPS co-ordinates every night on your Garmin, and give them to BB; he will send it to me and also to the regional authorities and the gendarmes.

Ahead of us, a gap in the hills frames a small oasis, with its tall green palms outlined against the mountains of Saghro, frosted in a thin crust of white snow. At our backs, the space-age tower of Noor, the world's largest concentrated solar power plant, stands tall in its immense field of panels turned towards the light. Noor sucks up the rays from the sun and stores them in molten salt so the energy can then be used when it's needed, mainly at night. It produces enough power to supply a city of 2.6 million people, or half the population of Scotland, and it saves the planet from the 760,000 tonnes of carbon emissions which would be produced by an equivalent fossil-fuel power plant.

We are about 10 kilometres away from it at this point, and from this distance it looks like a long wizard's wand gleaming with lightning at its tip. The two views encapsulate what we are doing with our whole expedition, turning our backs on the city and modern life to walk back into history in the old way with our caravan of camels, following the nomad paths, albeit equipped with some great innovations like solar chargers, GPS and wicking materials.

Soon, we are out of the desert plains and into the black rocks of the Jebel Saghro – the Mountain of Doom. This is the area that Addi comes from and although it looks bleak with its jutting dark mountains, it is actually home to the Ait Atta tribe and a big nomadic community

Addi is from a nomadic family and his mum, Lalla Ito, spends much of her time with her flock in these hills rather than in their home in Nqob. At twenty-three, he is the youngest of our crew. He is about five foot ten and slim but strongly built. He has a long face, a good strong nose and very white teeth. His hair is a curly black mop and he sports a sparse moustache. He always has terrible shoes, which fall apart, and socks that breed holes. He was brought up living in a goat's hair tent and from his earliest days he was out with the herd strapped to his mother's back. He never waits to be asked to do something but just does whatever is needed without ever complaining. He has a slight stutter which becomes pronounced when he gets excited and a really naughty side. We quickly establish a favourite aunt/nephew relationship. Addi does everything quickly but, like me, he is not naturally tidy or exact, which gets on BB's nerves.

BB is Addi's opposite. He is meticulous in everything he

does: the mess tent is kept clean and tidy and a tablecloth is spread on the ground for every meal. Even though he has only brought a small bag, he seems to have an endless supply of outfits and always looks dapper. He wears a vibrant blue embroidered tunic over baggy *sirwal* (trousers) with an orange or red *chech* and a cap. He is a wonderful cook and makes every meal special. He is also a talented storyteller, acting out all the characters and keeping us enthralled with immaculate timing. He has a gentle spirit and a kind of delicacy which brings a different quality to the group.

'Brahim Ahalfi is fine – like a gazelle,' is how JP described him to me, and it's true. He is slender and graceful and his movements are measured. He is from Ait Bougemez – Happy Valley – a rich agricultural region in the mountains and his father was a herdsman but he has given his heart to the desert. Although he is Amazigh (Berber), he looks Arab. He has a noble face with a full mouth and expressive eyes.

From an early age he loved learning and said that he would run to Quranic school in the mosque after ordinary school had finished. He has learnt the entire Quran off by heart. Every day he spends the free time after lunch reading and re-learning sections and he always leads the men in their prayers. He is a deep thinker and a great advocate of patience, a quality which he tries to teach me with occasional success, but he is also passionate about social justice and rages furiously (and at length, often reminding me of my father) about the inequalities in the world. He is a natural protector and – to my delight – makes me his project. 'We only have one Flower (*Zahra*), we have to tend her carefully,' he tells me on the third day, and I agree heartily.

As well as the human team members, we have our five camels. 'Who is this?' I'd asked Brahim pointing at the black one on day one. 'Alrum,' he said. I heard 'Alone' but was corrected the next day. Happily armed with a treat of orange peel, I approached Alrum, cooing at him and sure, now I had his name, he would warm to me. It took me about a week to learn that Alrum just means 'camel' in Tashlaheet and that Moroccans don't name their animals as we do. They use descriptors like *boutershweet* (the one with the white face) or Saghro (the one from Saghro), but, of course, I had to. The camels were an integral part of the team and I am very guilty of anthropomorphism.

All our camels were male as you cannot mix male and female camels because the males would fight for ownership of the females. Also, the males are bigger and stronger. Initially, I thought that I'd name them after various men I have a crush on or have been out with, but decided that would be a bit creepy, so I chose good Scottish names instead – ones that I thought were suited to the individual animals. Camels all have their own personalities, quirks, likes and dislikes, just like us.

Alasdair is Brahim's lead camel and is the strong, silent type. He is the largest of the males but is quite gentle, unlike Hamish. Hamish is my favourite. He is younger than Alasdair but nearly as big and has a black coat. He is a bad-tempered alpha and very prone to biting. Since a male camel can take your arm off, Brahim spends the whole expedition saying, '*Khatar*, Zahra! Danger, Zahra. Look out.' And I spend the whole expedition alternately trying to bribe Hamish to love me by feeding him treats and leaping out of the way when he snakes his neck round to take a lump out of me. Murdo is the last member of Brahim's three and he is the oldest member of the team, a veteran of long journeys. Addi's lead is Callum, who he loves dearly and is always sneaking extra delicacies to. Callum has the beseeching eyes of a Labrador and a permanent 'Feed me! Love me!' expression which is pretty irresistible. At elevenses time, he stands right over us drooling until we hand over our orange peel. Camels love orange peel. Sausage – or 'shashage' as Addi pronounces it – is second camel. He is of medium build but quite strong and comes into his own later.

The landscape is magnificent. We have left the golden plains and sparkling rivers near the dam for the intense, brooding dark mountains of the Saghro. Jagged peaks rise on every side and the colour palate ranges from steely grey to deepest black. We and our camels are tiny by comparison, little splashes of colour against the looming slopes.

The sharp rocks of the Saghro are not ideal for the camels, but there are narrow goat tracks to follow and Brahim and Addi constantly search for the best route. To Alicia and me, it's an impenetrable forest of rock, but Addi knows a good place to camp where there's a clearing and a crumbling *azeeb*, a stone-built shepherd's enclosure, with enough space to pitch our three tents. We'd got ourselves settled when we spotted two little figures approaching. Aicha, in a velvet pink jellaba with a black and blue headscarf wrapped snugly around her head against the cold, was carrying one little brother on her hip and had another little one in tow toddling beside her, his face covered in snot. It's hard to judge the children's ages, but I think she is probably around twelve.

The minute the baby sees me, a strange pink face, he bursts into tears and BB swoops in and gathers him up. He's chuckling again in seconds. His face is chapped red raw with the cold and Aicha asks us for some cream. Out comes my Lâncome and I smear it over the sore bits, wishing that I had brought something less perfumed and more practical, but reassured by the thought that, at the price they charge, surely it will do some good.

BB re-emerges from the mess tent laden with goodies for Aicha to take back to her family: sardines, Laughing Cow cheese, macaroni and flour. Generosity and sharing are absolutely core to the way Moroccans live their lives. It's a reflex for them to give and, during the expedition, I experienced that time and again. '*Douyouf* Allah, guests are from God,' BB told me, and it became one of our expedition catchphrases.

Aicha is a delight. She is fascinated by us, particularly Alicia, and shadows her as she films the bivouac, slipping her hand in its pink flowery glove into hers. She goes around the camp examining everything carefully, picking things up and putting them down while trying to wrangle her two little brothers, wiping running noses and shifting the baby higher on her hip.

Then, she starts pointing to the red scarf around Alicia's neck. It's actually one of BB's, so Alicia has to tell her she can't have it, but Aicha won't give up. She keeps gesturing, becoming more insistent. Thinking that she would just have to explain to BB later, Alicia unwinds it and hands it over, but instead of putting it on, Aicha pats the wall and gets Alicia to sit down. Frowning with concentration, she carefully covers Alicia's head with the scarf, tucking bits of stray hair and tying it into a traditional style for women – a *hegab*. '*Tashweet, tashweet*,' she crows, clapping her hands. 'Now, you are beautiful.'

Crossing the Saghro, we occasionally come across a small cluster of palm trees, fed by an underground spring and presumably grown from seeds dropped or excreted by men or animals passing this way. The date harvest is in October but sometimes there are still clusters hanging on the pods. Dates are an integral part of our diet as we eat them with our soup every night, contrasting the hot saltiness with their sweetness. We'd left Aicha far behind when we pass by a group of about four trees with a fair crop hanging above us.

Addi drops Callum's halter and starts searching around for suitable throwing stones. The trees are around 25 metres high, but he manages to get some hits and dates fall down like smarties. I have a go but fail comprehensively, so content myself with running under the trees in between Addi's sorties to gather the fallen fruits. Brahim has been making out he's too cool to join in, but his resolve crumbles as we shriek and praise Addi for his prowess. Then, things get competitive. Brahim and Addi vie with each other to get big bunches down from the tallest tree. 'Look at all those,' says Addi. 'I got more,' counters Brahim. 'Who is the best, Zahra? Who got the most?' Two faces turn to me and I feel like Solomon clutching the sword above the baby. 'You are both so strong and throw so well,' I say, avoiding a diplomatic incident. 'Look how many dates we have for supper.' They do taste good. There are two basic types: dried brown ones that are very sweet, and slightly unripened yellow ones that have a fibrous texture to them.

That afternoon BB summons Alicia and me to the mess tent. 'Zahra, Hanan, I am going to teach you how to make an orange cake.' We don't seem to have much cake-making equipment with us, but we do have a camping gas-fired portable oven, which is strapped daily into pride of place on top of Callum. Bread is the staple in Morocco and is eaten with breakfast, lunch and dinner, and every three days or so BB and Addi would pound the dough and produce home-baked flat loaves to keep us going.

No finalist on *MasterChef* has more panache than BB.

Alicia and I step into the mess tent and are motioned to sit down on the earth opposite him, sitting propped up on a flour sack beside the oven. The light is cutting through the murky gloom of the canvas. Alicia and I, the eager acolytes, have our phones at the ready to take notes and videos, and the cooking lesson commences. We have all the necessary ingredients, including a tray of eggs which are the last thing to go on the camels and the first thing to come off, tenderly placed in a safe corner at every bivouac, except for the time Addi stepped backwards and crushed nearly a whole tray.

The recipe: 5 eggs, 5 spoons of sugar, a sachet of vanilla sugar. Mix eggs and sugar and add a small pot of natural yoghurt and then the same pot full of vegetable oil. Mix. Add the rind and juice of one orange. Oil a heavy pan. Put 5 big spoons of flour in the pan. Swish till the base of the pan is covered. Add 9 more spoons of flour and 2 sachets of baking powder. The consistency is quite runny – almost like thick pancake batter or thin drop-scone batter. Bake in a hot oven for 15-20 mins. For the icing: In a pan, combine half a glass of orange juice, a sachet of vanilla sugar, 3 spoons of ordinary sugar and a heaped spoon of cornflour. Add a pinch of saffron and cook gently on the gas, constantly stirring. When both cake and icing have cooled, pour icing over the sponge. Do try it at home.

Before he started, BB said, '*Bismillah*. In the Name of God,' and while he was mixing, adding and stirring, he told us why.

'Iblis [the devil] was the greatest angel, God's favourite, but his pride was his downfall. When he created Adam, he told the angels they had to bow before him, but Iblis thought that Adam was beneath him and would not obey. God said he had to, on pain of expulsion from the garden, but Iblis refused to bow to an inferior being like Adam. So, although he had been the favourite, he was thrown out of God's kingdom. Iblis was seized with a great anger and hatred and now he works tirelessly to gather as many souls as he can to join him in Hell – and we humans are weak. He's married and has a family and he's helped in his work by some of the jinn – they inhabit a whole parallel world to humans. We cannot see them, but they can see us. Some are good, but some are evil. Praying and using God's name keeps Iblis and the jinn at bay. That is why we always say *bismillah* when we enter the house or the tent, before cooking or eating our meals and before washing.'

The smell of warm spicy cake fills the air and, with a flourish, BB reaches into the oven and pulls it out, absolutely perfect. It's so delicious that when Addi is given his piece, he sticks his whole face in it and is left with icing on his nose.

Our first discovery is at the hamlet of Tanamroute. Towering above it is a giant plug of rock. Its name means 'the axis around which a millstone turns' and it looks just like that, thrusting up out of the ground vertically towards the sky. The villagers told us that there were ruins on the top built by 'El Bortugese' – the Portuguese. However, although Portugal did colonise parts of Morocco, building ports and fortifications along the coastline, most notably in Essaouira, which is a medieval Portuguese city, there are no records of them having come this far inland. Prayers that morning are next to the outside mosque which has been traced in stones on the edge of the village. Eid Al Adha, the Feast of the Sacrifice, is the big Muslim holiday that commemorates the willingness of Ibrahim (Abraham) to sacrifice his son Ismail when told to by God. For the feast, it's customary in some places to pray outside, and these stones have been laid out for that reason.

The path up to the plug takes us past the pressed clay walls of the village, a little donkey standing alone in one corner. For the lower slopes there's a path, but we quickly leave it behind and are soon scrambling up the side of the rock. It's super-slippery and crumbling. Every time I put a hand or foot on something it breaks away. We persevere and get up to a point where a rock fall completely blocks our passage. Above us we can see the remains of a wall curling round the rock, presumably a fortification, and further ahead is a building which is still recognisable as a house of some kind with some visible roof timbers. We can't get up there, though, not even with ropes; the rock is too friable. We have to settle for what we have seen, clear evidence of some kind of fortified settlement, built in a strategic position high over the Draa, but it would be great to go back with a helicopter.

Our route throughout the expedition snakes back and forth to the Draa; sometimes we have to leave it behind to make better progress and sometimes we are right beside the river or in its bed. Alicia has left and for the first time I am on my own with the team.

In all the run-up to our departure I had been remarkably worry-free about the journey itself. I had great confidence in JP's organisational skills; I knew I was in good shape for walking; and I had a few adventures under my belt. The one thing that had preyed on my mind was that I might be lonely. I was a Scottish, Christian woman travelling with three Amazigh, Muslim men. I knew they all had strong religious beliefs and I thought they might disapprove of me and what I was doing – so far removed from what their mothers or wives or sisters would do.

It's crunch time. I'm walking at the back of the camels feeling a bit sorry for myself when Brahim shouts back at me, 'Zahra, come up here. Why are you walking alone at the back? Come and walk here with me. One hand can't clap.' I scurry to the front and take my place beside him, one of the gang. My worry about loneliness disappears.

2

THE HENNA PARTY

Agdz – not far from Hassi Bou Lham

15 January 2019

We're on the outer fringes of Agdz, one of the largest oases on the Draa, ahead of us a vast expanse of palm trees crowds the valley. On the left is the row of peaks called Jebel Kissan – Glasses Mountain – because they look like a row of glasses. In their lee is a string of villages, built of traditional red clay. Many of them are deserted or abandoned for the smart new concrete homes the villagers have put up next door. We turn down a dusty road through some houses towards the palms and Addi says, 'Tea. There is no doubt that there will be tea.' He must have a sixth sense, because within two minutes a small leprechaun-like man in green trousers and shirt, with a wide-brimmed straw hat and a long white beard, appears. He is carrying a tray with mint tea, clean glasses, olive oil and freshly baked bread wrapped in a blue checked cloth. We're all hungry and gobble down the bread, which is still warm. Delighted, our host runs back up the hill to bring us more. 'Everywhere there are good people and bad people,' says Brahim.

When our host gets back, he tells us he had seen us on the road and thought we were bound to be thirsty so had prepared the tray and run down to meet us. Suddenly, Addi gallops off with one of our little buckets and sticks it under Callum's back legs. Callum is, very obligingly, having a long, noisy pee and Addi needs to catch the outpourings. Our host has asked for some camel wee for his wife, who suffers from allergies. Camel hair, milk and camel pee are thought to have restorative qualities and people use them in traditional medicine.

After dinner, we always drink a glass of *luisa* – verbena – a herbal tea made from vervain leaves. It tastes delicately of lemon and promotes sleep and good digestion. I've become addicted to it and now grow a large pot on my terrace. It's our time to relax and someone always comes up with a story or a riddle. Tonight, Brahim has the floor and tells us the story of the Ait Atta and Ait Sedrat.

'In the name of God. In days gone by, there were two tribes, the Ait Atta and the Ait Sedrat. They were neighbours, but they were not living in peace. Between them was a piece of land and both laid claim to it. They argued and discussed and shouted and threatened and pleaded but could not reach agreement. Finally, when their voices were hoarse and their throats ached from talking, they went to the judge of the whole province and laid their problem in front of him.

'"O honourable Qadi," said the leader of the Ait Atta. "We are in dispute over land with our brothers in the Ait Sedrat and we cannot resolve the issue. We feel the poison of the devil between us and we want to return to the righteous path. Please tell us what we should do." The leader of the Ait Sedrat nodded his agreement.

'"Fear not, my sons," said the clever Qadi, "I have a

solution if you will both agree. Say the morning prayer on your own land and then set off. Travel as fast as you can, stopping not for food or water, and use your best camel and all your might as riders. When you hear the call to evening prayer, stop, and that will be your boundary."

'Both leaders agreed and went back to their lands. They set the date for the competition for the following Thursday.

'Thursday came and the leader of the Ait Sedrat arose before dawn and prepared his camel. He ate a breakfast of dates, oil and bread early so that the minute he had completed his prayers he could mount his steed and ride like the wind to win as much of the land as possible. His camel, the white-faced one, was saddled and waiting in the courtyard. The night before, he had been fed well with oats and watered at the well. The muezzin called "Allahu Akbar" and the leader completed his prayers, jumped onto his camel and opened the door from his courtyard.

'He could not believe what his eyes were telling him. There, sitting in front of his gate, drinking water from a gourd, and leaning against his couched camel, was the leader of the Ait Atta. "All your land is mine," he said.

'"What is this treachery?" demanded the leader of the Ait Sedrat. "It is impossible that you said the morning prayer on your own land and then reached this point. You have broken our pact."

'"By God, I have not," said the cunning leader of the Ait Atta. "I scooped up the earth from my land into this saddle-bag and travelled all night, bringing it here to 500 metres before your gate, where I scattered it. This morning I prayed on my land, as we agreed, and set off to reach here. Now I claim your land for my own."'

The Ait Atta is one of the biggest tribes in Morocco and

is based around the Saghro and Draa region. Ait means 'the family of' and is very similar to Mc or Mac in Scotland. Tribal life is still very important in many areas and land disputes remain keenly fought over. There are ancient and complex agreements in place regarding ownership of the land as well as grazing rights and seasonal use. The Ait Atta from Sahgro migrate every year in the summer to Ait Bougemez where they have an agreement to graze their flocks for the summer months that dates back centuries.

Every day I'm growing more comfortable with the men. They've given me a nickname, 'Tafilfilat harran' – the hot chilli pepper – which I would like to think is due to the warmth of my personality but am categorically told is because of my hot temper. 'Patience, Zahra, patience,' is Brahim's constant refrain. Walking through the dark rocks, I've started to search out all the little plants and flowers that grow in the crevices, many of them surviving on the dew that collects overnight. I stop and search a five-metre radius at one point and find about seven different species: a type of dandelion, a dusky pink flower like a mini hyacinth with spaghetti-like leaves and another one that has hairy leaves with white and maroon stalks and flowers. Addi picks up on my interest and starts pointing plants out to me.

'Zahra, Zahra, look at this one,' he breaks off a stalk from a succulent cactus. It's about the length of my forefinger. 'This is good to eat; it has water inside it.' I eye him dubiously, 'Addi, are you sure? It just looks like a bit of cactus to me. Isn't it bitter?' His eyes widen and he takes on the face of a latter-day martyr accused of blasphemy, 'Zahra, don't you trust me? Of course it is good. It is sweet like honey made by the wild bees. When I was a child, I used to eat it all the time.' To prove his point, he takes a big bite and munches away. '*Bisaha wa raha*, health and rest,' he says, handing me the rest of the stalk. '*Bismillah*,' I say, and eagerly bite in, ready for some honey sweetness. Ha! It's as bitter as I'd thought it might be before I fell for Addi's patter. I spit it onto the ground and swill my mouth out with water. Addi capers around, shrieking with laughter like a banshee.

We're crossing a large plain dotted with occasional small houses. A very fancy one stands in the middle, freshly painted and rather large. It's the primary school for the surrounding area and children walk long distances to attend. Primary school is mandatory in Morocco. Two little boys arrive on their bikes and race the camels. Spotting a foreigner, they chance their luck, '*Stylo*, pen,' they chant. 'I don't have any,' I say. 'No problem, what about some money?' they try. I shake my head. 'I know, I know,' they're undeterred, '*al bortable diyalak*, your mobile phone, that will do.' I like their style. 'No, I need it.' 'But don't you have another one?' When I decline, they finally accept my lack of gifting with good grace and ride alongside us for a while.

We are camped in the lee of a hill, looking out over a small canyon filled with yellow and purple gorse. Past that is a flat plain leading to a little oasis where palm trees and henna grow, with one house beyond. The owners had passed us earlier on their motorbikes and said I was welcome to visit, but I felt a bit shy and had gone to help Addi with the water instead.

I drank the water untreated wherever we were all through the expeditions and had no stomach problems, thankfully. I think the water was usually much purer than our town water, in fact, as it was from wells or pools of rain or snow melt. We always had a two to three days' supply with us, carried in 4 x 25-litre bidots (white plastic containers with red lids) or empty 5-litre mineral water bottles. The big bidots weighed 25kg when they were full, so carrying two was quite hard.

Addi and I fill up from the well next to the garden and stagger back with a bidot each. At camp I am met by a pretty young girl in a silver-spangled headscarf and jeans who says, 'You must come over to the house now and we will do henna,' so off I go hand in hand with Ghislaine.

Henna is a small privet-like shrub, *Lawsonia inermis*. It is grown as a cash crop in Morocco and the leaves are dried and milled and then ground into a paste. It's used traditionally on the hair and on the skin, both for decoration and for health. It toughens up the skin, so you will see women in the fields with henna on the soles of their feet and the palms of their hands to help protect them. The pretty designs that you get offered when you go to tourist areas are called *naqsh* and are used for celebrations like Eid and, of course, for weddings.

It was so cold at night and in the mornings that my hands had cracked and I had open cuts between my thumbs and forefingers, so I needed the toughening. Brahim had been treating them every night by rubbing them with raw lemon, which is fantastically good for the skin but stings like crazy.

Ghislaine chats to me as we walk across the plain. She's eleven and tells me she has 'lots' of brothers and sisters. She wants to go to school but can't because there isn't one in the area. She is not as lucky as the boys on their bikes. She's clearly clever and asks intelligent questions but constantly has to break off to pick up and throw stones at the two shepherd dogs following us. The dogs in the country are usually either guard dogs or sheep dogs and they don't tolerate strangers.

This house is a typical, low-lying clay building, but the inhabitants are clearly much better off and there are lots of women and children all together. The teenage girls are all in jeans and headscarves like Ghislaine. I'm led into the salon, a large rectangular room with a TV in one corner, playing a Mexican soap dubbed into *darija*, and a gas stove on the other side with a tea tray beside it and a kettle bubbling on top. I sit down on the rugs covering the floor and Ghislaine brings a cushion for my back. I am not at all flexible, unlike all the Moroccan women who can bend from the hips and sit cross-legged at will, and need something to prop me up. It's rude to point the soles of your feet directly at someone, so I can't always sit with my legs straight out, which is almost comfortable, and usually end up with them curled beside me and leaning on one arm. It's one of the things that's tough on a long trip because everything in camp is at ground level.

There are two young women tending the kettle, Oumaima in a black jellaba with shiny spangles and Naima in brown and gold. Naima is twenty-five and had married at seventeen. She has two sons: Mounir and Imran. We drink tea and eat fresh msimmin, a flat, square, flaky pancake which is lightly fried and is rather like a paratha. You eat them with oil, melted butter, honey and jam. They are about a thousand calories a bite and worth every one. Once I've eaten, Naima asks me if I'd like to come out and help her milk the goats. I jump up, very excited – I've never milked a goat before.

We go via her kitchen, of which she is justifiably proud. The fire has a large pot of couscous steaming on it, a separate bread oven and also a three-ringed gas stove fuelled by camping gas. Lots of utensils and basics in jars are lined up neatly on shelving on the wall. I say everything that is admiring and we leave for the back of the house, where the goats who have kids and are in milk have been corralled by the children. First of all, I watch Naima. The goats all know her, of course, and she just sets straight to it with a long-haired brown nanny who stands there patiently as she pulls the teats and milk streams out into a white plastic container.

'Me, me, me,' I'm keen to get started. Naima gives me up her place. Mounir and Imran go to the front of my victim and hold tightly onto her horns. Squatting on the ground, I start squeezing away. The nanny's kid comes up behind me to check out what I'm doing to her mother and climbs onto my back. Nothing is coming out. I pull some more; still nothing. My victim has started to bleat loudly and, although I don't speak fluent goat, I can recognise an 'Ouch, get off me, you oaf!' when I hear one.

Naima is a diplomat, 'That's enough, Zahra, we only take a little from each mother anyway so that they have plenty to feed their babies.' She leads me on to another nanny. This one is chestnut-brown and has shorter hair. To stop her from running off, I grab her by her left hind leg, then reach under and count while pulling down on her teats. The udders are very swollen and surprisingly hard, 'One potato, two potato ...' Gentle pressure, relentlessly applied has its effect and milk starts squirting down. Some goes into the container, some goes all over Naima and some goes in my eye, which is a feat of some dexterity. Everyone wails with laughter.

Back in the salon, Oumaima is mixing henna powder with water, oil and lemon juice to make a thick paste. This is where I make my tactical error. I should have gone to the loo, because once the henna is on, I won't be able to and there's more tea drinking ahead. The henna is from their garden and has the consistency of dough. Oumaima plasters it thickly over the palm of my hand and up and over the fingers to my first knuckle. She then encases my hands in two plastic bags, tied at the wrist to protect the henna and to speed up absorption with the extra heat and humidity. Another sister arrives and brings out her embroidery to show me. She sells it at the local market – napkins and table coverings.

Henna should be kept on overnight and the women are desperate for me to stay. 'Stay with us, Zahra,' says Oumaima. 'You can eat couscous and sleep with me and Naima and then in the morning go back to your camp.' At that moment, one of the children comes running in, 'There is a man in a brown jellaba coming. Is he yours, Zahra?' Brahim has come to claim me. More tea and msimmin are brought out and some of the menfolk arrive. We ask about schools for the children and they tell us it's a big problem for them. They don't have one and even if they had a building, because of the remoteness of the place, they can't get a teacher to come. There are four extended families living within a 5km radius. I count six children of school age in the house – if multiplied, that means over twenty children in the area are missing out on even the most basic education.

I can see that Brahim is getting restless. It's prayer time. He asks our hosts where he can pray and they point him to a corner of the room. I'm surprised that none of the men join him. His voice and the TV fight for supremacy and the chatter of the family carries on unabated. Prayer is such an integral part of life that there are no hushed silences or pauses in activity. '*Yallah*, let's go,' he says when he's finished and we cross the moonlit plain.

By now, my bladder is signalling extreme distress and I know I have to get these bags off. I have no idea how the women manage; presumably they get a sister or a mother to help them if they need the loo. Back at camp, BB says I ought to keep the bags on overnight but, with an agonised look, I insist I need them off. He understands my pain and roars into action. Addi builds a fire to help dry my hands off quickly, while Brahim makes the soup. BB takes off my plastic bags and holds my hands as close to the flames as I can bear. When the henna is baked dry, Addi pours water over my hands and BB scrapes them hard to get the paste off. My hands and fingers are a fluorescent orange. The longer you leave the henna on, the darker it dyes the skin and the more effective it is, but I'm happy. '*Ishwa*, beautiful,' says Addi. '*Bisaha wa raha*, in health and rest,' says BB. 'May God give you health,' I reply and rush off gratefully to the bushes.

3

THE LOST CITY

Not far from Hassi Bou Lham – north of Timtig

17 January 2019

'Zahra, do you know why donkeys bray in the morning?'

BB and I are walking behind the camels together through a narrow gorge stuffed with vibrant purple flowers which grow in sprays off large bushes that look like a type of broom. Hamish and Callum keep stopping to grab a mouthful and chomp noisily through it. I make some guesses: 'Because they are hungry? They like to sing to the sun. They want to wake up their owners?'

'No, Zahra. There is a holy reason. The morning prayers are very important and all good Muslims should get up when they hear the call and go to the mosque, but it is very early and Satan is circling. In those early hours, the devil and his cohorts gather up coverlets and walk among the sleeping people, laying the blankets gently over them. They are so warm and comfortable that their slumber deepens. Beni Adam, the sons of Adam, are weak and many of them would prefer to stay in bed under Satan's coverlets than get up and pray to Allah. These coverlets are invisible to us humans, but they are actually green, and to the donkeys they look just like bundles of delicious sweet grass. They bray in hope of being given some to eat. So, when you hear a donkey calling at dawn, you will know that Satan is circling.'

We are camped a few kilometres from Foum Chenna, where there is a collection of rock carvings. JP and Abdellah are coming in to rendezvous with us tomorrow. The sun is getting low when I hear some rocks tumbling and see BB coming down the side of the cliff. Every day, if it's at all possible, we have to send our GPS co-ordinates to the local authorities. This means that BB often has to find a high point to climb to in order to get signal. 'How is it?' I ask. 'Two bars, Zahra, if you go right to the top.'

I hadn't spoken to my parents for a few days and I wanted to check emails and messages. It was a scramble rather than a walk. Lots of it was straight up, clambering over big rocks and trying to avoid putting my hands on the thistles that nestled there. By the time I get to the top, I am panting and sweaty. There is a flattish plateau and the miraculous two bars appear. I find a handy flat stone and sit on it, then bury my head in my phone and tap away. Time passes quickly, and I am aware that the light is deepening from gold towards dusk. Night always falls fast and I don't want to have to scramble back down in the dark.

I've just finished WhatsApping my mum and think I should wait a few minutes to see if she replies. I look up and, straight ahead of me, I spot something. *That looks like a building*, I think. I get up and climb over the rubble of rocks. It's a rectangular room with a space for a window or door and beside it is another of the same. There's no roof or sign of any habitation and it's built of stone – a bit like an old crofter's house in the Highlands. We have passed dozens of crumbling stone shepherds' encampments – *azeeb* – on our journey but it definitely isn't one of those. This is much more formal and the shape is different.

The light is really dimming now but I want to see if there are any more. I turn and walk to the left, away from the descent to camp, and lying around the corner are several more of the buildings. These are in a much worse state of repair, but the overall impression is of an organised settlement, with spaces for alleyways and constructed buildings. Now, the light is critical and I have to get back down quickly. My battery is low on the phone and I haven't brought a head torch. Going down is always treacherous and I am usually quite tentative, but this time I slide over the ground as fast as I can, knowing that the men will be worried if I don't get back to the camp before dark.

As we are drinking our soup, I quiz them. JP does regular visitor trips out to Foum Chenna, which is just down the road, and they know this area well. 'What is the old city on top of the cliff?' I ask. Three puzzled faces look towards me. 'The old town, all the ruined buildings, what is it?' I am met with blank incomprehension. None of them have heard of it and BB had gone up a different route so hadn't seen it. I start to get excited. Have I found something 'new'?

That night felt long. Usually, I hog the last minutes in LPF, enjoying my sleeping bag before I have to get up and start the day, but this morning I am up and at it and making my porridge before the men have even finished breakfast. It feels like an age till JP and Abdellah walk up the valley to join us. I hasten through the formalities and then tell JP what I've found and ask him if he knows anything about it. He doesn't. 'There is nothing on the map, Zahra. It is probably just an *azeeb*.' I knew it wasn't and I had seen enough of them not to be put off. 'JP, we have to go up this hill. I want to show you what I've found.' He isn't keen at first as he wants to go straight to the rock carvings further down, but I insist.

When we get to the top, I drag Abdellah and JP to the spot. 'Look, these are ruined buildings from some kind of town or city, I think.' JP's eyebrows go flying up, his eyes pop wide open and he goes from sceptic to enthusiast in one breath. '*Impressionante*, impressive!' He starts climbing over everything, exclaiming and taking photographs.

In the daylight, the extent of what we are looking at is much clearer and it really is impressive. The settlement stretches over the hill in front of us right down the slope, which is much less precipitous on this side. It also winds round the corner that I had walked the night before. Turning to our right, there are further buildings on the next hill. We can clearly see the streets and alleyways between the buildings and even some spaces that might have been squares for markets or public gatherings.

By now JP's excitement matches my own. 'I think this must date from the same period as the rock carvings a few kilometres away at Foum Chenna,' he speculates. 'At that time, there would have been a lot more water to support a community and anyway the Draa River is not far away. It has been built high for defence purposes. When you see the rock carvings, you will see that there are many depicting war, so it would make sense to have your settlements in places that you could defend from other tribes. They would have kept animals and farmed but also at that time there was a lot more game, so they could have hunted too. There must have been a lot of people living here and they would have used horses or mules for transport to bring goods up. I guess the roofs would have been timbered and perhaps covered in grasses. I can't see any sign of kitchens or areas with cooking fire marks but there must be some.'

When I was writing up the brief for the Draa Expedition for sponsors and press releases, I blithely put in that I would be searching for lost cities, but (spoiler alert) I didn't actually think that I would find one. This is what makes exploring so rewarding. You do make discoveries big and small and you get to really think about what they are and what might have happened. You use all your knowledge and experience and that of those around you to work out as much as you can. In my case, my imagination runs riot and I have peopled the city and made up a whole series of wars, hunts, love stories and feuds – there was even a donkey called David – before I leave the hill.

Was the city really 'lost', though? And can I claim to have 'discovered' it? Nomads walk all over these hills and, of course, will have seen the ruins and probably sat on the same comfortable flat stone that I did, possibly also using WhatsApp, as mobile phones are ubiquitous here. In any inhabited, or formerly inhabited, area of the world, you would be a very brave person to say that you had 'discovered' anything like this. That feels like terminology that belongs very much to a different era of exploration, or nowadays to science, space and the depths of the ocean. Did I come across something unexpected and not widely known and that could definitely do with a lot more investigation? That I can say yes to with a clear conscience, and it felt fantastic. As well as the sheer fun of it, exploration is about finding stuff out for ourselves and using it to try to understand our world and our humanity better. There are quite a lot of hard days, monotonous days and physically crucifying days on expedition. These big days are few and far between and they are to be treasured.

We walk on to Foum Chenna. It is one of 300 documented rock-carving sites in Morocco and, because you can get to it relatively easily if you drive down the Draa and then hike in, it is well worth a visit if you come to the area. There are no custodians or tickets and no people, so you, too, can truly explore. There are hundreds of carvings, some at ground level and some further up. Researchers have documented over 3,000 in 300 different groupings.

One of the distinctive features of this site is that so many of the pictures actually are groupings: a hunt, a battle, a flock of ostriches and so on. They show humans, animals, weapons and some script and lots of them are very clear. Researchers believe that they were a way of communicating and that the sites were specifically chosen. The messages were to set out territories, proclaim ownership and to commemorate heroes and battles, as well as to depict the animals and tools of the time. They believe that the images may have two levels of meaning – one that is easily understandable but another that is more symbolic and abstruse. I had hiked up to the Yagur plateau in the Atlas Mountains previously and seen the large sun etched there on a plain inhabited by nomads. That carving seemed symbolic, whereas the rock carvings in Foum Chenna are more representative.

The rock is sandstone, baked black by the sun and the carvings are 'pecked' out. This is how archaeologists describe the way they are drawn, and close up they do look as though dedicated birds have had a go at them with sharp beaks, creating little dents in the hard rock. The colours range from cream, through red to dark ochre, and this helps to date them. They have been defined as Libyco–Berber, which is the term applied to this kind of rock carving all over North Africa and dated as 2500 BCE onwards.

Exploring Foum Chenna is like opening presents on Christmas morning. At first, I dash around, my magpie eye caught by first one thing and then another, taking photos, doing very bad sketches and just touching the stone, knowing that someone thousands of years ago has done the same thing. JP helps me by pointing out details I've missed or taking me to see a particularly fine grouping. Being able to take as much time as you want and to get up close and personal with history is the ultimate luxury. You may not understand everything as you would if you were in a museum with an audio tour but you have that immediate physical connection to other lives lived.

One of the most common depictions is of fighting. There are stick-figure men on stick-figure, or slightly fatter, horses with round shields and very long lances adorned with wicked-looking barbs. There are also foot soldiers with swords. Quite often it looks as though the men on foot have the upper hand. I speculate that they may have been the inhabitants of the valley, who the carvers are lionising, and the men on horse-back are the invaders.

There are lots of animals: gazelles with head-toppling giant horns, cattle and a whole flock of ostriches. The flock of ostriches has twelve clear members and then some damaged bits and bobs that may have been birds at one point. There are two big adults and a string of baby birds behind them of various sizes. There are also two giant eggs, although they are more football-shaped than oval.

My absolute favourite, though, is a bit ego-driven. I feel like it's a picture of me from centuries before. It is a camel train with two camels, various horses and what I think is a dog at the back. They are all heading in the same direction and above them are words in the Libyco–Berber script. Not only a caravan – but a writer.

Satisfyingly little is known about the Libyco-Berber script
and there is detective work to be done. Controversies rage
among linguistic circles about where it came from and when.
Inscriptions dating back to around the 7th century BCE have
been found on rocks in the High Atlas and on some pottery
shards from around the 3rd century BCE, but it emerged
clearly as the official language of the Numidian Empire,
which stretched from Morocco all the way to Libya, in the
last two centuries BCE.

It is still spoken and is found in the Amazigh (Berber)
languages of today. Some symbols from the Libyco-Berber
script, particularly in the Sahara, are used in neo-Tifinagh,
which is the alphabet which was developed in the 20th
century for use in the Amazigh languages. The Amazigh
can't necessarily read the Libyco-Berber script but they can
recognise some of the symbols and you can still see some of
those symbols woven into carpets or embroidered on shawls.

Back at camp, we wave off JP and Abdellah and BB who
wants to go back and see his two young boys for a couple of
weeks. I get the distinct feeling that he will not miss us as
much as I will miss him. In his place, we have Ali Ahalfi,
who is Brahim's cousin. Abdellah says that Ali would make
a great Jesus in Hollywood and I can see what he means;
he is very handsome, although to me he looks more like a
Moroccan George Clooney with an outdoor hardness about
him. A new team member brings in different energy. Addi
has become cook and does a good job, but there is no tablecloth that night.

I'm sleeping deeply, zipped up into my two bags, when
suddenly I am jolted awake. I hear men's voices speaking
quietly in the near distance, and they are not my men.
Immediately, my body goes on high alert. We are camped

several kilometres away from the Draa Valley and the nearest road is a good half day's walk away. There are no houses
nearby and no farms, so why would men be coming out here
in the middle of the night? I don't know what to do. My mind
races ahead and, of course, I think back to the two girls in
Imlil who were taken from their tent and beheaded. I know
that Brahim and Addi would never abandon me and would
put my safety above their own, but I don't want anything bad
to happen to them or me and I certainly don't want to end
up on a YouTube video.

Should I get out of my tent and go into the mess tent where
they are sleeping so at least we are together? The problem is I
don't know where the strange men are. What if they are just
outside my tent and grab me? My ears are straining in the
darkness. I don't want to switch on my torch but I have it in
my hand. Time ticks on very slowly. Then, cracking across
the silence, there are a couple of shouts and a shriek and the
sound of feet running followed by complete silence. I have no
idea what has happened and I am too terrified to go outside.

I spend the rest of the night hours in an agony of apprehen-
sion. Finally, at 5.30, I hear what sounds like Brahim rustling
around, boiling up the water so that the men can wash before
prayers. About twenty minutes later, his voice rings out, 'In
the Name of God, the Compassionate, the Merciful.'

When he finishes and brings me over my little bucket, I
have never been so glad to see anyone's face.

'Brahim, what happened last night? What was all that
noise? Why were there men's voices outside the tents? Who
were they? Why were they here?'

'The men, Zahra? Ah, they were a group of boys. They
were walking overnight so that they could watch the dawn
break in the oasis behind us and then have a barbecue and

a picnic. They were probably students from the college. A lot of people come to that oasis to eat and sing and play the drums – you know, friends or family – for the day. Then, they just about fell over the camels in the dark and they got a real fright. They didn't expect camels to be couched in the oued, the dried river bed, so they shouted and ran away. Did you hear them? Were you afraid, Zahra?'

He's grinning at me.

'Afraid? Me?' I manage a high laugh. 'No, no. I was just wondering. Thank you for the hot water.'

That morning we were lucky enough to spot a wild cat in the distance. It was running just beneath a long ridge of hills about 500 metres from us. It must have been startled out of its lair by the sound of our approach. Although hard to tell from a distance, after a Google photo search later on and with some convoluted descriptions in Arabic and Tashlaheet, I think it was a caracal. They have distinctive ears with long tufts of hair like a lynx but they are actually more closely related to servals in the cat family. They are medium-sized and – like most cats – are known to be very territorial and generally live alone. Their preferred habitat is dry steppes and semi-desert conditions, which is exactly what we are walking through.

And then, quite suddenly it seems, our time in Jebel Saghro has come to an end.

We reach a tarmac road, such a shock after the wilderness. Handily for us, there's a clearly designated bike and scooter lane, so we colonise it and I take photos of our camels walking over the picture of the man on a bicycle. No one seems to mind and cars all slow down or stop to marvel at this camel train which could have been plucked straight from a film set or a child's history picture book.

We are now in Morocco's date basket, the valley of the

Draa, with green palms stretching out for as far as we can see. At intervals along the route, individual farmers have set up tables, often manned by their sons, piled high with dates, hoping to sell to a passing car. We stop at one to replenish our supplies. Mohamed, aged twelve, is the proud proprietor and strikes a hard bargain. Ali actually has to do the old trick of walking away before he is chased back and a deal is agreed. I had a moment of anxiety that we really wouldn't have any dates to go with our soup at dinner.

Turning the camels out of the bike lane, we walk down into the green. We have to stop. Directly ahead of us a nanny goat is giving birth to her kid on a piece of empty ground. We all hold our breath as the baby emerges, covered in sticky goo. Almost immediately, it tries to stand up, nudged on by its mother who licks at the birth sac. We watch as the new little being takes its very first steps in life and issues a tentative bleat. 'Thanks be to God for a safe arrival,' I say. 'God is great,' replies Brahim.

Entering the oasis is like stepping onto a different planet. I have got used to harsh rock and emptiness and then suddenly we're in the midst of lush green gentleness. The temperature drops by about five degrees and it smells of plants and wet earth. The air feels slightly damp on my face. The light is no longer bright and clear but green with shadows dancing off the spiked leaves of the palm trees and patterning the dry dirt roads. It's the sound, though, that affects me the most. There are birds everywhere, chattering and calling and swishing through the trees, and there is the cool, delicious murmur of water running.

The gardens are watered by a clever network of underground tunnels and overground sagiyya – irrigation channels – which take water to every inch of ground and are communally maintained and governed. Each farmer has his own designated time when he can open a channel by means of a little iron gate, or big stone, in the main waterway. When it is your allotted time, you lift this up to let the water flow into your channels and garden. Each year, the farmers inspect the channels and any repairs that need to be done are usually organised by the community through the local mosque. Date palms need a lot of water – up to 60,000 gallons a year – and they don't like getting their leaves wet, so they thrive in the Draa where water is delivered to their base through the irrigation channels, but it rarely rains.

Dotted through the palmeraie are little villages and clusters of houses, sometimes guarded by a *kasbah*, a little castle. There are fairy-tale red buildings rising up among the green of the palms and donkeys and mules plodding along pulling carts or carrying whole families to market – one son on the front, Dad in the middle and a son on the back. They look picturesque but there are hazards ahead. We are walking through the streets of one of the villages when it starts to narrow, and then narrow further, to the point that BB's little rush kitchen stool which is tied on to Sausage at the back starts to bash against the walls. 'If we come to a stopped end, we are in trouble,' Brahim warns. 'If we can't go forward, and we can't turn around, we are stuck.' His face is set in a grim line and I don't dare to ask the next question, 'How easy is it to reverse a camel?' I suspect I already know the answer.

Our other hazard is donkeys. They are pretty and hard-working, trotting along on the paths with their humans and baggage, but there is one big problem: they don't like camels. In fact, they absolutely hate camels. We are trundling along on an unmade road through the fields and turn a corner. A dignified, robed elderly man is driving his donkey cart towards us. The donkey spots us and lets out a volley of absolutely outraged brays along the lines of, 'What are you? Why are you here? You don't look anything like a proper animal – a cow, or a horse, or a mule. Get out of my oasis.'

Our camels are unmoved, at which point the donkey decides that they may be donkey eaters and plunges into the field at breakneck speed, throwing his driver almost off his seat. Mayhem reigns. Addi thrusts Callum's halter at me and plunges into the field to try to help the *hajj*. Ali moves in behind to offer abject apologies and Brahim walks firmly on with me behind, getting our trouble-makers the hell out of Dodge. As I look back, I see Addi tenderly dusting off the owner, with Ali saying, 'Forgive us, O, He who has completed the pilgrimage to Mecca, we did not see you approaching. Forgive us.' '*Hashouma*, shame on us,' mutters Brahim, and I look sternly at Callum, who appears embarrassingly unconcerned.

I had imagined when we went into the oasis that we would camp in one of the cleared fields under the shade of a handy palm. I was dreaming about putting my hot feet in a water channel and setting up my chair in the shade to write my notes and enjoy the birdsong. I am, therefore, dismayed when we cut out of the green and up onto a familiar bare hill at the side, with little to recommend it.

'Why are we camping here?' I ask Brahim grumpily. 'Why can't we camp in the oasis where it is pretty and cool and fresh. It is horrible here, just sand and stones and acacia trees.' He looks at me sadly. 'I'm sorry, Zahra, but we have to camp where it is good for the camels. If we camped in the gardens, they would eat everything. You know the camels have the devil in them; they would go straight to the fields and . . .' At this point he makes a gesture with his hands which eloquently illustrates a greedy Hamish galloping into the field of a poor farmer, who has a large family to feed, and gobbling up every green shoot in site. 'This site may not be the most beautiful, but I will put up Le Petit Fromage in the shade of that acacia tree (the only one) for you and you can write in peace.' I feel like such a heel and vow to remove petulance from my tone of voice repertoire.

4

I Become a Bride

North of Timtig – close to Zawiya Moulay Ali Sharif

25 January 2019

One of the things that the men miss on the long trips is the chance to go to the mosque and pray, especially on a Friday, and the other thing they miss is their wives' or mothers' couscous. It was a Thursday night and they were all chatting away quickly in Tashlaheet after supper and looking excited. When I asked what was going on, Ali told me that the next day we were going to stop at a village where one of their fellow guides, another Ali, lived with his family. The men would go to the mosque and I would stay with the women and then we would all eat couscous together. A grand treat.

We get to Ali's house about noon and unload the camels. I am enveloped in girls and pulled into the house. I'm heavily aware that the girls all smell lovely and are dressed prettily and cleanly, and neither me nor my clothes have washed for quite a long time. In Morocco, you have to take your shoes off when you go into someone's home, and I flinch as I think of what their poor noses are being assaulted by. The family's

salon is long and rectangular with rugs on the floor and cushions around the walls. What luxury to sit with my back on a
cushion against a wall.

The men disappear one by one to have a thorough wash
before prayers, then we hear the muezzin call and they set
off happily for the mosque. No sooner does the last heel cross
the doorway than the girls pounce on me. Mama with her
daughters Fatima, Hassna and Miriam, baby boy Youness
chuckling all the way through the proceedings. There is no
point in trying to hold on to any dignity or modesty when
faced with a group of determined Moroccan women. Any
vestige of British reserve has to be cast aside. You have to go
with the flow and enjoy it. The girls obviously view me as
their own personal Barbie doll and are very dissatisfied indeed
with my outfit of khaki shirt with co-ordinated trousers.

'Today, Zahra, you are going to be a bride!' Hassna crows.
They disappear off into the back bedroom and come back
with mounds of clothing. 'Stand there, arms up,' I am told
firmly. I do as I am told and, regardless of the fact that it is
pretty warm, I am layered up. First an emerald green caftan
with paisley print is pulled over my head. Then, a long piece
of white satin is draped around me and tied at both shoulders
to make armholes, a bit like a toga. Hassna, thirteen, proudly
brings out a long, woollen red cord with three enormous
tassles on the end and spangles along it. 'This is mine,' she
sighs happily, stroking the belt. 'I made it myself for my wedding. Isn't it beautiful?' It's tied round my waist and the white
satin ruched up. Mama produces a red headscarf which is
hand-beaded all around the edge and ties it round my head so
that all my hair is covered and the beads hang down to frame
my face. The top goes up to a little peak. Fatima winds pearls
round my neck and then Mama adds a necklace of amber and

orange beads. To top it all off, a traditional Amazigh black shawl, with bright splashes of embroidery, is draped over my head and shoulders.

I feel like a giant parcel but we aren't finished yet. A large, jolly neighbour arrives. I can sense the force of her personality as soon as she comes in. From her bag she whips out kohl, lipstick and perfume. Kohl is liberally applied round my eyes and the lipstick rubbed into my cheeks as well as my lips.

The girls are ecstatic, 'Beautiful, beautiful, so much better!' They are fluttering around me like little birds, darting in to fold a piece of material properly, or make sure my head coverings are just so. It is such a moment of innocent fun and happiness.

But now on to the more serious issues of the day. I am pressed back into the cushions and the neighbour fixes me with a gimlet eye. 'You have never been married? No children?' I admit it. She gives me an exploratory squeeze. 'Hmm, good.' I feel vaguely worried. 'Now you have the clothes, you can marry Ali, and become his second wife.' I glance over at his first wife, who is sitting opposite me and nodding along in apparent agreement. The rumbunctious neighbour makes a circle of two fingers and pokes another one through it vigorously and with inescapable meaning. Just to make sure I understand, she carries on. 'You and Ali, lots of fucky fucky, and then you will have a baby.' Ali's wife and daughters all chorus, 'Yes, yes, then you can live with us always.'

I am wondering how to get myself out of an idea that appears to be gaining quite a lot of ground without causing offence when I hear the sound of the men coming back. Saved!

Addi and Brahim come in first and do a cartoon comedy double-take when they see me. Addi makes the clicking sounds in his cheek that are his highest form of approbation and Brahim says, 'This is good, you have changed for the better.' Couscous is served and we all eat hungrily. I am allowed to take my wedding dress off but gifted with the red beaded headdress and the necklace as we set off again.

We need more food, and Tamegroute on market day is the ideal place to go. Tamegroute is a bustling town famous for its potteries which make unique, green-glazed ceramics. The green roof and mosque tiles you see all over Morocco are made here. The market is buzzing, and when we arrive with our camels, we manage to raise the noise levels by about ten decibels. All the donkeys and mules who have been brought in to carry their owners' weekly shop go crazy. The men stop in their tracks and shout to their friends, 'Look at the caravan! It's like something from a movie.'

We settle the camels then hire a donkey and cart and set off for market. I'm so happy to be shopping for the first time in weeks. We start off buying several bales of hay for the camels and load them on our cart. Unfortunately, Brahim is not a browser, so I am pulled away from the jellaba and shoe stalls to the vegetables. The produce is laid out in big colourful mounds on the ground, with paths between for the customers. The owners sit on wooden crates or squat beside their wares. We spot a stall that has a big variety of produce. Brahim and I each take one of the plastic bowls and started filling them up: carrots (small ones), potatoes, turnips, tomatoes (hard ones so they last longer), chilli peppers, mandarins, bananas, apples, onions and cucumbers in great quantity. Brahim loves teasing me with my nickname, Tafilfilat harran. 'You choose those, Zahra,' he says, pointing at a pile of red hot chillis, 'they are your people.' Our donkey has been waiting patiently for us in a cul-de-sac. He has to do a three-point turn which involves us lifting the cart and the shafts off the ground and then turning the donkey as we shuffle round behind him.

Tamegroute is a real artisan town and the road back to our hotel is lined with little workshops for iron. The workshops are small, about the size of a normal sitting room, and long. Finished knives, scythes and palm-cutting tools hang on the walls. It is a sauna inside because the furnace is at the back of the room and is burning hot. I go in and meet the proprietor and his two young sons who are working with him. 'They go to school,' he tells me. 'But then they help me as well.' 'Do you like working with your dad?' I ask them, and they nod vigorously, their eyes glowing, and show me the knife they are beating out, red from the flame. The ironsmith takes over and hammers out a curved knife blade with quick, accurate blows. Once cooled, a wooden handle is tied firmly on with handmade rope. I try the blade and it's deadly sharp.

The potteries lie at the edge of the town. The process is still entirely traditional. It seems to me that nothing at all has changed for centuries. Smoke is billowing from the kilns as donkeys arrive laden with palm fronds. Men, streaming with sweat, shovel the hot embers into the clay ovens while others create pot after pot on the wheel with mesmerising speed. On one side of the world, automated factories are churning out tiny microchips, whereas here men are doing what their families have done forever. The pottery is a complex of buildings: a place for throwing the pots and tiles; a wide-open space for drying them; and then the kilns themselves which are small square huts filled with fire, with plenty of room in front for the donkeys to come in and out.

Local red clay is cut from the earth in the surrounding areas and brought in. Water is added and kneaded like dough to the right consistency for throwing. The potter sits on the edge of a hole in a ground. In the hole is a contraption that looks a bit like a bicycle, but which is actually a form of wheel that you have to twist round rather than up and down. This powers the wheel on top, where you cast your pot. The tiles are an elongated pot that is later cracked in two. Once finished, you take the pot outside and leave it to harden in the sun for three days.

Meanwhile, there is a man whose whole job is to pound rocks down into a black powder using a pestle and mortar. He calls them *kahal*, which means 'black' or 'kohl', and I wonder if it is the same thing that you put on your eyes. The potter explains to me that it is manganese and is what gives the pottery its distinctive green colour. The pots are covered in it for a glaze and then are put into the kiln for five hours at 90 degrees. The kiln is divided into two parts. The top part is where the pots go and, once they are in, it is sealed up with stones and clay, which is then broken to take them out again. The bottom part is the fire and there are two men who constantly feed it to keep it hot enough. As we are walking around, I spot a very modern-looking kiln and ask Omar, the chief potter, about it. 'Ah, yes. That was brought in by a German man from Germany a few years ago. It is powered by gas and it is very exact with the temperatures. But, when he put the pots in, they didn't come out the right green. He tried and tried but no luck. The old way is the only way.' We grin at each other.

That night, we are entertained by a group of traditional dancers and singers who have come to give us an injection of culture. There are ten of them dressed in white jellabas and white turbans, with white *babouches* (soft leather slippers) and black sashes with impressive silver daggers tucked in. They are carrying a variety of skin drums: tambourine-shaped ones about 500cm wide, long narrow ones and square ones that look 250cm across. They move from foot to foot rhythmically and sing in a low, melodious thrum. In front of them are the two main dancers, who are holding long swords. They approach each other and bow and sway, go forward and retreat, tap their swords together, thrusting and parrying in time to the music. All of it is performed very slowly and gently. At the end of each song, someone 'dies' very quietly. It is hypnotic, but I can't help making comparisons with the energy and whooping delight of a Scottish sword dance.

Days after Tamegroute, Ali asks me, 'Zahra, are you in?' 'Yes,' I say, 'but for what?' Generally in life I think it's best to say yes first and then find out the details. 'Brahim, Addi and I are all going to put 100 MAD [£8.50] in the pot and if you add 100 that will give us 400, which is enough to buy a goat for tomorrow. We need to eat some meat.' 'Yes, great idea. Where are you going to get the goat from?' Ali points to the herd of goats parading past the mess tent and I send up a little prayer for the one who is having his last supper.

Our route is always dictated by what is best for our camels, but I also want to see as much as I can. We have reached the Zagora, Ktaoua region and are proposing to walk over the hills to a large crater plain that was formed by volcanoes when the land was still shifting and settling. It is tough, so we have to recce the ascent first. It's been decided that Brahim and I will go up the mountain to recce, and Ali and Addi will stay at camp that day and attend to the goat. The camels will luxuriate in a day off and roam in search of tasty acacia thorns. They have very strange tastes.

Brahim and I set off at 8.30 across the plain towards the hill. On long expeditions, you spend all your days talking, and this is no exception. We cover eating your words, men having a physical violence urge in them that women don't, the story of Moses in the Quran, the name for an Adam's apple in English and why women are the fire beneath all problems. This got us to the foot of the mountain and love and marriage got us to the top.

'Satan works between men and women very cleverly,' Brahim starts. 'While they are getting to know each other, he is there with them all the time. He hides their faults from each other and blocks their ears so that they only hear sweet words. He creates magic to make everything good. Then, the minute they do the *khtouba* – get engaged – he disappears and all of a sudden everything he has hidden becomes clear. Satan's curtains are opened.'

As we are going up, Brahim is concentrating hard on the ground underfoot. We're following a faint goat's path which is blocked in various places. 'No good for the camels,' he mutters, moving a big rock to the side. 'It's hard for them to pass here; we would have to dig out a path,' when we come to a particularly narrow ledge. I am losing hope that we'll be able to get our boys up and over. We reach the top three hours after we left camp. The view stretches out below us for miles. We can see Le Petit Fromage, white against the sand, and the camels scattered out to graze. Old water courses have cut lighter paths into the earth, as have worn animal tracks heading for the wells. One of the ways to find water is to get up high and then look for where the goat tracks lead.

'Zahra, come and look here, you haven't seen this type of flower before.' Brahim has found a rather unprepossessing plant with green maple-like leaves and yellow heads which open out into white fuzzy clocks. When I turn over the leaves, they are a pretty purple underneath. Suddenly,

Brahim lets out a yelp. 'Thanks be to God. God is great!' I don't know what he's on about. 'Zahra, Zahra, it's a miracle.' He points to a leaf on the plant and there, clearly written, is 'Mohamed' (the name of the Prophet) in Arabic. 'It's a sign. Our expedition is blessed.' What are the chances of stopping to look at that particular plant of all the hundreds around us and then finding that a worm has left its traces across it in perfect Arabic script to write Mohamed? Nature is indeed miraculous. We take lots of pictures and then continue on to camp.

Addi and Ali have been busy. They've laid out the mess tent rugs under an acacia tree and a fire is lit. A goat skin, with the head still attached, is hanging up on the tree out of the way and Addi has lined up knives, kebab skewers and little bags of salt and cumin on a plastic sack with a big plate of offal ready to be cut. The teapot is steaming quietly and the glasses are on the tray. The brochettes are already cooked. Little cubes of meat sit on the skewers, very tender and fla-voured with woodsmoke. The men have made fresh bread too. We wolf down two skewers each with tea and then the real work begins. '*Titliwin*,' says Addi and bends to his task.

Addi is a good worker but I never see him concentrating as hard as when he has got goat offal in front of him. He loves it. First, he takes the liver and cooks it whole at the side of the fire in the ashes where the embers are still glowing. Then he cuts it into pieces and covers each one with the belly fat which he has stretched out to dry in lacy sheets on the acacia tree. These are put on the skewers and balanced on two lines of stones, into which the glowing coals have been pushed. As each skewer cooks, Addi takes it off and hands it round to us. We take two pieces each and eat them between the bread, dripping in delicious fat, and wash them down with tea. Addi keeps them coming for round after round. My belly is getting pretty full.

The rounds of *titliwin* end and I think we are done, but no. Addi is busying himself again. This operation is more complicated and somewhat gruesome. The goat's trachea is laid down and covered in something non-specific but that may be lungs. It's rolled up to form a long sausage, which is then tied up with strings of intestine, which have been squeezed to get rid of any residue. '*Cordass,*' says Addi. I look at Ali and ask with alarm, 'Do we eat those?' He bursts out laughing and then can't stop. Apparently, this is the *pièce de résistance* of the meal. After they've been cooked, Addi chops one into quarters and hands me my bit, beaming with pleasure. For the sake of his fine eyes, I bite into it and grin with (feigned) pleasure too. The trachea is crunchy. '*Immim!* Delicious!' I exclaim. Seriously, I am giving up adventuring and going into acting – that BAFTA would be mine. Addi is too busy munching to reply but just presses another piece on to me. Ali is still laughing between mouthfuls.

More tea is made and we all lie back on the rugs watching the sun as it begins to set. African sunsets tug at your heart. The wide plain is framed by the hills with one flat-topped acacia tree standing just beyond my tent. Hamish is munching contentedly on its thorny branches. Life throws up perfect moments.

But Addi isn't finished. He wraps up the goat skin, folding the head in carefully, and bundles it into a bag to take to the nomads. No piece of the animal goes unused. 'I'm going to pay them now,' he says. 'You pay them, Addi, and then we'll give you the money tomorrow,' says Ali, 'as long as we aren't sick. If we're sick then no money.' Addi's face falls. 'But I have to pay them.' Ali, with a totally straight face: 'But my

stomach hurts, maybe I will be ill.' Poor Addi. I take pity on
him and hand over the cash.

Having found a decent path for the camels, we wind back
up the hill the next day. Brahim is teaching Addi the call
to prayer. Addi grew up tending the goats and sheep that
his family owns. He didn't go to school at all and is illliter-
ate. Most nomad children now do; they stay with a family
member in the town during term time and get at least the
minimum education. In school, they are usually taught in
Arabic, not in Tashlaheet, and I think it must be extremely
hard to be confronted with the new concepts of reading and
writing in a foreign language. Arabic and Tashlaheet have
nothing in common as languages although many words,
greetings and religious phrases have seeped into Tashlaheet
and Tashlaheet has had a big influence on Morocco's Arabic
dialect. Addi, of course, grew up speaking his own language
and in his own community so had no reason to learn Arabic.
Every day, he prays with Brahim and Ali, but what I hadn't
appreciated until this moment is that he doesn't understand
what Brahim is reciting. The verses are from the Quran and
are all in classical Arabic. He would know the meaning of
the prayers used daily but not the ones that Brahim goes on
to. It is similar to the mass in Latin, I suppose.

Brahim sings out the *idhan*, the call to prayer, segment by
segment, and Addi repeats it. An obstacle for him is that he
is not used to any form of learning of this kind. Addi is quick
and clever, but this is new territory for him. He keeps getting
frustrated and trying to stop, but Brahim patiently perseveres
and Ali and I chime in with lots of encouragement.

The men in their robes, with faces covered by their *chechs*,
are silhouetted against the blue of the sky. The camels pad
up the glowing yellow cliffs with the luggage creaking

rhythmically on their backs. The wind blows away the heat of the sun. Cutting through it, Brahim and Addi call again and again to their God. That night, and every night afterwards, Addi proudly starts off the evening prayer ritual.

Brahim and I talk about religion a lot. He has been teaching me to recite some verses of the Quran, explaining the meaning if I don't know the word and choosing verses he knows will hold significance for me. He constantly surprises me with his tolerance and inclusivity. He hasn't read the Torah or the Bible, but has been taught by Islam that all the prophets and the holy books are part of the greater whole. They all lead to God. He is a man of unshakable faith but allows me my doubts and questions, never getting angry when I challenge something. It's one of the great riches of the expedition to spend so much time with him and to benefit from his knowledge.

We camp near a glade of tall lupins and white gorse, sustained by an invisible underground water source. Ali teaches me some of the stars that night as we eat beside the fire: the North Star, the Great Bear and one that we can't name but is multi-coloured and changes from red to blue to green to white as I watch.

The next day we descend into the *tafedna*, which means the basin where water collects in a hammam. It feels like a secret garden encompassed by the walls of the hills. We camp near a well which is surrounded by patches of spiky grass. The minute we've unloaded them, the camels go and roll in it, scratching their backs luxuriously. They roll just like horses, with their legs kicking comically in the air.

I am pulling up water from the well when I hear a rumbling. A string of goats appears and gallops towards me. A couple of them stop short when they see the tents and have a good look, but the rest are thirsty and head for me. There is a big tin drum and a trough by the side of the well and I pour the water in. I can't fill them fast enough and the goats fight to get their heads in, climbing over each other until it's a hairy mess of horns and top nolls. Addi comes out to help and we shout at each other above the cacophony of bleating and calling.

Two young boys, the herdsmen, walk up: Samir in a green turban and Hamid in a blue *boubou* (robe). Addi had been busy in the mess tent and brings out a chocolate cake and glasses of spicy coffee and we all sit down on the rug. There is a delicacy of manners to nomad hospitality, and part of that is that these boys are treated very much as young men and an important part of the gathering. Addi cuts off generous pieces of cake and Samir reties his turban before saying '*Bismillah*' and then tucking in. Nomad news is always long and detailed and Addi has questions on herd numbers, family tree, water availability, market prices and then who he and the boys might know in common. The family live in a low white house we can see in the distance and own nineteen camels, which Hamid is on his way to guard overnight. First of all, though, he has a good go with my binoculars, which he loves.

So far, we have been lucky with the weather, but one morning I wake up and stick my head outside the tent, only to have it almost blown off. The wind has arrived. I rummage in my bags and come out with my ski goggles. They are large and foam-covered on the inside with snazzy orange lenses. 'What are you wearing?' gasps Addi when he sees me, in admiration I like to think. Brahim tries to educate me in the different kinds of wind.

Comes with the sunrise from the east and lasts till noon.

Comes with the sun from the east but lasts all the way till sunset.

Comes any time and can last for three days.

The last one is the one we really have to worry about, he says, not telling me about the Saharan wind, which I will later come to know so well.

The wind is still up when we camp. We have established a routine where Brahim and I put up Le Petit Fromage and Addi and Ali or BB put up the mess tent. There is only one mallet for the pegs which Addi always gets hold of and he always gets the mess tent up first. On this day, Brahim decides to change that, 'Zirbi, zirbi, hurry up, Zahra, look at Addi. Hurry up with the tent.' I understand immediately and have unloaded Hamish in a trice. Brahim grabs Le Petit Fromage and I go scouring for the pegs. Addi has hidden the hammer as usual, but I find a perfect rock. Addi spots what's happening. 'Zirbi, Ali, zirbi!' he yells. 'Zirbi, Zahra, zirbi,' yells Brahim. Sparks fly as the pegs are hammered in at top speed. Our iron pole goes into the coping stone and I see my chance: Addi has put down the mallet; I run and grab it. Brahim hammers in the rest of our pegs and then I return it – very slowly. We are up. We are first.

'Oghir aytsh,' says Addi sulkily at lunch. 'I don't want to eat.' I think he's joking but he isn't. The whole of the meal is interspersed with 'But I had three camels to unload, you just had two,' 'The mess tent is much harder to put up than Le Petit Fromage,' and 'Ali was way too slow.' Brahim and I snort our way through the salad and sardines. Victory is sweet.

5

THE GIANTS OF THE DRAA

Zawiya Moulay Ali Sharif – Mdawwr Saghir

3 February 2019

We are not far from Zawiya Moulay Ali Sharif when Brahim points to the graveyard we're passing, 'Look, there are the graves of the *kubbar*, big ones.' Arabic being what it is, *kubbar* has a number of possible meanings including 'old', 'senior', 'big', 'great', 'the elders' and so on. Fortunately, I have a clue. The graves he's pointing to are about four metres long. In Islam, you're buried with your face towards Mecca with a stone at your head and a stone at your feet. So, does this mean that these are the graves of giants?

Addi scrambles over to have a look and Ali and Brahim tell me what they know, which isn't a huge amount. There are a couple of dozen of these graves in the Draa, including the famous one at Sidi Najji. 'Early men used to be a lot bigger than us and live a lot longer than us. How tall do you think Adam was? In those days, men had a lot more that they had to accomplish so they needed the extra size and years. Now, we have less to do,' Brahim tells me. 'Could it be that they were just important men in the community and so their heights were exaggerated as a kind of mark of respect?' I ask. There is no real answer to this and Ali points out that there are some very tall Moroccans, and that is why they have a good basketball team, which sidetracks us a bit.

The graveyards we are passing by are still in use, and this area is a halfway house between rich oases and dry desert. The waterflow is regulated by the dam, which benefits the agriculture higher up, but it also cuts out the floods that would have occurred in this area every two to five years. Then, the Draa would burst its banks and cover the surrounding flat spaces, soaking into the earth and rendering it cultivable. People would come and farm the land very intensively while the water lasted, setting up temporary encampments of clay and stone or just their tents, and then move on. Since the '70s, those areas have been drying out, and now, in the bottom of the valleys we walk through, we find only the remnants of clay cooking pots and sometimes a smooth oblong grinding stone, which would have been used to crush wheat and corn into flour. The last crocodile was seen in the area in living memory – around fifty years ago.

Black and white birds about the size of sparrows have been coming to our bivouacs every evening. The men call them Mulla Mulla birds. In the days of the great caravan trade, these birds had a very special role. They used to follow the caravans in great flocks, attracted by the fodder that was carried for the animals. As they are homing birds, like carrier pigeons, they would follow the caravans back home too and that is where they played their part. When they had almost reached home, they would fly ahead singing out their sharp song and then the children would know that their fathers were coming home and run out to meet them on the road.

We pass the last big expanse of sweet water we will see for

a few weeks, with colonies of birds at its far end. Now, we are heading into the dunes for some days, then across into the wilderness where we will have to find wells to restock on water. It is time for another reprovisioning, and Ali leaves us and BB comes back in. That night the mess tent is all tidy, a cake is baked and the tablecloth is back.

For a couple of days, the men have been getting excited. 'We're coming to the sands, Zahra, the real desert,' Brahim says. I know what he means. Even though we've been walking through lots of arid areas where desertification has taken place, and that would absolutely classify geographically, when you say 'desert', the mental image conjured up is one of endless sands in rolling dunes. What surprises me a little is that the team are looking forward to it so much. Sand brings a lot of hassle. You have to bag everything up really tightly to stop it encroaching into every nook and cranny, and walking – for the humans at least – gets much tougher.

Our route is taking us to the outskirts of the great dunes – Erg Chigaga. The top end has become a bit of a tourist enclave. Luxury camps have been set up where you can come out for one night and sleep in a tent with an en-suite shower, a five-course meal with wine, some Berber drummers and rose petals on your bed. I did it once as part of a review for Fodor's and I really enjoyed it. Only now, after weeks on foot and with a new awareness about how precious water is, and how simply the people here live, do I start to question it. Roses don't grow in the desert.

I'd taken my chair up onto the top of a dune to look over the *erg* – the sea. The sun was sinking gold and peach and the far mountains were blue-grey behind. It was the third day of the new moon and a thin silver sliver shone. The sand rippled and ruffled in lapping waves ahead of me to meet the darkening sky. To my left was our little bivouac, our home, and couched in a small hollow just behind it were our five camels. I sat in that still moment between dusk and dark when the sun finally disappears and heard Brahim's voice rise in prayer. I had learnt the prayers so that even though his voice was faint I could follow, 'God hears those that praise him.' Night was coming quickly.

We are in the centre of the dunes and when we hit the biggest dune of the *erg*, BB and I go off to climb, leaving the camels to go round it to save their energy.

BB and I bound up. We are only a couple of days into the sands, so still have plenty of energy for the slip-sliding up, when you take two steps only to slip back down three. The sky is blue and clear, and my gaiters are holding up brilliantly – no sand in the socks. It takes us about an hour to get to the top, but what a view. The waves of the *erg* sweep out on every side: sometimes big, crashing dunes and sometimes layers of silver-crested riffles. The wind is strong and we have to shout to make ourselves heard as we use our *chechs* like flags, waving them at the top in case Addi and Brahim can see us below.

Suddenly, screaming rips through the air. My heart stops and BB and I run to the far edge where it seems to be coming from. Then BB starts laughing, 'Zahra, look, it is yoga. Sometimes the foreign women come here to do that. It is part of their religion. They like to scream in the desert.' I look down and, right enough, at the bottom of the dune I can see a group of tiny figures sitting cross-legged on mats, screaming away. 'Everyone is different,' says BB. 'God hears us all.' I wonder what those women are going through in their daily lives to make them want to come all this way to scream.

We've entered a part of the *erg* called samra, which means

dusky, and the dunes are darker brown than the lighter sand further in. BB tells me that in April they look almost black, as that is the season when the scarabs die and their black shells cover the sands. We've been heading back down to the side of what had been the River Draa. Now, it's a dusty valley lined with tammayt bushes as tall as small trees. The wind blows the sand across the plains till it gets caught in the tammayt roots and lower branches, forming little pyramids with tufts of green popping out of the top. Acacias don't attract it in the same way as they are a tree with one trunk rather than a bush.

We can see traces of abandoned irrigation channels running into non-existent fields. I wonder if this is caused by the damming of the Draa at Mansour Eddahbi. The men think it is, in part, but that it is also because of the continuing decrease in rainfall in Morocco. There hasn't been a heavy, sustained rainfall of the kind that is really good for the crops since 2014. Every year there is rain but not enough to soak the ground. This is a problem which is afflicting the whole of the Sahel, not just Morocco.

I am thinking this through when I almost bang into Hamish's bottom. Brahim had dragged Alasdair to a halt and we had all concertinaed up. 'Stop,' he shouts. We all stop where we stand – I assume there is a snake or some other hazard nearby. 'Look, it's a bone,' says Brahim. 'A human bone; a leg I think.' The rest of us walk up carefully and crouch down. He's right, and as we look around, we see skulls, long leg bones and other less identifiable human remains lying exposed to the elements.

We've stumbled onto an old graveyard, presumably dating from the time that water still ran along the river. We are all tired and hot. It's nearly midday but Brahim is clear that we have to make this right. The wind has uncovered these people but we are going to rebury them. Addi couches the camels and Brahim takes out our hoe from the saddle baskets. He digs trenches for the bones and then moves them delicately into their new resting place and covers them over. Sometimes it's hard to see which bones belong to which person and, in some places, there are just piles of white shards. Addi and I search for stones to put at where we guess their heads and feet to be. It takes a long time and the sun keeps rising in the sky until we hit the real heat of the afternoon. Brahim is pouring in sweat but he keeps going until every fragment of bone is covered and every departed soul is marked with a headstone.

'La budda al mawt, there is no doubt of death,' says Brahim as we walk on. Addi is totally silent and all of us feel that shadow, not just for the death of these individuals and their disappearance into nothingness, but also for the death of a whole area, a whole community. Where there is water, there is life. Where there is no water, there is death, and we are walking across land that has lost its water.

The desert looks empty but it is hiding treasures every-where. Every day, the men find things for me: a fossil with the worm shape of its inhabitant from millions of years ago clearly etched, or shards of ostrich eggs from the time when they were plentiful on the plains. One day, though, Brahim presents me with something I just can't guess at. There are three of them. All are an elongated finger shape and are open, broken, at one end, with a brown crusted shell. I can slip them over my forefinger and they reach down just beyond the second knuckle. They are snakes' eggs, and Brahim found a nest that had just hatched in one of the creases of the dunes. He tells me that the snakes lay around fifty at a time and they would still be in the area somewhere.

I am carrying a snakebite kit with me and always have it

close at hand. If I was bitten, JP had told me, I had to inject the anti-venom in a circle around the bite and keep that area below the heart, and not move at all for twenty-four hours at least, in the hope that it would work its way out. The medicine would act as an anticoagulant and stop the fatal blood clots from forming. This would only work for some types of bite from snake or scorpion, though; if one of us was bitten by a fatal poisoner, we would die.

Snakes kill more humans than any other venomous creature. Each year, up to 5 million people worldwide are estimated to be bitten by snakes and around 100,000 die, with 400,000 more left disabled or disfigured by their injuries – and that is just those that are recorded. Many are not because they occur in such remote places.

In Morocco, there are eight recorded deadly species of snakes, of which seven are from the viper family and one type of cobra, although the cobra is very rare and in fact the only recorded bites are to snake charmers from Jema el Fna, where you can see these poor creatures, who love quiet and solitude, being exposed to the noise and crowds simply to entertain us humans. Of the vipers, five of them are found in the Sahara and in the conditions we are walking through.

When he gave me the kit, I had asked JP what an ordinary Moroccan who didn't have the anticoagulant would do if he got bitten. He told me that he had actually met a man whose young son had been bitten when they were far away from any hospital. There is a bitter gourd that grows in all the arid places; it looks like a small, hard melon, and it is believed to be an anti-venom. This man knew about it and had used it the traditional way. He had taken his knife and scored bloody lines horizontally and vertically across his son's scalp. He then split open the gourd and tied it tightly around the boy's head with his *chech*, placing the fleshy side down onto the open wounds. The boy was kept still and given lots of fluids and ran a high fever but after two days he rallied and recovered. I decided that the best thing all round was to try to not get bitten.

We are running short of water and I assume that we will head out of the dunes and towards the remains of the river and the towns that lie along it, where there were people and taps, but we actually do the opposite and cross further into the interior. After a few hours of walking, we have left all vegetation behind us and are in classic dunes. 'Can you see it?' BB asks me. I can't see anything except for big golden hills. 'Look, follow the tracks, its name is Bou Shintouf.' He points at a whole raft of camel footprints heading towards a dip and as I look along them, my eyes come to rest on a round structure in the middle – a well.

A mini miracle. The water is sweet and cool and great to drink. How can this well be here, though, right in the centre of the sands when there is no visible water source for kilometres and no trees or bushes or any kind of growing thing? It is concrete and has a heavy iron pulley with a rope and an oval-shaped bucket made out of recycled tyre rubber to lower down. At the sides are a series of containers: from a stubby barrel with a wide circumference for the camels to smaller bowls, and a 5-litre oil holder with a narrow neck and its base cut out to act as a funnel into our bidots.

The camels are all thirsty so we fill up the barrel first. Camels have no table manners. They all cram their heads in at once and slurp like crazy, sucking the water in. Then they lift their necks up and shake their heads vigorously, spraying droplets everywhere and soaking you before they bend to the water again. It makes me smile every time. Once we have watered them, we start filling up all our water carriers and drinking ourselves. I drink till my stomach swells, it is so cool, and then pour the rest over my *chech* and cap. It takes about half an hour to get ourselves sorted but just as we are about to leave, BB pours a little into the very smallest bowl and rests it carefully on the lip of the well. 'It's for the birds,' he says. 'We have to look after all of God's creatures.'

Brahim and Addi stop the camels and start pointing and I run up to join them. They have spotted a desert fox in the distance. It's gone by the time I get there. 'Don't worry, Zahra, we can follow the tracks. We will find it,' says Brahim. The fennec is right at the top of the list of things I am hoping to see on the expedition. It is an unbelievably cute-looking animal about the size of a domestic rabbit with enormous ears, a foxy face and silky blonde fur. Its body has totally evolved to cope with the desert conditions of North Africa. The big ears are to dissipate heat and also to listen out for the insects and small mammals that make up its diet along with the occasional bird. Its lifespan is around ten years and it can live with almost no water as it has specially adapted kidneys. Its predators are the eagle owl, jackals and (inevitably) man, who trades them as exotic pets. Fenneko in *Zootopia* and Sonar in *Sonic the Hedgehog* are based on fennecs and is the nickname for the Algerian national football team – Les Fennecs.

What I didn't know, and it would have been very handy, before I set off in pursuit with Brahim, is that fennecs are very sociable animals that live together in groups, and that fennec families dig out large burrows – sometimes 120 metres squared – to live in. These have multiple entrances and exits and adjoin the burrows of other families. They are basically huge warrens under the sand.

'Run, Zahra, run,' yells Brahim, and takes to his heels. If

you've run over sand dunes you will appreciate that it is not easy. The sand sucks you down on the way up and pushes you on the way down. I've developed my very own style over the years in which I resemble a camel spider, hunched over on my tiptoes going up and then leaning back and plunging on the way down. Brahim had told me proudly many times that he weighed 50kg and usually accompanied that with a squeeze of my arm and a cheeky, 'What are you? Double that?' and he runs like a gazelle. He is 50 metres ahead of me in no time. As well as being much lighter, he also has better balance and has no compunction about running along the very tip of the dunes where they fall down sharply on either side. I have to walk as it makes me feel giddy.

He runs on ahead and spots the fennec again. 'Come on, Zahra! Hurry up. What are you behind for?' On he sprints tirelessly. Half an hour later and I am starting to feel it; we've already done about four hours' walking and I am struggling to keep up with his pace. Brahim waits for me at the top of a hill. He looks at me critically, 'Shhh, don't run so heavily, Zahra. You will frighten the fox – it has gone into its burrow down there.' *All very well for Mr 50kg*, I think bitterly.

We slide down and there is the burrow with lots of tracks in and out and small entrance holes. Brahim plunges into a thorny bush and tries to peer inside. I stand behind trying to catch my breath quietly. I know there is no way that fox is coming out and, after waiting for ten minutes and then scouting around for fresh tracks, Brahim finally gives up and we head for camp. 'Don't worry, Zahra, we will see one next time *inchallah*, if you can run better and more quietly.' I doubt my chances.

When JP and I had been plotting the route, I had got very excited about the prospect of the Iriqui Lake, imagining a big expanse of water surrounded by teeming wildlife as promised on its Wikipedia page: oryx, gazelles, hyenas and flamingos. What I found was a poster boy for climate change. The lake and its surrounding area of 23,000 hectares was set up as a national park in 1994 as in times of rain it becomes a richly bio-diverse wetland, but those days of rain seem far behind.

We reach it in the morning and for the whole day we cross it – 25km of dead flat sand. The surface is slightly sinking and crunchy, leaving clear footprints where we pass. The only wildlife we see is one fat green caterpillar with orange horns and legs – *tafanoust n taleb*, the cow of the student. He is making a valiant attempt to move across the top of a ridge of sand, convulsing his body together and elongating it to make progress. He gets about 50cm forward and then a gust of wind comes and blows him over sideways and he has to roll back up and continue. Brahim had been here twenty years ago and said he remembered when it was green. I ask him if it's because of the damming of the Draa, but he says it's just down to lack of rain. Intellectually, I know that climate change is a reality and I understand that this part of the planet is drying out, but that day we walked across 25km of evidence. Erasing the mental picture of flamingos standing elegantly in the water and replacing it with the reality of flat empty sand was a sobering experience.

Addi, at least, spends the time productively. Since he has learnt the call to prayer, he has been encouraged to learn his letters. Walking with Brahim and BB, both of whom are intelligent, educated men and value learning highly, is an ideal opportunity for him to break through and start to read and write. We walk along together chanting, 'Alif, ba, ta. A, B, C' and drawing the symbols in the sand with our sticks.

A new bird joins us called Beloved of the Wind, Aziz

Ar-Ruh, it has a very distinctive flying style, plummeting suddenly to the ground and then bounding up again as though on a trampoline. The countryside has begun to look almost American, with big plains broken up by the occasional jutting mountain.

I know nothing about the way the earth is formed, but my cousin, Charlie Mackenzie, is a geologist and he's always willing to explain what a certain type of terrain may have been caused by, or to point me in the right direction. Morocco is located at a triple junction between a continent (Africa), an ocean (the Atlantic) and an active plate collision zone (the Alpine belt system). Africa is actually moving north towards Europe at a rate of 5mm a year and so, unlike the middle of Australia, which is apparently very static, there is lots of shoving and pushing going on. You can actually hear this in some areas as sand and rubble shift with the infinitesimal movements of the earth, and it is one of the reasons that there are so many rockfalls in the mountains.

The plain we had reached had once been underwater and we found some fantastic fossils etched white against a hard black stone. The most common finds were single or groups of Orthoceras. The Orthoceras lived more than 400 million years ago and was a predecessor of our modern squid. Its name means 'straight horn' and the fossil does look like a unicorn horn impressed into the stone. When it was alive the squid's head would pop out of the fatter top end. It was a carnivore – a hunter of the Paleozoic seas. The Orthoceras operated on a kind of jet-propulsion system. It had an internal tube which ran through all its chambers and when it forced water through it and out the back end, that pushed it forward. It could also go up or down by releasing water and letting air into the tube, which gave it less or more buoyancy. As it successfully hunted down Trilobites and its body grew, the Orthoceras shell would be too small so it would simply grow a dividing wall and build a bigger cell. I have a great example of this, which is forefinger-sized with three distinct and differently sized segments.

Cousin Charlie had told me that the main way that mountains formed was either by being squeezed up from the ground, or by being the remnant of an area that had been heavily eroded. The plug-like mountains we are surrounded by had almost certainly been pushed up by movement from the tectonic plates on the earth's crust. Ahead of us is one characterised by pretty alluvial fans caused by water running off down the sides into the flat beneath. It is called Mdawwr Saghir – the round small one, Amtiti Mzay in Tashlaheet, and is the site of an old army encampment with outposts trained on the Algerian border. It forms a kind of transition from the dunes that we have just come from and at the top we can see the next stage of the journey ahead of us, the wilderness section. From here it looks forbidding: long and flat and empty.

6

THE SPACESHIPS IN THE DESERT

Mdawwr Saghir – south of Ain Ouine Mesdour

14 February 2019

Climbing Mdawwr Saghir is like crossing the Rubicon. We have moved into the Sahel, deeper into Africa. Having done the small version, we turn towards the big one, Mdawwr Kabir ('the big round one'). We're heading west now, towards the Atlantic, and the wind is helping us at our backs. 'From the east it is always cold,' Brahim tells me, and I am glad of it because the sun is hot. Addi is in fine form and hitches his camels behind Hamish so that we can all walk together and he can tell us a story. For the full five hours of that day's walk we are regaled. There are a lot of elements, including nomads, sheep, a baby left in the wild, dates, a serpent and a miracle. But it doesn't end there. There is an engagement, accusations of pre-marital sex possibly leading to the baby in the wild – which causes Brahim and BB some consternation when they have to translate for me – and a reconciliation. This is the pleasure of walking. The sun's heat is mediated by the cool breeze on our backs. There is no person in sight, just the fringes of the mountains and outbursts of acacia (amrad) trees in the sand. There is the sound of Addi's voice bubbling over with laughter or dramatic tension, BB and Brahim's gentle teasing and an occasional harrumph from Hamish. There is nothing to do except walk and be.

The narrative stream is interrupted when BB stoops down and picks up some hard brown pellets. 'Gazelle droppings. They must be near here,' he tells me. We search the landscape. All the men have fantastic eyesight and see things that are absolutely invisible to me. BB spots movement. 'Look over there, in the amrad trees, can you see it?' It must be a good two kilometres away but, with the binoculars, I can just make out a solo gazelle running the length of the thicket. 'It's seen us and is frightened. Now it will run far before it circles back to its family,' BB says.

The whole plain is littered with black stones. I find one which has fossilised clams prettily etched across it but put it back down as it weighs about a pound and the camels are carrying a lot of water. Brahim finds me a single white one called *an-nasr* – the eagle – which is very common in this area. The fossil is well named because it looks exactly like an eagle's head.

We have the plain to ourselves but there are signs of human habitation: round stone-built corrals with roofs made of wood and palm fronds. Cooking utensils are hanging outside, left for when the nomads return. There are also skeletal tent structures with just the wooden branches anchored in the ground, ready for a cover to go over the top. The area is dry with the occasional amrad, but has one narrow strip of green which extends out for quite a distance. When we get nearer I see that it is wild camomile, *ifsi*. The yellow flowers bob around merrily and it smells delicious. We gather it up in armfuls and stash it in the saddlebags for our after-dinner tea. I also put some in Le Petit Fromage under my pillow that night to enjoy the perfume.

Walking uphill is actually a treat after days on the flat, and although Mdawwar Kabir is big, it isn't steep and the camels take it easily in their stride. At the top, Brahim teaches me what I should say every time I reach a summit: 'Allahu Akbar kabiran, wa alhamdulillah kathiran, wa subhan Allah, bukratan wa asila' – a big 'God is Great', and lots of 'Thanks be to God' and 'Praise God' in the morning and the evening. It's a great one to shout out to the wild in Arabic.

The top is covered in enormous porous black boulders that we have to wind between. The rock is sharp and looks like it has been spat from the centre of the earth. It's quite unlike anything we have seen before and I think it is a'a lava which is also found in the Canary Islands. Lava, particularly the basaltic one, comes in two basic types: pahoehoe (pronounced paw-hoey-hoey) and a'a (pronounced ah-ah). Both names come from Hawaii as do lots of other volcanological terms. Cooled pahoehoe lava is easy to walk on because it is smooth, like solidified chocolate, but a'a really isn't. It has a rough, rubbly surface made up of broken lava blocks called clinkers. I can climb over the clinkers – although I'm glad I have my heavier boots on because they are spiny – but Brahim has to snake the camels through them, or they will tear their pads to pieces. Going down, we enter the belly of the Mdawwar – I translated it as 'round one' but dawwara also means 'to circle'. Here it is a ring of hills rather than one on its own, like Mdawwar Saghir, and now we are crossing the centre.

Addi is mid-sentence in his tale of adultery when he turns to our right and runs off at top speed, leaping across the sands and pushing through the scrub. 'It's a hare, look.' Brahim grabs my arm and turns me in the right direction and there is a white tail bobbing ahead of Addi. I send up a treacherous prayer for the hare's escape. We keep walking and about half an hour later Addi catches up, empty-handed. 'No *titliwin* for us tonight,' he says sadly. '*Alhamdullilah,*' I say silently.

Our camp is particularly lovely. It is in the natural bowl of the hills, with three perfectly shaped acacias casting their shade for us and providing food for the camels. There is wood for a fire too. After supper, Addi, refreshed, continues his story and even BB starts to nod off, his eyelids drooping down in the flickering light.

The next day is a short one as we have to meet up with JP. He is taking Brahim away from us for a week to help him with a group of Sufis who come to study and pray in the desert every year. They want Brahim to recite the prayers and the Quran with them. JP converted to Islam many years ago and this group is very important to him. He tells me he has found much solace and peace in the faith and that it gives him a good structure to live his life by. He has always enjoyed joining in the prayers with his men but he confides that some clients don't like to see him doing it. 'I have had a lot of criticism. People say to me that I am weak and brainwashed and that I shouldn't believe in Islam, that it is a religion of war and terrorism. Some can be quite angry and hostile,' he says. 'They seem to see me as some kind of traitor.'

To replace Brahim, we have a young man about Addi's age called Mohamed, and Alicia has come back to join us too and do some more filming. I am delighted to have my friend back and she has also brought us the best gift – a box of very posh 'Explorer's Biscuits' from Fortnum & Mason which includes the magnificent Chocolossus. The clue is in the title. BB's eyes light up at the tin and Addi simply says, 'Zahra, Hanan is better than you are. She should stay with us and you should go.' I hope he's joking. I carry Alicia off to Le Petit Fromage and we make Earl Grey tea on my tiny Esbit stove and catch up while the wind howls outside. The weather has turned cloudy and blustery, the beginning of tempest season.

Mohamed fits right in. BB likes his good manners and politeness and Addi, at last, has someone his age to chum around with and someone more junior than him to boss about. Mohamed wears a peacock-blue *chech* and speaks quite a lot of English, which is great for Alicia. As we walk, he roams off looking for interesting stones, of which he has a good collection, and any interesting plants or wildlife.

Departure the next morning is a little less smooth than normal without Brahim. At break time, we come across a man sitting with a small fire and a pot of tea. Greetings are exchanged and then we all squat down to drink with him. He has one spare glass and we share it round. He tells us his daughter is out on the hill with the goats that we can see behind us and that his family are camped a day's walk away. We had actually met them the day before. A tall, slim man – presumably our new friend's son – had come out to have a chat with us. He knew Brahim and they had exchanged news. He had given us fresh goat's yoghurt and a bottle to take away with us. His pregnant wife was very shy and had stayed half-hidden beside the goat's enclosure, but two of his daughters came over to kiss my hand and say hello.

I begin to feel a little like our little caravan is part of the moving neighbourhood that makes up nomadic life.

From time to time we pass a pit that has obviously been cut into the ground and is blackened at the sides. These are for making charcoal. The wood from the amrad trees is brought over and lit and then the trench is covered with rocks and sand so that the wood can burn very slowly and create the charcoal. The pits are obviously still in use, although it seems to me that wood would be very scarce in this area.

We see our first water since before the dunes. It is a sludgy long tributary with palm trees and vegetation growing round it, originating at some point from the Draa and then popping up from its subterranean course. It isn't good water, though; it is very salty. The banks are completely encrusted in white where the water has dried out and even the camels shy off. They can drink salty water but don't unless they are really thirsty, and they had had water from a well the day before. There are a few extraordinary yellow plants around the edge. They look like rockets and have obviously forced themselves through the dried mud with great force. Piles of cracked mud lie at the bottom of their stems. BB tells me that there may also be fish in the water. The desert fish lay their eggs in the mud and they wait there dormant until some new water comes along. They can stay there for years. When there is a heavy rainfall and a puddle or a small lake forms, they hatch and live until the water evaporates.

'Zahra, ZAHRA!' Addi's voice has a note of urgency in it so I uncurl from my mat where I have been having a sneaky siesta and poke my head outside the tent. I am nose to nose with an enormous green lizard. It flicks its tongue out at me and bulges its eyes. I squawk and retreat into Le Petit Fromage. 'No, no, come out, Zahra. It's fine, I've got it on a string,' Mohamed is beaming at me. The lizard, a *halis*, is the size of my forearm and fat. Its tail is the same length as its body and Mohamed had tied a piece of string round its back legs to stop it escaping. It is trying its best on the ground to get away while Alicia tries to get in for a close-up. Its body is a mixture of greens ranging from bright neon to a darker olive, with dark greyish legs and a mint-green head. They do come in different colours and later on we see a fine red one. The skin is different on his back where it's smoother and has a mesh-like quality, and on the legs where it is armoured. It has a tail straight from the crocodile family. The *halis* is vegetarian but it has strong teeth and jaws and will bite if provoked.

'*Titliwin, titliwin*, kebabs, kebabs, they taste really good. I'll cut his throat and then we will put him over the fire.' Addi's hopping around in excitement. 'No way, Addi.' I don't want to kill this gorgeous thing and I have no idea of its status in the wild. It is the first one I have ever seen. Addi takes the blow in his stride and Mohamed picks it up firmly by the neck and walks out of camp to release it; he had only brought it in to show us. He must have lightning-quick reflexes to have caught it in the first place as the minute he unties the string, the *halis* rockets off and scurries across the stones with a very distinctive undulating movement.

In order to get Alicia to her transport home, we have detoured to a small hamlet right on the banks of the Draa. Palm trees and cultivated fields herald the proximity of the river. The fields are occupied by makeshift scarecrows. Some have trousers, some are sticks with a *chech* and one is a jacket over a tree stump with a pair of trousers wound round his neck – but no head. There aren't too many birds around, so perhaps they work.

Two young women see us and come up to say hello. Addi and Mohamed do a quick rewrap of their *chechs* and straighten up their jellabas in preparation for these pretty visitors. BB hands out biscuits and candied peanuts. There's much giggling and eyelash fluttering and smouldering and then they go on their way, leaving Addi and Mohamed with a spring in their step. Three older women in sequinned skirts and black shawls with the traditional colourful embroidery of the desert are carrying water on their backs from the well back to the village. Each has one large bidot like ours which weigh 25kg. Their backs are bent double and the bidots are rested flat on them, held in place by a strap round the women's foreheads which goes under the base of the container. They move quickly, chatting as they go.

When it's time for Alicia to leave, Addi tries to load me into the truck instead. 'Zahra, you go, we will keep Hanan,' he chortles. 'I love Hanan, she is very, very good. Zahra is *shwiyya*, so so.' When I lunge at him for some physical retribution, he dodges behind Mohamed, laughing all the way. The theme is returned to often.

We are a studious little group in the afternoons after we camp, have lunch and finish our chores. Mohamed is keen to learn English and has a notebook and a phrasebook that we go through together. I am painstakingly writing out all my Tashlaheet phrases and trying to work out the grammar. BB is a good teacher and the day I do my first verb conjugation is a happy one. Mohamed is teaching Addi to write his name in Arabic and Addi shows off his progress. BB looks on benevolently and at around 4 o'clock brings out afternoon tea: spicy Berber coffee made from hot milk with cinnamon, pepper, nutmeg, ginger and, of course, lots of sugar, and fresh pan-cooked bread (*arkhsis*). We sit on the rugs under the shade of a thorn tree and relax before the evening routine of bringing in the camels and organising supper starts. Afternoon tea is a common ritual in Morocco and at home in Imlil, in my family compound, the women do exactly the same thing with hot buttered pancakes and honey.

BB is a master of organising our food so that we eat the fresh stuff first and have something a little bit different every day and save the dried foods till the end when we need them. Addi, on the other hand, comes from the nomad tradition of feast and famine and caters with abundance. 'He has no idea of economy,' sighs BB one lunchtime when he had cooked eggs and Addi still opens the tuna. 'But better no economy than no faith.' He settles himself in for a story.

'There was once a woman who worked very hard. She sowed her seeds and tended them all year round, watering her fields by hand and making sure that no weeds grew. God smiled on her and she reaped a great harvest. She looked over her bounty and was happy. "I will be prudent," she said to herself, "and measure out my grain and my vegetables so that they will last all year long." She created a parcel for every day of the year, carefully measuring out the exact amount and making sure each one was equal. When she came to the end, she realised that she was one day short of a year. "Hmmm, I am one day short so tomorrow I will fast and then I will have enough food for the whole year afterwards."

'The next day she didn't eat anything and she was really hungry. She worked hard, as always, cleaning her house, and sang to herself knowing that she could eat the next day and every day of the year thereafter. That night, she went to bed early to try to forget her empty belly. But God is the Ultimate Judge. In the night, death came for her and she never woke up. Her food for the year went uneaten. You see, she had erred, because she had no faith in God's bounty. We always eat today, because we are Believers and we know that God will provide for us.'

Overeating was about to prove a bit of a problem – not for the humans but for the camels. Camels are greedy. When they are grazing that is not usually a problem, as the sheer logistics of roaming large distances to pull thorny branches off an amrad tree means that they can't really overeat. However, on expedition, we also supplement their diet with oats, which they love. Hamish had overdone it. He is a bit of a bully anyway and had threatened and bitten the others in order to get more than his share. Then, he had drunk copious amounts of water at the well. The end result of this was that his stomach had swelled up like a balloon and when I got close I could actually hear the water swishing around.

He is standing listlessly at the edge of the camp obviously feeling very sorry for himself. This behaviour is so unlike him that we know something is seriously wrong. Normally Hamish is quite rumbunctious and seeing him so quiet, looking at us with big, sad eyes, is terrible. Colic kills in bad cases. Hamish is a biter and has strong teeth so he has to be approached with caution. Mohamed takes the lead and grabs him by his bottom lip at which point Hamish vomits all over him. Addi, avoiding the sick shower, gets him to couch. BB is holding the cure in his hand – warm olive oil, collected in an empty mushroom can.

Nomads have two cures for everything: lemon and olive oil. The oil is going to make him poo and ease the congestion in his stomach. Mohamed holds on firmly to his lower lip and lifts his upper lip and BB approaches with the oil. Hamish promptly bites the can in half and shakes Mohamed off. BB unbends the can and Mohamed takes a stronger grip, getting tossed about as Hamish fights the constriction. Addi takes the can and goes forward. This time he manages to get it down Hamish's throat. Mohamed lets go and Hamish stands up, spraying everyone with bits of oat sick and roaring in indignation. The boys go round to the back end to make sure nothing is obstructing his bottom so that the oats can – with a bit of luck – come out quickly.

'God willing, he will be well,' says BB. 'May God grant him a cure,' says Mohamed. We all leave him to it.

While I am waiting to see if the patient recovers, I set about my notes and it strikes me that on this adventure I get to do the thing that I always dream of: to simply sit under a tree in Africa. I am doing it right now, under an amrad tree. It is cool, almost cold in the shade, whereas in the sun it is still baking hot. Little yellow camomile flowers are growing in clumps around my feet and I can hear the labels on my chair clicking against the metal legs in the breeze. There is birdsong and a hornet buzzing round me hopefully. The delight of it makes me put down my pen. In this moment it is important to *be*, not to *do*.

About three hours later, I go in search of Hamish, following a line of poo and acacia trees. There he is at the end, his belly unswollen, munching happily on a thorny branch, ignoring the sick which is still stuck to his face.

Mohamed continues to bring me different creatures to see. First is a brown locust that was alone (or seemed to be) and surviving on fairly meagre rations. Locusts do swarm in Morocco, wreaking havoc on crops, but this lonely chap poses no threat. The next offering is an Attidor. It's a large iridescent green beetle about the size of a kingfisher but oblong rather than round-bodied. It has two sets of wings and hovers when it flies. It has sparkles of yellow gold on its green carapace and its head is blackish-green with a yellow streak down the middle. It rests quite calmly on Mohamed's hand and lets us look it over until it is ready to fly away.

Addi is getting a bit jealous of Mohamed's prowess and manages to come up with a perfect hawk feather for me with broad brown and beige tiger stripes with stipples of brown on the lighter segments. Mohamed immediately ups the ante. 'Zahra, look over there, wild donkeys.' Away to our left is a herd of about fifteen animals, including foals and a couple of pregnant females. When they see us, they immediately kick up their heels and gallop further off into the hills. Donkeys need water so it is one of the signs that there will be a well nearby. They must have belonged to nomads at some point but had obviously made good their escape and are now living wild. We come across several herds in the area but they always stay well away from us.

One new guest in camp is the giant white moth which is prolific in this region. These come out at night, attracted by our lights, and swarm around us if we eat outside by the fire. They are lovely and will sit on my arm for a moment. Their heads look exactly like an owl face and their wings are a dusky white and grey. Addi hates them and swats and flaps around, trying to get them away from his face and head.

Then, Brahim is returned to us full of stories of the Sufis and applies himself to the day's prayers with renewed passion. Mohamed is sad to go. It has been an adventure for him too.

At camp, we are near a well and I need to do a wash. I am pummelling away when a young woman trots up with two donkeys to get water. She has a toddler with her grandly called Salah Ud Din, the Sword of Religion. He is very small for such a big name. She also has a two-month-old baby strapped to her back. He is tightly swaddled and both his legs are tied together with cloth. This is common practice in Morocco; Abdellah told me he had done it with his son too. It is thought to stop the legs from going bandy and also to make the babies comfortable. The young woman says that she gets quite lonely as her husband is out all day with the flock but that she has everything she needs for life. I can't imagine the depth of her solitude so far from her family or any other young women to share life as a young mother with.

As well as washing, I need to cut my toenails. They are not a thing of beauty. Ever since I massacred my feet by running the Marathon des Sables (MdS), which is six marathons across the desert in six days, my toenails have resembled my dad's, and he is eighty-four. They are yellow and horny and pretty grim. I am trying to get my cutters to widen enough to actually chop them when Brahim sees me and comes hurrying over. Addi arrives to watch. 'No, no, no, Zahra, you need to do it like this,' says Brahim. '*Khatar*, danger!' grins Addi. Brahim cuts them right down to the nub and I flinch and shriek dramatically at requisite points. I thought my whole pinkie toe was going to go at one stage. Then, he carefully collects the clippings, digs a little hole and buries them. 'They are a part of you and they are dead, so they should be buried,' he tells me solemnly.

Water is starting to become a real issue for us. We can't always find it and sometimes have to detour longish distances in the hopes of a well or a pool. Our route becomes a series of zigzags. On this day, we need water badly and actually have to double back when we realise that there is no hope of anything ahead of us but there could be water behind. It is anathema to all of us after a hard morning's walking. We pass a series of walls surrounding the fields made of palm fronds, standing around chest height. They are to keep the sand from blowing in from the desert and swamping the smallholding.

For me, this is to become a place of shame. What do you think the worst crime you can commit is when you are travelling hundreds of kilometres on foot through the desert, surviving from well to well? When you need water for the camels and for yourself? When the sun is beating down mercilessly and you last found water two days before?

It is to drop the bucket down the well. And I plead guilty.

We'd finally camped in a heavenly little oasis about 200 metres from a well of sweet water and the future looked rosy. The tents were up, we'd eaten lunch and it was time to wash both myself and my clothes. My socks were beginning to form their own little exclusion zone. I headed to the well with my little purple bucket in my hand for backup because our big, black bucket was already there.

Depending on the well, sometimes people leave a container or bucket and a rope attached or by the side and sometimes you have to take your own. At this one, we had to take our own and Addi had already been and filled the bidots for camp and watered the camels. Our bucket situation was that we had three of the small sandcastle buckets for washing. I always washed after the men had finished their ablutions. We had two big buckets for all the other things we needed to do in camp including washing the vegetables, doing the washing up, doing our clothes and so on. For the dishes we needed two buckets to help preserve water and maintain good hygiene – one for soap and one for rinsing.

When I got to the well and found our rope and bucket I felt full of confidence in my burgeoning desert experience. I had been on the road a while so felt I could claim a certain expertise in drawing water. *I am an Adventurer Extraordinaire*, I thought to myself, forgetting that old adage about pride and fall. I plunged the black bucket on its blue cord down into the water 10 metres below and waggled it furiously to fill it up. Fill up it did; I heard it *glug glug glug*. I began to pull it to the surface. Only one problem: the rope felt light ... very light ... too light! My heart sinking, I peered down over the lip into the depths and was just in time to see the silver handle disappear below the surface, lost forever. My heart sank further than the bucket.

I rushed back to camp. 'There has been a disaster!' I told BB. 'I've dropped the black bucket down the well! I am so sorry.' That night, supper was spent plotting how we could get it back. 'Tie Addi to a rope and lower him down,' suggested BB. 'The water is too deep,' said Brahim. 'It's actually Addi's fault,' said BB. 'He didn't tie the bucket properly onto the rope.' Addi defended himself vociferously and with my socks unwashed, I sat sadly and stinkily at the back of the tent. 'Zahra, it's the stick for you!' said Addi, softening the threat with a flashing smile and some dates. Washing up had to be done in the big cooking pot and I felt my humiliation keenly.

As we continue, the men, with remarkable self-restraint, restrict themselves to mentioning my crime a mere three to four times per day.

A week later, we are walking through some scrubland in low hills and BB is slightly ahead. Suddenly, he lets out an almighty shout, 'Zahra, Zahra, come quickly, hurry.' I run up, dodging Hamish's teeth as he tries to bite me in passing. I think it might be an animal or an interesting rock, but it's something much more exciting. There, clutched in BB's hand, is an ancient black bucket. It is very worn but it looks sound. 'Praise be to God. It is a miracle!' BB says and I agree wholeheartedly. 'Hmm, it's very old – like you Zahra – and bashed about and it won't hold the water,' says Addi, raining on my parade. 'Trust in God,' says Brahim.

I can't wait to get to camp to try it out. Rarely, in fact never, has anyone looked forward so much to doing the dishes. When the time comes, I fill the miracle bucket to the brim and not a drop of water leaks out. 'Ha!' I say triumphantly to Addi. 'Thanks be to God, the Merciful, the Compassionate,' says Brahim.

Every time I use that bucket I smile and wonder what

the odds are of us finding an intact bucket in the middle of a vast wilderness. I also make sure I tie the rope securely. The bucket is still with me now, with pride of place on my terrace in Imlil.

For a couple of weeks, we have been walking through the empty spaces of the wilderness, with the heat increasing and the wind gathering strength. I am ready for a break by the time JP arrives in a cloud of dust for a little sidebar expedition. Two things you need to know about him is that a) he doesn't need any sleep and b) he is a man who brooks no opposition. With that in mind, there is no snooze button for me when the phone beeps horribly in my ear at 4.45 a.m. I had prepared everything the night before and had told BB that I would just have bread and oil for breakfast to gain time. Grumbling inwardly, in a very un-explorer-like fashion, I stumble to the mess tent and squeeze out a vaguely, and totally falsely cheerful, '*Sabah al Khayr. Taginnt mizayn?*' (Morning. How did you sleep?) Brahim looks at me with sympathetic eyes, Addi smothers a giggle and BB moves his kitchen stool and does a virtual 'Ta, da!' He had got up even earlier than me to make my porridge and coffee. 'I can't let you go for the day with JP with just bread. I know you are Scottish and need your oats,' he whispers.

After prayers, we get ready to set off and the men go back to have some extra snooze time. The arrangement is that we will head off for our detour in the van and then come back late morning and set off together for the day's trek to the next bivouac.

I do a last check of my bag: water, medical kit, wet towel wrapped in plastic to put over my head later in the day and the GoPro with extra batteries. I clamber into the van, squeezed in the front between Ychou and JP. Ychou is a tall, slim streak of a man. The light has that gentle pre-sunrise softness and the cool breeze soothes me. We are in the Draa Valley proper, which comprises a very large flat plain, flanked by two low ridges and dotted all over with waist-high bushes and flat-topped acacia trees. I'm idly scanning the landscape when I catch something out of the corner of my eye.

A flash of red streaks across the valley about 500 metres ahead and to our left. A fox, a fox! At last I have seen a fox after my failed dash in the dunes, although not a fennec. He is a big one, like an elongated and slimmed down Pointer. Fluid as water, he races ahead of us, easily keeping ahead of the van. His red coat flashes and shines, bold in the muted colours of morning. His brush is tipped white and I can see patches of white around his neck and paws. He runs long and low to the earth, the king of his domain, temporarily startled by our noise and strangeness. For about two minutes he stays in range of my straining eyes and I watch this creature enjoying his absolute freedom.

We stop at a pair of acacia trees and JP gets out his Garmin and sets the arrow to the exact spot we need. He had got the GPS co-ordinates from Jacques Gandini's guidebook on 4x4 routes in the area. Ychou stays with the car and as we head off I see him wrapping his *chech* over his face as he stretches out in the shade. The land, which had looked flat from the van, is actually riddled with channels up to about 2 metres deep that were carved out when the rain caused water to flood. They are so deep and narrow that they are almost like tunnels. The earth is dark red and there is lots of vegetation. The green is a welcome relief after the days of dryness and I even find some patches of residually damp ground. I can almost visualise mud. JP's course is straight ahead so I am soon panting as we cross the channels, lunging to get myself over the lip and then scooting down on the other side or taking a big leap and landing in the bottom. All I can see of JP is his head bobbing up and down in front of me. We're heading towards the ridge and as we reach the foot of it, I can see a small cairn or tumulus poking up at the top. JP picks up the pace and we crest the hill.

There is something extraordinary extended out in front of me. A 250-metre stone wing is laid out, with the sun glinting off the stones like mirrors. I stand breathless, completely taken aback by the extent of it. It's so clear and so unexpected, here on the top of a flat ridge in the middle of an empty valley, this vast winged structure formed of carefully laid stones and small rocks. JP sees my face. 'Ha!' he says. 'You see? You see? Now you are glad you came. I know you weren't sure yesterday.' I give him his triumph. He deserves it. This is truly amazing. My heart is thumping in my chest as I look at this strange monument created so many thousands of years ago out here in the wilderness by people whose names and stories have disappeared forever, but whose work bears witness to their existence and their need to create and record. The hair on my arms stands up and I can feel the vibrations of the history of our kind all around me. The quiet is suddenly filled with faint echoes of voices from long ago.

The next couple of hours are spent properly investigating what we can see. We pace the different parts to get an idea of size and use the GPS to fix the important points. The structure is composed of two giant antennae which each stretch out for around 250 metres. They are wing-shaped: wider at the top and narrowing down to a tip with a gentle arch shape. The stones that are laid to make them up are roughly the size of a palm to a fully opened hand and are more or less intact. Between the wings at the top, there is a collection of larger stones forming a body which brings the wings together. These stones are much bigger, but mostly still of a size that I could lift them up (not that I did). At the very top, the structure sharpens into a triangular point with slightly bigger stones again to make it a distinct shape. Then, right in the middle of the body part of the monument is a cairn or tumulus, and this is made of large rocks up to half a metre wide. The other thing we note is that the structure is precisely oriented. The wings are laid out to the north and south and the head points due west towards the sea and the setting sun. I draw rough sketches so that I can remember the shape and use my handspan to measure the stones and the rocks.

JP and I stop for a biscuit and an orange. 'What do you think they are?' I ask. 'I don't know,' says JP, 'but I think they must date from around 7000 BCE and there are three of them on this ridge, but this is the biggest one. They're so impressive; imagine the people who built these. Why did they point them west and how could they get them so exact? There were no drones or GPS in those days but judging from our pacing, the wings are totally symmetrical and we can see from the compass that the head points exactly to the west.' 'It's amazing,' I agree.

What were they? It's so tantalising. Are they ancient temples or graves? Their orientation towards the setting sun and the scale of them give them a god-like feel and they are pointing to the west. Could they have belonged to a cult that worshipped a bird god? Could there be some link to the ancient Egyptians, who had several birds in their pantheon? This last theory feels unlikely purely because of the different nature of the craftsmanship. These structures look firmly Stone Age, made out of the natural materials to hand, unlike the exquisite workmanship and art of the pharaohs. I speculate that the large cairn in the middle could be a tumulus with a grave beneath it. There are tumuli scatted all over the Draa, but they usually stand alone. The orientation towards the setting sun would certainly be appropriate for a grave.

As I'm sitting there, sketching and thinking about what we are looking at, a theme tune pops into my head, 'Da da da dadddadadaaaaa ... Space: the final frontier. These are the voyages of the starship *Enterprise*. Its five-year mission: to explore strange new worlds ...' and the light dawns. *Eureka! I've got it,* I think, *I know the answer. I am Einstein watching the apple fall.*

The structure looks exactly like a spaceship. It has the enormous wings you would need to fly through all of those light years. The cairn in the middle is obviously the bridge where Captain Kirk, or his like, sits in his big chair, and the triangular bit at the front is where the pilots steer through the stars. The filled-in body could be the main part of the ship. I warm to my theme and share it with JP. 'Possibly,' is his dampening response. But I am actually starting to believe myself. There are three of them depicted on this ridge and they all look identical but are of slightly different sizes. It could have been a spaceship patrol heading west and the people of the time just built what they had seen. Who needs Google when you have an imagination?

As it happens, Google would not have been much help to me. When I got back, I started searching for any information I could find on the spaceships – or antennae as they are more often called. Scientists have very little on them. What I could glean is that they are found in reasonable concentration in the Draa and there are some further afield in the Sahara. They are thought to be burial sites and the orientation is considered important. It's believed that many are from the days when the Sahara was greener and inhabited by non-nomadic groups of people (8000–5000 BCE) but some of the structures catalogued could be newer, as recent as 1000 BCE. There is so much still to learn about the history and prehistory of this region – all sorts of jewels buried in the sand.

7

THE FOREST OF STONES

South of Ain Ouin Mesdour – the sea

15 March 2019

Water has now become our major preoccupation. We are nearing the sea and the end of our journey but the Draa has disappeared underground or dried up and wells are fewer and further between.

I am learning how to try to find those occasional wells. The first and best way is to ask a nomad. We pass a person every couple of days or so and after greetings and enquiries about their health and the health of their family, we ask where the nearest well is. The directions are always brilliant. 'You walk for half a day towards the sun with the wind on your right. When you are entering an oued between two lines of hills, look to your right and you will see a *tafrukht* (palm tree). There, you will find water.'

The second way is to use animal tracks. Camels and desert foxes, as we know, can survive long periods without drinking but most other animals can't. If we are in an area where nomads still have flocks, it's relatively easy, as the tracks from the herd will lead us to a source. Another good guide is the wild donkeys, who never stray too far from water. Palm trees are also a sign. They need water to grow, so there is a chance of finding it there. The only problem with that is if there isn't an associated well and the water hasn't surfaced. Then, you need to dig. Fortunately, we never got to that state of emergency.

On this day, the terrain is flat with canyons eroded into it where water has been at one stage but no longer exists. It's getting near bivouac time and we're down to our last bidot of 25 litres. We're now in March and the temperature has risen into the late thirties Celsius. Ahead of us, a grove of palms emerges and we all get excited. It's quite big so surely there's water there, but when we arrive we find we were wrong. There's none. We hadn't passed any nomads or animals that day and there are no visible animal tracks. We are running out of options. Addi and I are left with the camels and BB and Brahim take to the hills on either side of us to gain some elevation and see what they can. They come back with nothing and we carry on.

There is a well shape in the distance and we aim straight for it, but when we get there it's been concreted up. There are lots of different reasons for wells to be concreted over – usually it is when the water is gone and it's been made safe but sometimes it is because of water wars. At one camp, we had been told that the well was disputed between two tribal families. Both wanted exclusive rights and they started to fight each other over it, carrying out raids. Attempted negotiations failed and eventually, to stop the violence, the authorities came in and poured concrete into the living well. Each family then had to dig a new well in their own undisputed territory.

Beside the concreted well is a square metal container about a metre and a half across and a metre high. It is covered in cloth with plastic on top. It's a cistern and Brahim explains that if there are nomads in the area then the military will come and fill it for them. Addi wrestles the top off to check if there is anything inside but again we are disappointed.

By now, we're all really tired and the canyon that we've been following has deepened and widened. It's filled with acacia trees which could mean some kind of source. We still have 25 litres and since both the team and the camels have had enough, we stop and set up camp. Addi takes off straight after we have done the tents to scout and arrives back, drenched with sweat, just as the rest of us are finishing up lunch. He has run all the way and is flushed with success, as well as the heat, because he has found a well. When I ask him how, he laughs, 'Don't you see them, Zahra? The nomad tracks. They took me straight there.' I can't see anything.

Immediately after prayers, he and Brahim set off again carrying the bidots and an hour and a half later get back with them full. They must be exhausted but neither complain. I would have been moaning like mad if I had had to do it, but they are just happy to have got us what we need. Not only that, but we also each get a full bucket of water heated over the gas – the miracle bucket, not the little sandcastle ones – to wash in. I find a secluded bush, strip off and scrub.

It is tough, experiencing the lack of water so viscerally, and the next day I record a short piece to camera on my iPhone:

'Everything is dead. There's no water. There are the stubs of palm trees behind me. I'm actually sitting on the lip of a beautiful concrete well. There's no water in it, just sand at the bottom. We've been walking for days now across a landscape that is dying or dead. Even the acacia trees can't live where there is absolutely no water. There has been a drought here. The nomads are gone. We haven't even seen any little mice.

There are no words really to describe what it feels like to be walking across a landscape that's not only dying but is dead. It still has its incredible beauty, but if I think about what it means that twenty years ago there were people here, there were nomads here, there were flocks here, there were camels here, there was a whole infrastructure and way of life and now there is nothing and that is just in twenty years.'

One of the chief aims of the expedition is to see what effects the damming of the Draa in the north had on the more southern reaches, and clearly it has deprived them of water. Before I had started this journey, I had cast human intervention, by building the dam, as the villain, but, in fact, the dam conserves resources in many ways. The bigger story, the more important factor, is the lack of rainfall over the past few decades.

Most of us believe that climate change is happening. We've been shown its effects and read about it too often for it to be in real doubt. Morocco dries up, Britain floods, hurricanes sweep across the Pacific and we are inundated with information in the media. It can be very overwhelming and confusing and all sides on the argument use statistics to fight their own case. Doing this long, slow journey across a large distance over a lengthy period of time, I was able to actually observe and feel what is happening close up.

When we started, we had water every day and even though the landscape was sparse – barren to my uneducated eyes – it supported a lot of life. Then, we'd walked over the graveyards of fields that no longer had any water and the actual bones of ancient communities that could no longer live where they had for millennia. Now we were in an area where even the hardiest of trees were dying. The statistics are just a numerical way of proving what I have seen with my own eyes. Due to its geographical position, Morocco is vulnerable to the effects of climate change. When China or the EU or USA pump out climate polluters, the effects are felt in Morocco. It has two seaboards and then it stretches into the Sahara.

These statistics from the World Bank (they are for Morocco from roughly Layoune northwards with the disputed area of the Western Sahara calculated separately) confirm what I had encountered by walking across the country.

Morocco has a diverse climate, as you would expect from its varied geography. There are the desert conditions of the Sahara to the alpine conditions of the High Atlas Mountains.

The temperature is rising fast. The mean annual temperature has increased at an average rate of 0.2°C per decade. But that number is zooming up. Current predictions are that the annual temperature will increase by 1.1 to 3.5°C by 2060, and that will happen more intensely in the interior than on the coast.

In a double whammy of misfortune, rainfall is decreasing. The mean annual precipitation is just 318.81mm (1901–2016) and that is predicted to go down by a whopping 17 per cent by 2050. Droughts are happening every three years instead of every decade. To give an example: in 2016, 70 per cent of the entire wheat crop of the country failed because there wasn't any rain.

What that means for humans, according to the UN, is that by 2025, over a third of the population will be suffering from water poverty. They simply won't have enough of something that none of us can live without.

Climate change and water scarcity are really high up on the Moroccan government's agenda and they are the leader in Africa and, I would argue, one of the leaders in the world – coming second after Sweden in the Climate Change

Performance Index (CCPI) in 2019 – in driving through national change. Morocco actually passed a Water Law in 1995 and projects like the Noor Solar Power Station, the Green Morocco Plan to help small farmers, and initiatives like the National Drought Observatory all help. However, Morocco cannot cut the emissions of the big, industrialised nations which are contributing to the change in climate. Until our individual consumption, which fuels those emissions, is slowed down – and that basically means buying less, using less and throwing less away – it seems inevitable that Morocco will continue to dry out.

These gloomy thoughts and my realisation of the part I play in it all – I like shopping and have way more clothes than I need, I eat more food than I need and I like travelling and fly a lot – are not helpful at all as I'm trudging across the rock-filled plains. What is extremely helpful is BB's genius in the camp kitchen. 'I am making something special,' he says, and dives into the boiling heat of the mess tent.

At 5 o'clock, we are all called over to the rug which has been set out under the shade of an acacia tree. The tablecloth is laid and on it our battered teapot full of spicy Berber coffee and three tea glasses. There is also a mysterious plate, clearly piled high, covered in a red checked cloth. We all sit down expectantly and BB whips off the cloth. Underneath is a mound of hot *svenj*, Moroccan doughnuts. These are big triangular puffs of fried dough. You pop the puff with your spoon and then dollop in strawberry jam. A jam doughnut is a treat at the best of times; imagine what they taste like to us after weeks of expedition and on the toughest stage. We all stuff our faces, even Brahim. Addi and I end up with jam everywhere and none of us have much appetite for supper. My love for BB grows.

A new type of tree makes an appearance. It's yellowish and short and stubby. It produces a fruit that looks like a watermelon for mice and when I peel it, it's brown and fibrous inside. I taste it with my tongue and it tastes sweet but the men tell me not to eat it so I leave it after a couple of licks. It has thorns the size of medium carpentry nails. That brings my thorn count up to six:

The ones as big as nails from the new trees.

The round spiky ones that look just like a morning star – the medieval weapon used by knights to create maximum damage.

Amrad thorns which are thick needles.

The little fine hair thorns that you can barely see but that rub off on you from their host plant and irritate anything they can find.

The big round spiky ones like a WWII naval mine.

And finally, the Big Daddy of them all, the 'one that puts the lion to sleep' (*msagn izm*), so-called because tradition has it that it entered a lion's paw and killed him.

Walking around barefoot for me is not an option as getting an injury in my overworked feet is not an attractive thought. My rather charming plastic, pink, Hello Kitty sandals are my footwear of choice in camp but I still have to keep my eyes open while walking in them as the bigger thorns go right through. One enjoyable evening task is pulling off all of the type number 2 that have got stuck there throughout the afternoon.

We have had several days across an area of spirit-breaking black stones. The heat has ramped up, the wind has ramped up and it is hard underfoot with my feet slipping and ankles twisting over the kilometres of rocks. The one consolation is that when the wind is strong, there are no mosquitoes. We see the occasional bird of prey circling above us, and BB spots a chameleon hiding in full sight one morning.

Sometimes we find a small oasis and at one of these there is a ruined house on a mound, with some water beneath and clumps of palm trees where we stop for our elevenses.

'Everyone's left; they've gone to the town. It's finished,' says Brahim sadly.

'I'd like to live here in the wild,' I muse.

'No,' he says. 'You wouldn't. You say you'd like to live in the wild but you don't really want to live in the wild. You would bring everything with you: your computer, water from a tank, a kitchen, power . . . You just want the peace; that is not the reality. You don't truly want to live here. Imagine if you are a nomad and you have your sheep and goats and they get sick. They are all you have. What do you do? In the morning, all you have for breakfast is some sweet tea. At supper you just have some bread. You will have to marry because just looking after the goats is a full-time job and how would you also have time to cook? Or to go to the market? You have to have two people at least.'

BB tries to inject a more positive note: 'You could sell two goats at 500 MAD each [£40] and buy everything you need: flour, gas, sugar, tea, lentils and porridge.'

Brahim: 'Porridge? What is this talk of porridge? Where are you going to buy porridge here?'

Me: 'And seeds, don't forget them. I could plant a garden with carrots and turnips and tomatoes and I could have chickens and have eggs.'

Brahim: 'The goats will eat the garden straight away. You are going to have to choose – goats or garden.'

BB: 'Choose the garden. You can eat lots of different things and it is nicer.'

Me: 'The garden.'

Brahim: 'And what if there is a hailstorm and you lose everything?'

I can't help but think this is a tad negative or, given the fact that it looks like it hasn't rained here since 1902, perhaps it is positive in some ways.

Brahim has the last word: 'Gardens cost money. Yours has just been flattened by a hailstorm. How will you pay for sugar and tea? You want a dream – but the reality is very different.'

It keeps getting hotter and we're walking longer and faster because we want to make our finishing date. I'm getting to the stage where I am so tired and heat-ridden I want to be cross with someone. This feeling is inevitable in any long, physical journey and is the payback for all the peace and calm you feel while walking and being part of nature. Unfortunately, the men are so kind to me I have no one to be cross with. This makes me even crosser. BB has taken to soaking one of the kitchen blue-checked dish cloths with water at around 11 a.m. and putting it on my head over my cap and *chech* to try to keep my head cool. It really works but the downside is that it smells of old onions. Addi comes bounding up at intervals to offer me water. In camp one night, he had adapted a couple of our day water bottles nomad-style. He had cut up a bit off the old rug, wrapped it round a Sidi Ali mineral water bottle and sewed it on with thick green twine. Then, he had drilled a hole in a sweetcorn can and attached it to the bottle with more twine. Once the outside rug is soaked it cools down the water inside and every time you drink, you just tip a little onto the top of the bottle and it keeps the temperature down.

Desperate for something to grumble about, I say to Brahim, 'We are walking so fast I have no chance to pee. If I do then it's too hard to catch up with you again.' '*La budda* – no doubt about that,' he laughs. 'Look, there is a good tree. Go behind it and we will wait for you.' I'm foiled of my rage again, and, what's more, I am so dehydrated I can't even wee.

The landscape is flat with hills on one side and the ground underfoot is reasonable. Every so often, nature offers a little gift for us to enjoy. 'Zahra, a *tammamayt*,' says Brahim. A perfect brown hawk is sitting slightly ahead of us to our right watching us with unblinking eyes and stretching out her wings. I don't understand the significance of this but Brahim does; he searches the ground and finds her nest. She has two blue eggs in it and it's right in our path. We detour the camels to avoid it and when I look back, she is settling herself down on her babies.

Addi, unlike me, does have a target for his expedition frustration – his mobile phone. It is an ancient model which he had bought in the market very cheaply and which works only intermittently. It won't hold a charge and, in spite of our best efforts, using my biggest solar battery and an adapter that actually fits, it finally decides to stay dead. Addi lets out a long stream of Tashlaheet words which I am glad to say I understand none of and then dashes it down onto the rocks, where it shatters. 'What are you doing, Addi?' asks a horrified BB. 'You could have taken it to an engineer when we got back home and maybe had it fixed.' 'It's rubbish. I don't want it. I will buy a new one,' retorts Addi. BB's thrifty soul is mortified. 'You have no patience, Addi. Shame on you.'

That afternoon, Brahim comes back into camp after rounding up the camels from their grazing and calls, 'Addi, come here, I have been to the *hanout* [small shop] and got you a present.' Addi takes the offering and starts laughing. It is a stone shaped exactly like a mobile phone. We charge it up with a twig and after that Addi intermittently pulls it out of his pocket and phones friends and family.

We have settled into 40°C heat by 10 a.m. and I am wishing we were camped up. Three hours of trudging later, two birds fly past. 'Water chickens! *Tafaloost n aman*,' shouts Addi, and sure enough, they quack. Where there are ducks, there must be water. Our spirits rise. At last, we see a small clump of palms and Addi spots a trough and a group of camels close by. When we get there, the water is salty but our camels drink thirstily and at least we have enough water to wash and do the dishes.

We camp under a couple of amrad trees with Le Petit Fromage and the mess tent on opposite sides of a rough track. Lunch is a very simple salad, but after the long trudge it tastes fantastic and we eat it outside on the rug in the shade. A big flock of goats comes and surrounds our camp looking for scraps. They are obviously intrigued by Le Petit Fromage and I have to dissuade a couple of them from home invasion. A trio of black and white spotted ones with good-sized horns hit payday with the onion skins and pepper seeds and hoover them up. I wave at the girl who is shepherding them from her donkey and she waves back but won't come any closer, so I pour a glass of tea and set off over to her.

Her name is Mbarka – the blessed one. She is sixteen, dressed in a thick fluffy pink jellaba and leggings and has a big scarf wrapped over her cap. It must be hot in there, but it is a good defence against the sun. Her donkey is small with lambent eyes and long furry ears that he doesn't mind me stroking. She has no bridle and a carpet as a saddle, with two saddlebags from which she produces some soured goat's milk and water and offers it to us. I try to give her the tea but she waves it away. 'I don't like tea,' she tells me. She is the only

Moroccan I have ever met who doesn't. Brahim had seen what was happening and comes over with some more welcome alternatives, oranges and chocolate, which go down a treat. She is happy to chat away with me and wants my phone number, which I give her. She spends most days out with the goats on her donkey with some bread, water and the *aghro* (drinking yoghurt).

The people of this region are Arabs and speak Hassaniyya. Because of the proximity to the Algerian border, as well as the disputed territory of the Western Sahara further south, there are lots of connections to the military. An old soldier comes to visit us in camp. He arrives carrying a black and white baby goat who is too young to roam with her mother, and is riding up front with him in his Land Rover while his herd is out grazing. Mbarak had retired after thirty years in the army. He tells us he had fought in the 1970s wars in the south and that his children live in Tan Tan on the coast. After so long in service, he couldn't settle with them, so he lives out of his Land Rover and spends his time in the wilderness caring for his small flock. I sit in the shade playing with the little goat and feeding her scraps I've begged off BB. She nestles on my chest and butts up under my chin just like a cat. I don't want to let her go. I love goats.

At supper, Brahim is very thoughtful and talks about how he sees Mbarak's life. 'He had thirty years in the army. He paid all that time for his wife and his children. But now the children are grown and in Tan Tan. They stay with the mother. They always go to the mother. After all that time and work, he was left with nothing. How many more men like Mbarak are there in Azilal, our main town in Ait Bougemez?'

I wake up feeling refreshed and surprisingly unsweaty and stick my head out of the tent. Mist. I haven't seen mist for months. The wind is blowing inland bringing the cooler, wetter air from the sea. It feels so good on my face and arms. The sun is rising over a flat-topped mountain through a miasma of clouds. We're heading for the hills again after a long stretch on the plains. The vegetation changes too. There are deep channels in the ground where neon-green shrubs live in the shade sucking their moisture from the air. These support families of tiny birds. The amrad trees have given way to argan trees, which the camels also eat.

The land underfoot is still dry and we're happy when we see a tannoutfi in the distance. This is a type of underground concrete cistern which is filled by rainwater. There is a concrete runnel leading into the cavity and this lets the surface water drain in. In front of it is a basin that collects twigs and detritus before they roll into it. It's covered by a heavy iron lid and is unlocked. Some wells are locked and have a guardian nearby and some have pitched 'roofs' so that the water can run off into the channels and not be wasted.

A little white and grey donkey is waiting beside it. We bring our camels up and she, surprisingly, stays close and doesn't go galloping off braying as donkeys normally do when they see our boys. 'She's thirsty,' says BB. Addi wrestles off the lid. 'It's empty.' Fortunately, there's another one not far off. The reason for this abundance is that we are close to the shrine of Tafraoute, and visitors need water. The little donkey trots after us.

Luckily, the next tannoutfi has water in it. We get out the ropes and the miracle bucket and the men start pulling the water up. The first thing they do is cut down one of our five-litre water bottles to make a deep bowl. They fill it up and bring it to the little donkey. She sticks her muzzle in as far as it can go and drinks it up thirstily. Addi filled that makeshift bowl up ten times and the little donkey drained it down every time until she was full. Then, she shook her head, lifted her tail and trotted off. Since then, I have always kept a bucket and a piece of rope in the car, just in case I come across a thirsty animal when I'm on the road.

I am enjoying the coolness of the humidity but it has brought its own particular share of problems. Two of those are creatures. My tent is infested with Ami Wislan – My Uncle (on my father's side) of Two Claws. My two-clawed uncle is an insect with a long, slim body and two big pincers on the ends of his forelegs. It is very disconcerting to lay my weary head on my pillow and come face to face with those pincers waving at me. The men are entertained in the evenings by a series of shrieks as the creatures crawl and scrabble over my legs. In the end, I decide to sacrifice my dignity and ask Brahim to come in and clear Le Petit Fromage before I go to bed.

The other creature is worse. Ticks. Really big ones. Ticks are the opposite of donkeys; they love camels and apparently they can smell them from a distance. The minute we halt to camp and start unloading, the ground starts to shimmer. It is an optical illusion created by the fat grey ticks running towards us. They must have some kind of bush telegraph – 'Feasting ahead, lads, ETA: twenty minutes.' They differ in size according to how much blood they have managed to suck up, but some of the big ones were the size of my thumb nail and nauseatingly plump. I wear all my clothes, all the time, with trousers tucked into socks so nothing can crawl up inside anything. It is torture for the camels. They are covered in them. Enormous grey ticks cling to the corners of their eyes and behind their ears and under their necks, eating their fill. 'They make the camels sick,' Addi tells me. 'They don't want to eat and it is very bad for the pregnant females and the babies.'

We don't have to worry about any babies with our all–male caravan and they certainly don't seem to be suffering from lack of appetite, galloping up eagerly whenever Addi lays out the tarpaulins of oats for them, and stripping any argan tree they see of its yellow blossom-laden branches. However, prevention is better than cure and so Addi and Brahim gather the boys up to be tarred.

The tar used to treat ticks is a thick, black, oily liquid made from the bark and sap of the juniper tree. It is called 'Ouijane' or 'Qatran' and it smells of the pine of the juniper and engine oil. It is a very strong scent. It not only kills the ticks that are already on the camels but repels any new ones. It is caustic, though, and burns, especially if there are any small nicks in the skin.

Addi wraps his hands in plastic bags and ties them at the wrists with twine. All the camels are brought into a circle, couched and have their halters put on – they fit over the bottom set of teeth. The tar is poured into a cut-off water bottle and then Addi takes another plastic bag, douses it in the stuff, and approaches his first victim: Sausage. He starts in the armpit of his left foreleg. Sausage immediately leaps up and bares his teeth. He is not at all keen. Addi follows him round and scrubs the tar hard into his fur where his legs meet his body and under his neck, then under his belly. Sausage lets out a kick sideways from his left hindleg and Addi leaps out of the way. Camels are double-jointed and can catch you unawares. Brahim manages to couch Sausage again, who is grumbling and roaring, and Addi goes back in.

Now it is the hard bit – round the bottom. Addi grabs up Sausage's tail and scrubs around his bottom hole. Sausage lets out an almighty bellow of protest, with which I have a great deal of sympathy. I certainly wouldn't fancy someone putting that nasty stingy stuff in a sensitive region. He leaps to his feet but Brahim wrestles him down again. His tail is swishing round and round like a helicopter's rotary blade. 'The ticks are leaving – direct! Straight away,' says Addi as he scrubs. Back to the delicate area and Sausage is up like a shot and running in rings round Brahim. Addi goes to the front and grabs him by the lower lip. Camels have quite a long bottom lip and you can get a good hunk of it if you need to stop their heads moving, or to open their mouths. Sausage is in full-on roaring mode by now as Addi does his face, avoiding the eyes. The tar is so strong that it must be stinging Sausage's eyes; mine water every time I get anywhere near it. By now, poor Sausage has lost the will to live; he lays his head on the ground and just looks at us, his torturers, with immensely sad eyes. His fluffy poll on top of his head and behind his ears are done last and then he is freed and takes to his heels immediately, wanting to put as much distance between him and Addi as possible.

We'd had some bad news. Military exercises meant that we had to do a detour of around 70km to avoid the area where the army were shooting and fake fighting. That added three days to our journey and meant we had to pick up the pace. We could hear the boom of shells firing in the distance. Walking across a landscape that could not support life, the irony was not lost on us.

At lunch, Addi, who is by far the youngest of us at twenty-three, decides to do a bit of stirring.

Addi: 'Zahra, how old are you?'

Me: 'Older than you.'

Addi: 'Brahim, how old are you?'

Brahim: 'I'm forty-five.'

Addi: 'What? Nearly seventy?'

Brahim: 'No!'

Addi: 'But it's kind of the same.'

Brahim: 'No, you have to think of each ten years as a stage. At ten, twenty, thirty and forty everything is perfect. At fifty, sixty, seventy, everything goes down. And the eighty means it is all over. It's the end.'

Me: 'Hmm, but you have to change that for women. We live longer than you, so even in the fifties we are still on the up.'

Brahim: 'That's because you drive more slowly.'

I have no idea if he means that we actually drive more slowly or whether it is a metaphorical reference.

The sea is coming ever closer. Sometimes we walk through the mist till mid-morning and although the vegetation is greener with more succulents, it also saltier and not good for the camels to eat. My favourite plant is one that looks like a small pink starfish, all plumped up and juicy, but inedible. Rain clouds hover overheard but still no rain. We have not had a single drop in the nearly three months that we have been walking.

Inevitably, we all start to think about the end and what will happen next. Our expedition bubble is about to pop. BB is unreservedly excited. He can't wait to get back to his two young sons and to some creature comforts. Addi is more in the moment. He is speculating on what he can buy when he gets to the market and he's looking forward to seeing Lalla Ito, his mum, and the rest of his family. Brahim expresses my own feelings, 'Separation is hard, Zahra. What awaits us behind the sea?'

I am dreading the end. By now I am physically tired and

want a break from the daily challenge of the expedition. I know that I can't just walk forever with my gang, but we have become such a unit I don't know how I can part with them. I have lots of exciting things ahead of me, including seeing my own family back in Scotland, the launch of my book *Adventures in Morocco* and festivals to go and talk at, but when I think of waking up to an alarm instead of Brahim's prayers, I feel overwhelmed with gloom. Ending an expedition is always like this. It is God's little joke: the more you have enjoyed it and immersed yourself, and striven and learnt, the more you will suffer after the end.

But the days run past and finally, with two to go, JP arrives full of excitement. He is ending with us as he has been such an integral part of the organisation and expedition. He'd set off – as was his wont – at 3 in the morning from Ouarzazate with Abdellah, who, after saying his hellos, heads straight behind the mess tent and lies down to sleep with his *chech* wrapped over his face, exhausted. JP bounds up to me, clutching maps. 'Come into the tent. We need to talk.'

BB has tea and cake ready. We sit down on the rug and JP spreads out the map. He traces his finger along the route we have just come, all the way from Ouarzazate, 1,500km winding along the Draa, leaving it and coming back, and ending up here at the edge of the Atlantic at Oued Chbika. But there are two other lines traced on the map in red and in green.

'What are these, JP?'

'They are your next expeditions, Zahra. What do you think? If you do this leg across the Sahara in the autumn and then you can do across the mountains of the Atlas from the Mediterranean to Ouarzazate in the late spring of 2020. That would mean you would have walked the whole of Morocco.'

'With the same team? And Hamish?'

The Draa Expedition

9 January–26 March 2019

The Mansour Eddahbi barrage is bathed in golden light at the end of the first day of our expedition.

Plotting the route for the trip ahead, with Addi (far left), Brahmin (left), JP (centre) and BB (right).

Addi and Callum outside the village of Tanamroute.

Addi gets ready to take a bite out of a succulent cactus he claimed was as sweet as honey. I fell for it.

Rock carvings at Foum Chenna, some of which have been dated back to 2500 BCE (left). An oasis filled with date trees, after the barren landscape we had been going through, this felt like we were on a different planet (right).

While the men went to the mosque, the women decided to dress me up as a Moroccan bride. You can see the big red tassles of the belt Hassna made for her own wedding.

Addi preparing goat kebabs after Brahim and I had been on an expedition.

In the midst of the desert, finding a well can be a huge relief – and you really don't care what size of container you drink from.

Sometimes it's worth getting up early to catch the sunrise.

The last leg of our journey to the sea.

We've made it to the sea, after all our adventures – and it is time to say goodbye to our camels and the rest of the team. But happily JP has an idea for the next expedition.

The Sahara Expedition

26 November 2019–12 February 2020

After eight months away, it was good to be on my adventures once more, but our journey was sure to throw up many challenges.

These intriguing structures, near Batiha, had been built by soldiers to teach them self-reliance.

In the first part of our Sahara expedition, the land was scrubby, with little for our camels to enjoy.

Professor Mouloud proved a handy guide to the ancient artworks we found carved into the stone, like this elephant.

A lovely welcome from a young girl in the Museum of Sahrawi Life in Smara.

This young camel has been lifted onto the back of the truck by the nomads, who will take him off to market for slaughter.

'Of course, with the same team.'

'I'm in, if I can find the money. Yes! Fantastic idea.'

And that is it. I know that I can't guarantee it until I have sponsorship financing in place, but I know absolutely that I want to do it. I feel very strongly that my journey is not over and that I have more to do. I hope that Brahim, Addi and Brahim Boutkhoum will think so too. I have discovered so much on this first leg of the trip and experienced Morocco in such a deep way that I need to know more. I thought I knew the country before I started, but every day has taught me something new. The past few weeks of walking through a land where water is disappearing has shocked me, but I want to find out more and I want the buzz of standing on a windy cliff looking at stone structures built millennia ago. I've also become addicted to the rhythm of the journey. I love the routine and the simplicity. I feel truly alive as I walk across the land. Sometimes I am bored and cross and tired but underneath that I know that I am doing what I am actually designed to do, that I am following the path laid out for me. I don't want to stop now.

Our last day has arrived. I wake up with a mixed bag of emotions.

There is every shade of green along the banks of the oued and in the water itself. Trees and plants grow in abundance and there are swarms of midges rising and settling on the slow-moving or still water. A duck flies past and then a heron. Brilliant dragonflies dart and hover. Two days ago, we could see no water anywhere; now we are surrounded by it. I've been smelling the sea for hours and am sure I can catch the sound of the waves. We crest a small hill and there it is: endless blue touching the sky and swelling up and down like a heartbeat. Our goal is, literally, in sight. We all cheer and chatter. 'I'm going to swim,' says Addi. 'He can't swim – he's a nomad,' says Brahim. 'God give you good health,' says BB. 'We can tie two of the bidots under his armpits to keep him afloat,' is my helpful suggestion, although Addi doesn't seem either grateful or convinced.

The autoroute lies ahead, blocking our way, and even from a distance we can see the big trucks hammering up and down. We send Addi off with a phone as outlook man and gather our boys up at a gap in the barrier. They flinch and dance every time a truck speeds past. When there is nothing in sight, Addi calls us. JP goes on one side and stands in the middle with BB on the other side. Brahim and I lead the camels over and down to the dunes and I hear the waves swishing in and out.

Addi, JP and BB run down and we get to the flat. We have 500 metres to go. My face is wobbling. I am smiling so hard that my lips hurt but at the same time I am having to fight back tears, whether of joy or sadness even I don't know. It is an overwhelming, heart-stopping moment. My heart is beating more loudly than the waves. Then, Addi starts singing, *'Allah, Allah, ya Mama!'* We all join in and our voices scare the seagulls into raucous flight. We link arms, moving forwards with all those kilometres travelled now behind us. Together, united and singing, we walk straight into the sea.

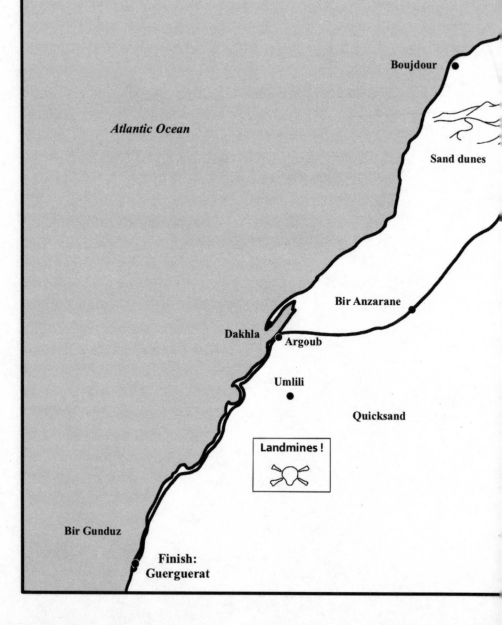

PART TWO

The Sahara Expedition

Atlantic Ocean

Boujdour

Sand dunes

Bir Anzarane

Dakhla
Argoub

Umlili

Quicksand

Landmines !

Bir Gunduz

Finish:
Guerguerat

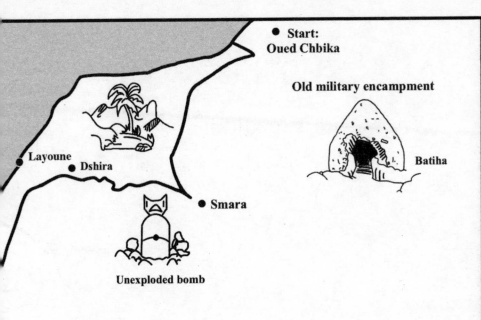

Start:
Oued Chbika

Old military encampment

Batiha

Layoune

Dshira

Smara

Unexploded bomb

8

INTO THE SAHARA

Oued Chbika – Smara

26 November 2019

It had been months of separation and all I could think about during the eleven-hour bus ride from Marrakech to Tan Tan was what it would be like to all be together again, and if Hamish would remember me and let me pet him or just try to bite me. I had brought a whole orange for each camel as a bribe. The baby in front of me cried for the entire eleven hours, exhausting all of us and driving her poor mother to the brink of despair. As we pulled into the station, I saw BB's dapper figure waiting with a big smile and JP beside him. It was a happy reunion. 'Have you learnt to make tea yet?' BB asked me as we drove to our first bivouac, and I told him that I had been holding Amazigh Ladies' Coffee Mornings and using his spicy coffee recipe, thereby dodging the fact that my tea-making was still rudimentary.

It was pitch black as we drove into the bivouac.

'Ahh, that's Brahim,' said JP, and there he was, waiting patiently on top of a slight rise so that he could guide us to our tents.

'Peace be upon you, Zahra.'

'And upon you be peace, Brahim. How are you? I missed you.'

'I am well, thanks be to God. How are you? How is Jeem and Fareeda and Rooby? Are they well?'

'Thanks be to God; they are all well. They send you greetings. How is your health and the health of your family?'

'May God give you health. We are all well, thanks be to God. Addi is sleeping already. Now you must sleep too.'

With our greetings over and promises to catch up tomorrow, Brahim ushered me into Le Petit Fromage, my home from home.

I wake up to the sound of Brahim's prayers and realise how much I have missed it, but I'm dying to be reunited with Hamish, so I quickly dress and bound out to find him, armed with my oranges. Hamish eats his appreciatively but I decide it is too risky to essay a neck stroke – I'll wait till his halter is on. We have a slightly new crew. Hunter is Brahim's new lead camel, who he has named after me, and we have also substituted Hector for Murdo. Hector is from Addi's neck of the woods, Saghro, so we call him Hector Saghro. Addi has finished breakfast and comes loping up and the greetings ritual is recommenced.

Striking camp and loading up, I feel clumsy. It's November, so nearly eight months has passed since we'd walked into the sea and my skills need brushing up on. '*Bismillah*, in the Name of God,' says Brahim, and off we set towards the site of our last Draa camp and the real start of the expedition. 'Look, Zahra, sea goats,' says Brahim, pointing to the flock of gulls paddling in the shallows and wheeling up shrieking with horror when they see the camels coming towards them. We reach our end-of-Draa spot, reminisce briefly and then the expedition proper starts as we break new ground.

I'd agreed to the expedition almost on the spur of the moment when JP had suggested it back in March. The thought of joining up the Draa with a Sahara and an Atlas Mountain stage to walk the whole of Morocco was a fantastic aim and I was blithely all in. In the intervening months, as we got into the detailed planning, I came to realise that this stage was going to be much more complex in many ways.

The Sahara itself was the biggest thing we had to plan around. Water and supplies were going to be tough to get and we needed to make sure we had enough stops and drops scheduled and also back-up plans if we ran out, or got too close to running out for safety. The weather, the sand under-foot making walking harder, and the prevalence of deadly snakes and scorpions all had to be factored in. After the obstacles created by nature, though, was the political issue.

Our route was planned to take us through the Western Sahara. This region is designated as a disputed territory by the United Nations, who officially recognise neither Moroccan nor SADR (Sahrawi Arab Democratic Republic) sovereignty. The area we were to walk through is governed by Morocco. It is one of the least densely populated areas on the planet and the Sahrawi people reflect a highly mixed heritage from Amazigh, Arab and sub-Saharan communities. Sovreignty of the region is very much a live and vital issue and extremely sensitive, provoking passion, and often bitter anger, on all sides.

For me, I wanted to go with open eyes and ears and just see what I could and listen to what the people who lived there were saying.

We cross inland, beginning our journey by heading south

and east towards the desert capital of Smara. This is our first goal. We pass an inland sea lake which is filled by very high tides supplying the sunken bowl not only with water but with fish. This makes it a perfect hunting ground for flamingos and a colony of about 200 of them are situated on the far bank. These ones are more white than pink, but when they fly we catch a bright flash of blush rose on the underside of their wings.

The flamingos are not the only fishermen. A bright-eyed man in a tan corduroy coat with a black *chech* tied high on his head into an impressive turban approaches us. We exchange polite greetings and he asks where we are going. 'If God wills it, we are going to Smara,' says Brahim. 'If God wills it. That is a very long way,' he chuckles. 'Is this one going too?' he points at me. I set aside the indignity of being called 'this one' and confirm that I am. He breaks into surprised and, I hope, delighted laughter. 'May God bless you,' he says. Then it is down to business. He squats on the ground and takes off his satchel, bringing out three fish which are still flapping. They're a reddish colour and quite thin and spiny. BB bargains him down to 20 MAD for the lot (about £1.80). In the meantime, his son has arrived on a motorbike and after money has changed hands and with good wishes for our onward journey, they speed off together flying over the bumps in the track.

Underfoot is a mixture of sand, packed earth and white rock. Embedded in the white rock are thousands of fossils, mainly of clams, scallops and common tower shells or their ancestors. At intervals, there are big indentations in the earth which expose the red underneath. I can't work out what they are. 'That's where the camels couch,' Brahim tells me. 'They like it here because the earth is soft.' I count about two dozen of them and look up to see a herd in the distance. One has a white face. 'Beautiful like Hunter, you are a *boutershweet* and so is Hunter,' says Brahim. *Boutershweet* means 'the one with the white face'. I am not sure if I am being deeply complimented or just compared to a camel (I do have a longish face) – or both – because being compared to a camel is a rare compliment indeed. I decide to test out Brahim, and bear in mind that we have already established that Brahim can't lie. 'Brahim, who is more beautiful? Me or Hunter?' He takes on the look of a man trapped in a corridor with burning doors at both ends. He looks from Hunter (who is rather gorgeous) to me and back again till his head has the blurred effect of something from a sci-fi horror movie.

Brahim is saved by the owner of the camels who approaches on his motorbike. He enquires if ours are the camels that were bivouacked on the dunes the night before and then goes on to ask detailed questions about their heritage and worth. He wants to know where I am from and when I say Britain he looks at me firmly. 'The British? You colonised Saudi Arabia, Qatar, South Africa and Egypt. Colonialists. That is what you are.' He then turns to JP and gives him the same treatment but the French version. I try to put forward that I am a Scot and that we had also been colonised by the English in our history but he is having none of it and finishes by telling me not to photograph his male camel. I am not sure why colonialism and a camel-photo ban go together.

Teeth is the matter under discussion in the bivouac after supper that night. BB has a sore, wobbly one. 'I'll take it out for you,' offers Addi. 'I have the pliers,' Brahim adds. I don't know if they are serious and am very relieved when BB declines. The general consensus, though, is that if you have a sore tooth, the best thing to do is to whip it out. The idea of going to a dentist is roundly pooh-poohed by Addi. 'You can get it done in the suq, Zahra. There is a tooth man there. You go to the pharmacy first and he gives you an injection. Then you go to the tooth man and he pulls it out – direct, straight away and then you put some betadine on. It hurts.'

My stomach is roiling at the thought and the memory of the old man who sits in Jema el Fna in Marrakech with his table of human teeth that you can buy singly or by the set for dentures. Brahim chimes in by tapping his chipped front tooth. 'My boys gave me that,' he laughs. 'They aimed the slingshot badly.' All the men have actually got nice white teeth, although BB and Brahim are missing some back ones, but I ask them why so many people in Morocco have truly terrible teeth and why they don't brush them so they can avoid having mouthfuls of rotting stumps.

Brahim: 'It isn't brushing them, Zahra. It is the water – that is what turns them black.'

Me: 'Not the sugar in the tea?'

Brahim: 'No, no, it isn't the sugar. There are old people in some villages who have perfect teeth because the water is good, but where it is not good our teeth go black.'

We wake up to a thick mist. I can't see the mess tent from LPF it is so dense and the camels loom up suddenly like giant ghosts. Brahim is undeterred and sets off with vigour and without consulting any directional aid; he just knows his way. It burns off and the heat sets in. We pass an encampment with low-lying clay houses. One of the men comes out to meet us but doesn't offer us any hospitality. He tells us that the family lives there permanently and drives in and out of Tan Tan. The well has a solar-powered motor and we fill up the trough for the camels, who gulp it down. He has five children and says that they haven't had any rain but there is still grazing for the animals in the oued.

'Do you think it is a hard life?' I ask the men. 'Not for them, they are used to it. Everyone is used to their own life,' he replies. There's something that is bothering me. 'Why didn't he ask us for tea? It's the first time we have ever met someone who hasn't asked us.' They reply, 'It's hard here because we are being watched and followed by the government and it would be a "heavy tea", *chay taqeel*. They think they might get into trouble – that the authorities might come and ask about us and then about them. Also, maybe it is a status problem. We are visitors so we should go to the qaid's house or the muqaddim's house not just an ordinary person. Or maybe they just don't have enough tea or sugar. Maybe they are just shy. If we came by the well two or three times, then they might offer us tea.'

We head for a gap in the mountains past the village of Batiha to our left. Far in the distance lies a set of ruined buildings and some beehive-shaped clay structures. As we approach, BB explains that it is an old military encampment. We go up the hill through a ruined gate. The first group of structures is three lines of crumbling square huts/rooms on three sides and past that the beehives start. They have entrances like igloos and, once inside, you find yourself in a circular, domed room. They are all different: some have windows; some don't; and one has intricate geometrical brickwork. BB tells me that the first thing the soldiers have to do when they get to camp is to make their own shelters from what they have to hand. This teaches them self-reliance. Here, there's mud to make bricks and compressed walls but no timber and that's why they prefer the domed roofs. Perhaps the man who had built the room with the geometrical brickwork had that trade in his family and learnt it from his father. There is also a ruined mosque which we can see because of the position of the *minbar* – which is used by the imam.

We leave through a series of small gorges and exit on to a high plateau. To our left is a modern military camp, the rows of tanks contrasting oddly with the beehives we have just left. There are lots of donkey tracks criss-crossing. 'They bring food and supplies and the herdsman use them,' Brahim tells me. A jeep with two men in it comes whizzing up. I am worried that they might stop us, but I have reckoned without our superpower – the camels. In the jeep are a soldier and a gendarme and they greet us quickly and then go straight to the boys and start patting their noses and tickling their chins. 'Look out for that one, Hamish, he bites,' I feel obliged to warn them. The soldier turns to me. 'You do know that you are in a forbidden military zone. Civilians are not meant to be here.' I look chastened. He smiles kindly. 'Never mind, you are very welcome. It is not a problem. Do you need any water? Do you need any food? If you need anything, let us know. If you need anything at all, just call us. I gave Brahim my number. We are ready to help you with everything. Can I have a picture with you and the camels?' We part after extensive farewells.

It is bread-making day in camp.

Addi: 'Zahra, today you need to make the bread.'

Me: 'No, Addi, that is your job. My job is to sit on this comfortable chair and drink tea and write.'

Addi: 'No, no, no. You are a woman. The women look after the children, make the bread and make the soup. I am a man. The men do everything outside the tent. They work outside and the women work inside. This is the law.'

Me: 'In Scotland, the men make the bread.'

Addi (outraged): 'That is illegal! What kind of a system is

that? That is no good. We need to abide by the Qanoon Ait Atta, the Law of the Ait Atta. Under this law the women do all the household chores and make the bread.'

Me: 'No, no, no. On the Sahara trip we have to abide by the Qanoon Ait Morrison, where Addi makes the bread in the hot *giton* [mess tent] and Zahra sits in the comfortable chair in the shade and writes.'

I need that comfortable chair. It is very hard-going. From the very first footstep this expedition is proving a lot tougher than the Draa. There are lots of factors. It is hotter than I had expected it to be and near the sea there is a lot of humidity. I have gained weight in a summer of laziness and whereas I had started the Draa in great shape after running round Everest, I had let myself get unfit for this Sahara leg. The walking underfoot is more difficult too. Sand is hard to walk in. It pulls your feet down and I have aching Achilles' tendons on both sides but worse on my right. At night, I lie in Le Petit Fromage with my muscles complaining and stiffening. We are also walking a lot more quickly than we had before. Instead of doing an average of 20km a day, we are going for 25km – but still in the five-hour period. We have further to cross and, with water scarce, Brahim wants us to cover the land faster.

After the military zone, we cross into an area that has no water and no people in it. We have to stay within walking distance of the tarmac so that we can beg water from petrol stations, or Addi can go up to the road and stop a passing water truck. In this region, water trucks are common, supporting the tiny communities in the wasteland and refuelling the service stations. The land is dead flat and our points of reference are mobile phone masts. These are quite handily positioned about 25km apart so we use them for our daily reference.

Worst of all, though, we have trouble in camp. BB does not want to be on the expedition. He had agreed to come because I had asked for him, but in truth he doesn't want to spend three months walking through a difficult area far from his two sons, whom he adores. BB is also a very sociable man and excels in a big group where he can host and entertain. 'Why didn't you bring any friends, Zahra?' he asks me sadly. I feel for him. When you are doing something that is tough and long, you have to want to do it and to be present and enjoying it. Short spurts of hating the experience are fine, normal in fact, and you can put up with anything for a time, but for the long haul it is very hard to reconcile yourself, voluntarily, to do something that every fibre of your being says you don't want to do.

BB tries to keep his spirits up, buying us little treats of Coke at the service station and reciting the Quran to himself over and over, but he can find no comfort. His mood rubs off on all of us and the mess tent becomes a place of tension rather than respite. When you are in such a small team, there is no way to have a break from each other and it's impossible not to be affected by the way everyone feels. You are connected in every way and it's not the same as daily life where there are outside influences and a wider pool of people. You have to be satisfied with your companions, every niggle becomes magnified and then unbearable – an untreated blister that you keep walking on.

We have a long talk and I tell BB how deeply I value him and love his company and how important he is, but that if he wants to leave I totally understand. He keeps trying for a few days, but the months ahead stretch out too long and he calls JP to ask if he can swap someone else in when we get to Smara. With an end in sight, BB is free to enjoy the rest of the journey and all our hearts lighten.

The landscape is still flat with small shrubs and the masts ahead as our beacons. It is at best featureless and at worst rather ugly, with a soupy sky and endless scrub. Instead of focusing on that, I search every day for the hidden treasures. Pretty snails nest in the shrubs. Their shells are brown and white caramel swirls with blobs on top of something that looks like white glue. I discover one perfect alpine flower with succulent leaves sheltering six white petals and bright yellow stamens. Some things are definitely hiding – a brown and golden striped lizard almost gets trampled on as he sits as still as death till we pass by. His five-fingered toes and fingers are completely translucent.

There is very little, though. One day in my notes I write, 'There was a spider in camp this morning and two crows circling overhead this evening. These were the only living things I saw all day.' The low point of this section comes when I start counting ants, and I can actually keep a tally of them.

At last, an amrad tree appears. It is almost bent double, blasted by the north wind. Behind us, storm clouds are gathering. From blue, the sky goes to black and the air feels electric. We quicken our pace as we want to bivouac before the heavens open. The amrad is guiding us towards an oued and a trickle of grazing for the camels. The radar post which signals our 25km is approaching on the left and the clouds, which were behind us, are now above us and rumbling. Our living being count is given a boost with a striped snake about three-quarters of a metre long which I ban Addi from killing.

The clouds still haven't broken when we camp and Addi sets off immediately for water from the service station under the radar. They don't have any to spare so we go down to emergency rations for washing ourselves and the dishes. What this means is that the men use stones for the ritual washing before prayers and I use wet wipes for my worst-offending areas. When it comes to washing up, BB pours out my water ration into the two buckets. It is the equivalent of about three mugs of water for the soap bucket and five for the rinse. This is to do dishes for four people, which include two large pots – the soup pot being my favourite as it always has turmeric-coloured gunk stuck to the bottom. I devise a system of least dirty first and then pour the filthy water at the end from the bucket into the *gameela* (soup pot) and scrub like mad with a stone.

Water aside, it's a great bivouac. The clouds have moved on and the sky has washed itself blue with a golden light glowing on the trees. The camels are delighted to graze on the thorns after days of unsatisfactory shrubs and I relish the shade and also the beauty of the trees themselves. Deprivation is the road to appreciation.

The boys' mood of satisfaction does not last forever. Our camels have undertaken lots of expeditions together but nature is stronger than nurture. Any good relations and warm feelings that the months working together may have brought them crumble under the impetus of testosterone. We are walking right through their mating season, which means they are all fired up to a greater or lesser degree. One of the ways this manifests itself is in a desire for dominance. Our alpha males need a pecking order. Up until now the caravan had been Hunter, Hamish and Hector in that order on Brahim's string and Callum, Alasdair and Sausage on Addi's. This meant that Hunter was the number one male of the group.

It's just before 8 a.m. and Brahim and Addi are rounding them up to start loading. They all have their head halters on and are milling around in a group quite normally. Then, Hunter knocks his head against Hamish, trying to bite

132

his ear. Meltdown! Hamish launches a counter-attack on Hunter. He lets out a loud roar and snakes his head over to grab Hunter's right foreleg. The two of them spin round and round with Hunter trying to shake off Hamish's jaws, which are firmly clamped. Both of them are bellowing as they fight for supremacy. Hamish's aim is to force Hunter onto the ground. If Hamish succeeds, he will then kneel on Hunter's neck, lower his chest down and smother him. He is going for the kill. Addi chooses his moment and leaps up, grabbing Hamish's halter close to his mouth. He drags him off Hunter and pulls him through the others into the open space. Hunter runs off in the other direction with no obvious limp or impairment. Disaster has been avoided by Addi's quick actions.

Hamish has actually got what he wants, and from then on he leads the caravan. 'He beat Hunter,' Brahim tells me. 'This is the way. Now Hamish is the leader, even though he is younger and his teeth are not so strong, he is a good fighter. He must go first or he will just bite Hunter all the time.' Sadly, violence sometimes does pay.

9

SMARA AND THE RED RIVER VALLEY

Smara – Sakiya al Hamra

8 December 2019

Hamish is looking smug as we set off with him at the head
of the caravan. He spends almost his whole time weeing and
then flicking it up onto his back with his tail and splashing
poor Hunter in the face. Hunter, unlike me – his namesake,
is of a very equitable nature, or perhaps he is just broken by
his defeat, and he does not retaliate by biting Hamish on the
backside, which Hamish definitely deserves.

Our mood is sprightly as we're heading towards the city of
Smara and a camel meat feast, plus some rock carvings (for
me). However, I am soon irritated by a drone buzzing overhead. It's following us as we navigate the shallow channels
and shrubs and keeps coming down almost to head level. I've
been told there is a big military presence in the area – around
20,000 soldiers – but I can't imagine why they need to spy
on us. Huffing to myself, I carry on. It is only about three
months later when I am talking to Abdellah about his foot-
age that I realise that the drone was his; the military have no
interest in us whatsoever.

We come across a barbed-wire fence and banked up walls of sand. The fence surrounds a vast plantation of dead trees. My soul withers inside me as I look at the rows and rows of carefully planted acacias. It was part of a big re-greening initiative by the local authorities. I wonder why they would choose acacias, which don't really produce anything, but Brahim says that it was for the camels grazing here – there are a lot – and the acacias were the trees that needed the least water once they were established. They never even got that chance. They are all dead, just grey withered sticks in the soil standing like ghostly sentries warning us that the climate is changing fast.

It wasn't always this dry. The Sahara has actually fluctuated wildly between wet and dry over the past few 100,000 years. This is due to a 41,000-year cycle, in which the tilt of the earth changes, called the Axial Tilt. This tilt affects insolation – the amount of sunlight on a particular area at a certain time. There is lots of evidence that the Sahara used to have wide areas of grasslands that supported game and hunter-gatherer societies, but scientists have not yet agreed on whether the drying out of the Sahara was a quick, catastrophic event or happened over a long period.

In the last glacial period, the Sahara was even bigger than it is today. Between 8000 BCE and 6000 BCE the end of that glacial period brought more rain, but when the ice sheets in the north had finally gone, the desert, which had transformed into grasslands, dried out. It took longer in the south where the monsoon counteracted the drying out, but gradual desertification means that the Sahara today is as dry as it was about 13,000 years ago. If the planet survives that long, and if the Axial Tilt cycle maintains, it is expected that the Sahara will become green again in about 15,000 years. Maybe rhinoceroses and giraffes will roam once more.

I'm on the hunt for evidence of human and animal presence in the Sahara from eons ago and I am meeting a professor of archaeology at a rock-carving site on the outskirts of the city. I'm excited and get there early. I'm poking around along a long, low ridge of black rocks when two children, who are coming up to the nearby tap for water, see me and come over. They are Hassina, who is eleven, and her older brother, Mohamed. They introduce themselves very politely and gravely tell me that they are here for the weekend with their parents and that their tent is pitched over the ridge. They live in Smara but they like to come and camp on days off. Hassina has gained confidence with me and holds my hand, chattering on.

'I am the baby of the family, the little one, which is very good. I love school. I have one teacher who tells me that I am clever. She is always encouraging me and explaining everything to me. I want to be an engineer when I grow up.'

They want to know all about me and are very pleased with pictures of the camels on my phone and gear up to help look for rock carvings. Mohamed has the first win with a ball and then Hassina sees a long-horned bull. Things get competitive and we scramble over the rocks yelling out our finds. 'A gazelle, but it only has one leg.' 'Do you think this is an elephant?' 'I've got a sheep – it's fat.' Each one is celebrated with a high five and some major self-congratulation.

A car carrying our professor and some local officials draws up and my new friends go off to fill up their water carriers. Professor Mouloud is small and neat. He quickly realises that he has a fellow enthusiast on his hands and drops the formal manner to give full rein to his passion. It is a linguistic mishmash. The exhibits and explanations in the centre, which is a large room built for the purpose, are in French and the Prof and I are speaking in Arabic but all the words are derived from Greek – Neolithic, Paleolithic, Mesolithic. Some of it is going way above my head, but I'm hanging in.

It transpires that we are in a prime spot for finds. Smara gives on to Sakiya al Hamra – the red river course, and this whole area had rivers flowing through it, lakes and grass-lands, during what the Prof calls 'The Sahara's Damp Patch'. There is a programme underway, under the patronage of the King, to explore and map the rock-carving sites and Smara has had archaeologists and rock-art specialists visit from all over the world.

During the Draa Expedition we had found several stone tools and weapons, and I notice a case with some in it that look really familiar. The Prof brings out a whittled stone shaped like the head of a spoon and explains that this was one of the earliest spear heads. Then he shows me arrowheads from 2,000 years later which are much finer and have serrated edges. He also has a number of rounded stones that he says were used as sling shots. When I ask how he knows which is older, he says that with these ones it is the depth that they are buried in the ground – the older ones are deeper.

He also explains something to me about the carvings. We study the carvings of horses, which are dated from 10,000 BCE to 1000 CE on the museum's chart. The Prof shows me that the older pictures are actually more finely drawn and more representative than the newer ones. It seems counterintuitive that, as the centuries spun past, people carved 'worse' than they had at the beginning. Surely they would have made the animals more detailed and more representative. 'Ahha,' says the Prof, his eyes lighting up, 'that is what most people assume, but in fact they were moving towards a script and in the later period start to use symbols as well as pictures – as you saw at Foum Chenna. You need to think about these carvings as a kind of precursor to hieroglyphics, or as an early hiero-glyphic.' Hassina and Mohamed have crept into the room and are listening wide-eyed and finding their discoveries from outside represented on the boards.

Then, we reach a set of pictures which show my Draa spaceships. There are different types but the elegant, winged version is there. It is confirmed as a funerary monument, with some of the details that we had noted highlighted on the board. It is called 'Construction funéraire en forme de lune', and as well as the moon there are other forms variously described as 'the fly' and 'the heart'.

The Prof and I go out and walk the ridge together. It is perfect. I have already had a chance to explore for myself and make discoveries and now I'm being shown all the best bits and having them explained to me by an expert. There are lots of the long-horned cattle, fish and what we think is a boar. Some are carved in graceful flowing lines – these are the older ones – and some are punched in points into the rock, which are later. The Prof definitely prefers these. My favourite is an elephant with his trunk curled under him and his stone being encroached by sand. A figure at the side could be a hunter. 'They want to save things and restore them, which is good,' says the Prof. 'But we need to be careful. We don't want to ruin the original by making it "new", sticking everything together.' We are deep in discussion about the pictorial his-tory of human and animal development which lies under our feet, when JP comes running up. 'We have to go! We have been invited for tea with the governor.'

This is a big deal. The authorities have been very support-ive of our trip, as have almost all the people we have met along the way, who appear to be tickled by the idea of this

caravan train crossing the Sahara in the footsteps of the caravans of old, but I am always aware that we are walking over
land that is disputed. We drive into Smara itself and up to
the governor's residence. It has a lawn. I find this even more
impressive than the battlements and flags. We are shown into
a salon and all sit rather nervously on the pristine banquettes.
The governor comes in, dressed simply in a navy jellaba and
yellow babouches, and greets us all warmly. I am instantly
aware of the fact that we smell bad and look like a band of
rogues, but he doesn't flinch and shakes hands with everyone,
regardless.

Trays of fresh juice and pastries emerge. I try not to gobble
down too many, but I drain my avocado and milk juice in
one. Abdellah whispers to me, 'If only Addi and Brahim
were here, they would love these.' 'Who? Forget them!' I
say, biting into another pastry. The governor is charming and
talks openly about his passion for the region under his care
and the people in it and about trying to find opportunities
for the younger people. He hopes that tourism, drawing on
the region's rich history, can be part of that. He tells us that
the area is currently very calm, 'as you can see'. I want to ask
him more about the political situation, but know that it would
horrify the men and JP and cause deep embarrassment, so I
don't. He asks us dozens of questions about our trip and grants
us permission to bring the caravans into the city the next day
and camp outside Ma'a Al Ainayn, the old city walls. When
we get back to camp, I tell Brahim that I was desperate to
bring them some pastries but that Abdellah wouldn't let me
steal from the governor. Then I run away to the sounds of
Abdellah's outraged protestations.

We are all up early for our triumphal entry into Smara.
Our pace is brisk and Abdellah is having to run like mad to

catch up with us if he stops to take shots. 'I don't know how you do it, Zahra. You are going much faster than in the Draa. It is really hard!' I do a mental fist pump as he says this in front of Brahim, who has been vehemently, and in my opinion fraudulently, denying that we are going quickly.

At the top of a low hill, we spot Smara in the distance, and as we approach, the rubbish that sticks to humans like glue starts to appear. We all keep our eyes open for glass or rusted tins which might cut the camels' feet. Smara has a landmark of a big water tower with a globe on top that looks exactly like a giant golf ball on a tee. Before we get into the town proper, we pass through some houses on the outskirts. There is a group of boys playing football and the second they see the camels they abandon the ball and come running over. They form our unofficial honour guard as we process along the rough street lined with houses. Being boys, they are racing in and trying to touch or prod the camels and some pick up stones. Addi puts a stop to that.

Their mothers and sisters come out into the doorways of their houses dressed in the brightly coloured *milfahs* (wraps) of the region, laughing and shouting exclamations and questions: 'Blessings of God be upon you. Where are you from? Where is she from? Come and have tea with us. Where are you going?'

We are on the tarmac road, which has palm trees lining it, a contrast to the dead acacias we had passed. All the traffic stops or slows to take selfies, including the driver of an articulated lorry, who parks it blocking the entire road. He leaps out and begs me to take his picture on my phone and send it to him. 'Forgive me, pardon me, I want to show my children.' Then, a local TV crew arrives. Addi and I are loving the attention, but Brahim grumbles about the camels being disturbed and how they are not created to be walking on roads. I reckon that Hamish is actually very happy to be made such a fuss of – his neck is positively arched.

We pass the giant golf ball and leave the roads, cutting past a military camp to get to our bivouac on the square right outside the crumbling walls of the old city and the shrine of Ma'a Al Ainayn – 'the water of the two eyes/wells [tears].' Brahim is not happy as the camels are going to have to be tethered, but they are compensated with large bales of hay. The walls are stone-built, like dry stone walls, and about three metres high with the domes of the shrine, white-painted or in the original clay, poking up above them. The entrance is through a mint-green door and to the right are the remains of a mosque, a row of colonnades. Inside, there are plain rooms to receive people and some fine examples of brickwork. Women and men are constantly going in and out to the shrine. From the top, you can see right across Smara and the beehive tops of the military camp over into the desert.

We are all excited to be in a city and the promise of camel meatballs for supper in a café. First, though, I have been invited to go and see the Museum of Sahrawi Life set up by a local woman, Maymouna. She is waiting, plump and beaming, at the door to the small museum, which is one large corridor. In the centre is an alarming toy caravan of camels and riders which would give Chucky a run for his money. She has amassed a wonderful collection of everyday items – exactly the kind of things that get used and thrown away and are actually fascinating for future generations. She has included lots of cooking equipment and household brooms and cleaning gear as well as old knives and saddles, lamps and teapots, owari game boards and the block-printed cloth from Mali. There are woven cushions in neon colours and hand-tooled leather cushions with long fringes; rugs and *milfahs*, old and new, piled up against the walls. Sitting on the floor is a little girl all dressed up in her best with a gold-beaded headdress pouring out tea. Three older women are beside her with drums and we drink and have a sing-song and JP buys lots of handmade jewellery for his daughters.

After our goodbyes and lots of kisses, I set off to the suq with JP and Abdellah because I want to buy Christmas presents for the men. We dive into the narrow streets as it is getting dark and mingle with the crowds of people checking out the piles of shoes and racks of fluffy pyjamas. Just like Brahim, neither JP nor Abdellah is any good at shopping. I want to wander and look at everything and maybe pick up a few things that I don't even know I need yet, whereas they are goal-oriented and demand a list.

My *chech* has worn out. 'That is no longer green, Zahra; it is the colour of the water for the dishes, after they have been washed,' Brahim has told me, so we head for a shop with long bales of thin cotton in every colour. JP advises 4 metres in length and I buy a green one for me and a smart maroon one too as a Christmas gift. I've brought a long pink, orange and red tie-dyed one from Imlil for Addi. For Brahim, I umm and ahh and after consultation with JP and Abdellah I settle for some wooden prayer beads and a prayer mat with a picture of Mecca on it. Then, I am bundled away from the shops and to the café.

We crowd round a table outside and our mouths water at the smell of grilling meatballs. The camel meat is spiced and rolled into balls and then put between two criss-crossed mesh paddles and grilled over charcoal. The whole place is filled with the smoke of roasting meat, so thick that I can't even see the cook behind the brazier. A big bottle of Coke is produced. Fresh bread, small pots of salt and cumin are put on the table. Then, an enormous mound of camel meatballs arrives. Brahim is still wandering about the suq, but we all tuck in ravenously. It is such a treat. We order a second round and are waiting for it to arrive when Brahim runs up. 'Stop,' he says. 'What? Why?' we ask. 'Did you know that the camel meat is not local. It comes from Australia. I just spoke to the butcher and he showed me the packages in his freezer. What if it isn't *halal*?'

Consternation reigns. We are all amazed that the meat has been imported when this whole region is inhabited by nomads who make their living from camel herds. JP and Abdellah do some Googling and we all agree that if the Australian meat is produced for export to Muslim countries then we think that it will be killed in the proper fashion so that everyone can eat it. Brahim tucks in. It turns out that Morocco is the biggest importer of camel meat in the world, taking over 35 per cent of the market, with (amazingly to me) the USA in second place and Saudi Arabia in third.

BB has left us. We both try to disguise our feelings as we wave goodbye. I am really sad to see him go and he is dancing with joy – inside only because he is a very courteous man – to be going back to his sons. Smara has been exciting and full of discoveries, but I am glad to get back to just us and the emptiness. Ychou Benobayd has joined us for a spell – I know him from when he drove us to the spaceships. He is from Nqob – Addi's hometown – so they pair up. On the second day he is with us, I tell Brahim that I am going to go back and spend some time with him and Addi. 'No, Zahra, they need to get all the news. They still have three days before they have caught up on everything about their families, the goats and sheep, marriages, prices in the suq – everything. This is the nomad way. They can always talk.'

And it's true. I tease Ychou about having brought a huge sack of news with him that is never going to be empty. He gives me a pet name: 'Zuhour', flowers, which makes me feel special, and he adds a big dollop of easy-going good humour to the camp. He is also a good cook and the first thing he does is abolish our separate eating bowls. We still have some meat left and he makes a pot full of stew then empties it out onto a communal dish. He gives me a separate bowl – thinking that as a Westerner I won't want to eat from the common bowl – and I immediately empty it back. 'Thank you, Zahra,' says Addi. We kneel or squat round the plate with our bread and eat. It immediately binds us closer together; there is a very powerful psychology around sharing.

Our bivouac is under a grove of acacias and the camels are off and happy. Brahim sets up my chair in the shade and I get writing. It remains in my mind as one of my favourite camps. It is cool and we are all comfortable and relaxed; it recaptures the spirit of the Draa. But there is also a discovery, a dark one. I see Addi gathering stones and laying them in a circle and go over to investigate. 'Be careful, Zahra, it's a bomb,' he says, pointing. There is a missile, half-submerged in the sand. It looks like some kind of rocket and is the length of my forearm. It is clearly unexploded. Nomads who had camped here before us had put a few stones round and Addi was piling up more so that nobody would accidentally walk on to it.

'What about the camels?' I asked. 'Don't worry, Zahra. They pay attention to their feet and also they are on the other side of the camp because the oued goes in that direction and we will couch them tonight on that far side.' We regularly found bullet casings and some shell casings as we were walking, but this was the first one that was unexploded. 'I don't know why Man is in such a hurry to kill other people. He just needs patience and then God will do it for him,' was Brahim's comment.

I am back in my spot, stretched out under an acacia tree having a short siesta when I become aware of someone. I open one eye and there is Brahim, crouching down and looking at me earnestly. 'Zahra, I have found a goat. I saw the tracks and thought it was a gazelle because they were single hoof prints so I followed them and I found her, going round and round in circles. I have brought her back.'

My knowledge of goats is not extensive, but I know that they are never alone. I get up and follow him to the side of the mess tent. There's the little goat, standing with her head in our box of vegetables. She is thin, but her coat is thick, and she has one broken horn. She stands completely silent, seemingly comforted by the parameters of the box. I reach out and touch her gently, murmuring softly so that she can hear a human voice. She is quivering under my hand but gives no other reaction. 'Is she blind?' I ask Brahim. 'No, but I think she isn't right in the head. She must have been left behind by the herd. They will all know where to go to eat and where there is water, but this one is all alone.'

We go and fill one of our sandcastle pink buckets with water and I put it right in front of our little goat. She doesn't react until I actually put the water over her nose and mouth and then she drinks thirstily. Brahim raids the camels' larder and brings over some oats which she snuffles up. Then, she retreats back to the box. As night falls, she bleats and starts circling until she falls over. I pick her up and she leans against me heavily. I think my legs give her the same feeling of security as the box.

Addi comes back from the camels. 'Zahra, what are you doing with this mad goat? She isn't right. She has to be killed.'

I immediately switch on the Labrador eyes. She is so defence-
less and sad I can't bear the thought of just killing her for no
purpose. Addi is clearly all talk, though, as the next thing
I see is him taking one of the blankets off his own sleeping
pile and wrapping the goat in it to keep her warm. As we eat
dinner, I ask Brahim what we are going to do. I know that
he won't just leave her here where she will die alone of thirst
and hunger. 'I'll find a solution,' he says.

The next morning, I go straight to the little goat. She has
got up and shucked off her blanket and drinks a little water
but won't be tempted by any of the delicacies we offer her –
not even orange peel, which I had saved from the ravenous
lips of our camels. 'Are we going to take her?' I ask Brahim.
'Yes, Zahra. We will do our best. There are some nomads on
the other side of the oued. We will take her there and see if
they know who she belongs to.'

She certainly finds her voice when we tie her legs and
balance her on the very top of the baggage on Hamish and
protests long and loud. She seems to get used to the rocking
motion and eventually quietens down.

About an hour later, we arrive at the nomad encampment.
There are five tents and some of the big plastic water containers that help the nomads live in this waterless area. Best of all,
there are several small enclosures full of goats. A smiling man
and his little boy come out to meet us and I leave Brahim to
explain as I am carried off by his wife, Fatima, to have tea
and *goufiyya* – goat's milk mixed with a type of brown grain
and sugar.

I bring out some tea for the men who are watering the
camels. The water is thick and cloudy and I ask our host what
is wrong with it. 'We put old grain or flour in it to help feed
the flocks,' he tells me. He says that he will ask around his

neighbours and friends to see if anyone has lost the goat and return it to them and, if not, he will keep it with his and feed and water her. Of course, she is destined eventually for the pot, but at least she is close to her own kind and won't die alone in the desert.

Hector has a blister. He is limping and keeps falling behind so that his halter, tied to Hunter's back, is stretched to its full extent. We try to limit his pain by unloading some of the heavy stuff and redistributing it, and also by choosing to walk where there are as few stones as possible. This means our route is even more meandering than usual. We think that he cut himself on the rubbish and glass that we had to cross when we were going into Smara. It is a real problem. We need all six camels as we are entering further into a no-water zone, and are heading west and south far from any tarmac and possible water trucks. Water is heavy, and we have just reprovisioned for a long stretch so our food bags are heavy too. The men confer after lunch and decide to operate.

We are under acacias and we build up the fire and leave it to burn until the embers are glowing. Brahim goes and brings Hector in from his grazing and couches him. Ychou ties a rope around his left foreleg, where the sore is, over his thigh and shin to keep the leg bent. He then passes the rope over Hector's back and does the same on the other side. Now, both legs are immobilised with his sore pad exposed. By this time, Hector knows something bad is up and starts booming quietly and looking at us with questioning eyes. Brahim is squatting directly in front of him at his head with his hand holding firmly onto the halter close to his mouth, bringing the head low to the sand. He has a calming effect and spends the time picking burrs out of Hector's muzzle and forehead.

Ychou and Addi are busy at the fire. They are heating up

147

the hoe head and two iron tent pegs until they are as red hot as the embers. They have also spread out a chunk of yellowish-white animal fat left over from our meat supplies. This is thick and leathery and is called *shahm*. They press a palm-sized gobbet of the fat deeply into the hole in Hector's pad. The bad bit is about to start and Brahim takes hold of Hector's bottom lip. When Hector starts thrashing his head about, if Brahim were still holding the rope it would cut through his mouth.

Ychou gets the hoe head from the oven, wrapped in cloths so he can hold it, and Addi holds Hector's hurt pad up. Then Ychou presses the hoe hard against Hector's foot. Hector lets out a roar of pain. Smoke from the fat and the smell of burning flesh fill the air. Brahim croons to Hector and holds his head firmly down. Ychou presses again and again, going back to the fire to get the heated pegs and laying these flat against the fat. Hector is being so good. He cries but doesn't thrash until the very end. Suddenly, he obviously can't take any more and lashes out violently with his back legs. Ychou and Addi jump out of the way – a kick would snap their bones like a twig. The aim has been to use the fat and the heat to cauterise and seal the wound. By pressing deep into the flesh, it will burn away the damaged tissue and harden it so that the wound doesn't continue to deepen and split Hector's pad.

Ychou unties him and Brahim lets go of his bottom lip and takes off his halter. Meanwhile, Addi has laid out a feast of oats on a tarpaulin under a tree for shade. Hector surges to his feet and Addi guides him over to the treat. He munches away and when I look over half an hour later, he has couched himself beside the tarpaulin and is still looking a bit sorry for himself.

It turns out that Ychou is quite the card. We are sitting

eating our lunch salad when he comes out with, 'I'm in pain. I have a big problem.' When we anxiously ask him why, he says, 'I wore the wrong underpants. And now . . .' He stands up and, bent double because he is so tall, walks around the tent with his legs spread wide, cowboy-style. 'It is a bad position to have chafing in.' We all howl with laughter. 'I'll tell you what, Ychou, Addi and I will heat up the *shahm* and the hoe and we can cure you, like we cured Hector,' suggests Brahim kindly. More gales of laughter. '*Khatar!* Danger!' yells Addi, clutching himself.

Hamish is misbehaving badly. His hormones are getting the better of him. We have to hobble him even when we are walking because every time he smells a lady camel he tries to take off. All the boys are in heat and they are distracted by their hormones. When a male camel in heat wants to attract a female, he uses some very specific techniques. First of all, he roars like a lion. Then, he puffs a balloon-sized pink bubble of skin filled with foaming saliva out of his mouth – his sex bubble. Now that he looks and sounds gorgeous, he slaps on the aftershave. He stands with his hind legs spread and pees, whipping it up onto his back to make him feel good.

This is all very inconvenient when you are walking in a train with the camels attached nose to bottom. A male camel can smell a female from a long way away – estimates from the men vary between 1 and 3 kilometres. In the mating season, a male camel actually eats less because he is so focused on finding a female and his stomach contracts. Hamish has to be tied to an acacia in camp because otherwise he will disappear in search of a woman and we will never see him again. The aggression is real, and Brahim tells me that one year, Callum was in the throes and tried to bite his head off, but he was saved by his *chech*, which came away in Callum's mouth. He is very offended when I get the giggles at this near-death experience.

Apparently, I'm misbehaving too.

Brahim: 'I hope there is going to be no grumbling today.'

Me: 'What do you mean?'

Brahim: 'You know, when you start saying – aren't we there yet? How long do we have to go? That place looks good for a bivouac? It's hot.'

Me: 'You are safe till 12.30.'

Brahim: 'Is that when the light goes red?'

Me: 'Yup, directly. 12.30 exactly.'

Brahim: 'From green to red – no amber?'

Me: 'Exactly.'

Brahim: '*Khatar*, danger!'

Me: 'If you were very intelligent then you would always bivouac at 12.25, then there would be no danger!'

That day we bivouac at 11.30.

When I get into LPF, I almost gag. My tent, my haven, smells of rancid fox. I start sniffing everything and soon find the culprit – my mat. This is always perched on Hamish's back, rolled up in an open-ended plastic cover. Clearly, Hamish's pee-flicking is reaching it. I drag it outside and wipe it down, using my smelly soap, and leave it to dry. I spray rosewater all around the tent. Rosewater is a disinfectant, as well as smelling good, but it still doesn't mask the stench. After that, my mat goes on Hector and I envelop my bags with a waterproof cover.

Sakiya al Hamra, the red river course, is teeming with life in comparison to the waste we have just come from and what lies ahead. There aren't any pools of water, but the earth itself is moist and there is lots of greenery. When we walk, we constantly have to weave to avoid deep, muddy channels that the camels would flounder in. The place is well named. The earth is different shades of red from russet to terracotta and there are lots of bushes with red or purple pods and berries on them. The air is cooler, as it is mediated by vegetation, and there is shade in the deep tunnels dug into the surface by the passage of the water. At times of rain, there are still floods here and we can see how high the water has reached on some of the neighbouring cliffs.

We come across a well with a trough. The water is salty but good enough for the camels, who slurp it down. Three nomads turn up in their *watta*, open-backed Land Rover. They are thin and tense. We greet each other and tell them where we are going and they ask us for a series of escalating things: a bidot, shoes, my phone, a job. I feel rather intimidated and Brahim gives them a bidot, telling me afterwards that he did so to get rid of them, even though we need it. We part and walk on alone until we come to their camp, which is a square tent with no sign of women or children or goats. There is a big group of female camels. 'It's like the army,' says Brahim. 'The men come out here and live alone so they can look after the camels for a week or a month. Their families are in Layoune.' 'Isn't that really hard for them?' I ask. 'What choice do they have?' he responds. Two of the men come down to meet us and offer to fill a couple of our bidots. They ask Brahim for help.

They want to take one of the young camels to market to sell. It will be bought to slaughter either immediately or fattened up for later consumption – I hope that it is the latter and he gets to have a longer life. They need help to catch the camel and to get it into the truck. Hamish and co. are bellowing and bubbling with excitement at the group of ladies standing so tantalisingly close. It is just like a school disco: a line of boys on one side and a line of girls on the other, both sides preening and posing but neither taking any action. After a few minutes, two brave girls break ranks and trot towards our boys. Addi shoos them away, flapping his hands at them to prevent a rape.

Meanwhile, one of the nomads has got out a sack of stale bread and is spreading it out for his camels so that they will come in close. The other four men move out among the camels with ropes in hand and wait to be told which one they are going for. It is a young brown one. The men close in and immediately the camels get suspicious and bolt off to stand about 50 metres away. The men circle them and go in again. They grab the young camel and separate him. His poor mother trots after him bellowing, clearly distraught. It is actually horrible to watch, even though I eat meat and I know how it has to be got. All the other camels mill around. Then the men have to lift him up to get him in the back of the *watta*. They are all strong men, used to this kind of work, but they really struggle to get that dead weight lifted up to waist height and into the back. Once in, he keeps calling disconsolately but it is of no use. His mother waits beside the *watta*, calling back, and then the nomads drive off and he is gone.

We park up in a bowl of low hills in a juncture between two river valleys: the big green and red one of Sakiya al Hamra and a smaller one that looks golden as the sun hits the striated trees that flank it. Directly ahead of us is a small clump of palm trees showing us that there is water underground. Small, crested birds with flashes of black and white under their wings are attracted into camp, and while we are walking the perimeter, we find boar tracks.

I sit outside LPF writing and watching sneaky Hamish. He is tied to an amrad tree, exiled from the tribe for fighting and running off to debauch lady camels. I felt sorry for him so took him some leftovers after lunch, but his eyes were trained on the oued and a female camel beyond it. She was standing on a small hill, batting her long eyelashes at him. After prayers, Brahim untied him from the tree, but kept him hobbled, so that he could go to the oued and graze on the trees. He dutifully trotted off and snacked on some thorns but kept an eye on the camp.

As I watch him, I see him looking round to find out where Brahim is. When he sees Brahim going back into the mess tent and that the coast is clear, he creeps up over the bank and starts galumphing with his hobbled legs towards his lady. I am afraid I whistle blow and he is recaptured and retied to his tree.

The greenery and the cooler air are invigorating and I stride out fast and strong. Although there is a lot of foliage, there aren't any goats or sheep. Brahim explains that it's because the water and the plants are all salty and so the camels can eat them but they're not good for the sheep or goats. At our break for elevenses we're joined by a local gendarme. He is full of bonhomie and sits with us for biscuits, saying, 'By God, I had to drive like a Formula One racer to catch you up!' We had had no signal to send in the GPS co-ordinates the night before so he needs them now.

There is a very tasty clump of amrad trees across the oued – which at this point is about 2km wide – and we decide to go over to them so the camels can graze well. We set off and cross a section of earth that looks like the victim of an earthquake. There are deep cracks in the dried, crazy-paving soil. They are so deep I cannot see down to the bottom of them. I learn that camels' eyes are set in such a way that they can't look straight down. They are always looking two to three metres ahead and I worry they might stumble into one of the cracks. We are stopped by a wide body of mud and water that is too deep for the camels, so turn back, hoping, and failing, to find as good a clump of trees. But at camp, a consolation prize for me is a handful of perfectly fossilised shells and a new riddle as we eat our soup that evening in the mess tent.

What keeps coming back more and more the more you chuck it away?

(Answer at the end of the chapter.)

'The water is in God's hands,' says Brahim as we set off. We are running really low and only have enough drinking water for today and tomorrow. It has all been salty for the last few stops. The camels drank two days ago but we couldn't digest that much salt. One of the team tells me that last time he was in Layoune he was caught up in clashes. He had gone into the town to do some shopping but when he got there he walked into a confrontation between the authorities and the citizens. 'Cars were on fire and the bank was set alight. Then the troops opened fire and I ran away directly. I ran until there was a soldier pointing a gun straight at me. But when I spoke, he understood I was not from there. Thanks be to God; the soldier was from my region. He told me to get out of there and also to take off my robe because I looked like a Sahrawi. And it is true, many people tell me that my face is Arab. I took it off and went back to the camp. The next day I came back and everything was peaceful. I could finish my shopping.'

I haven't had a phone signal for days and am missing it.

'You need it here,' Brahim tells me.

'Well, I don't desperately need it,' I say to him, 'but I do want it.'

'No, you do really need it for safety against the mafia.'

'The what?'

'The mafia. Didn't you hear the shots last night?'

'No, what do you mean?'

'There were shots fired and two cars in the oued in the darkness. What were they doing there? We were lucky we had camped up on the hill out of sight. If we had crossed the oued as we had planned we would have been in danger.'

The camels are hungry and we decide to camp in the oued where there is a dense thicket of acacia trees and they can have a really good feed. Usually, we camp higher up because if it rains the river can flow with incredible swiftness and go from zero to a torrent in minutes. Many people are swept away and killed by flash floods. We can see the debris from previous deluges: tangles of grass and wood trapped against the trees. However, there is absolutely no sign of rain so we take the risk. That night, the moon is full and I hear wolves howling in the distance. We have seen numerous tracks in Sakiya al Hamra and the men have all heard them before, but I must sleep soundly. Ychou tells me they hang round until a camel gives birth and then go in to grab the baby.

10

DESERT CATS

Sakiya al Hamra – Dshira

16 December 2019

When I am asked what I miss on expeditions, the honest answer is my cat, Squeaky. I have often wanted to bring her with me but she is not a good traveller. If you believe in manifestation, then a prime example of it is the hot springs at Gilb an Naaja – 'Heart of the Sheep'. Quite early in the day, a Land Rover had rolled up driven by a well-filled-out man in his fifties called Mbarak. He directed us towards his well and invited us to use it. 'It's good. I dug it. It is nearly 700 metres deep and the water is hot. Come, I'll meet you there.' Mbarak invites me for a tour of his control room. He switches on his pump and the water runs out in two directions: to a pipe which we fill our bidots from; and to a water tank which then cools it and feeds the trough. 'It is absolutely fine to drink when it is cold,' Mbarak tells us, 'but don't use it for your tea.' The Sahrawis are very particular about their tea and will only use certain types of water: rainwater or mineral water. Even in the cities, they will collect rainwater in a cistern specially for the tea rather than use tap water.

As we are setting up camp, a resplendent ginger and white tomcat appears over a dune and pads towards us. He comes straight up to me and allows me to stroke him. He then inspects everything we are doing in camp and, after satisfying himself that all is OK, he joins us in the mess tent for lunch. I make him up a little dish of sardines and rice in an empty sardine can and take it outside. He accepts it graciously and eats up half of it. Then, he takes the other half and buries it in the sand, obviously keeping it for later.

I can only guess that he has come from a nomad's tent and established himself near water. Mr Cat and I siesta happily together and I start to make long-term plans to take him with us. That night Mr Cat sleeps at the entrance of the mess tent. 'He was by my feet all night, Zuhour,' Ychou says smugly the next morning, causing me a pang of deep envy. He gets porridge and milk from me for breakfast and repays me by purring loudly. We leave lots of bread dipped in milk for him and I get in as much cat time as possible, deserting my camel-loading duties. I think he knows I have designs on him, though, because he leaves us about ten minutes before we are due to set off. Obviously, he is quite happy where he is.

A flock of birds, fatter than a pigeon but smaller than a seagull, fly overhead and we see a hut made of brushwood for a herdsman and, beside it, what I think is an enclosure also made out of brushwood, but Brahim says is probably a mosque. From behind the sun, a rider on a camel approaches. When he gets close, he is a smiling, slim youth of perhaps seventeen. He doesn't have any shoes on, just black socks, and his female camel is piebald with white rims round her pupils. He's riding on a simple wooden saddle, covered in white sheepskin, with saddlebags made of leopard-skin blanket behind it. He tells us he lives in the area and is just over to check on his herd. It's the first time I've ever seen anyone riding a camel to work as a herdsman. His steed is bridling and prancing and braying to the boys who are, predictably, bubbling away.

'Is she fast?' I ask. 'Very,' he flashes me a grin. 'Do you want to try her?' He couches her and I get on. She's very different from the male camels, much slimmer and more comfortable, and the saddle is good. *I could get used to this*, I think. Brahim later tells me she had probably come from Mali and that the name for a female riding camel is *tibirit*. I hand her back reluctantly and our camel cowboy leaps on and canters swiftly into the distance.

It's sultry weather and at lunch I can't seem to drink enough tea. I gulp it down, scalding my mouth, but I feel thirstier after each glass. 'Haven't you noticed, Zahra? The water from the bags today is salty. We can drink it but it has salt in it,' Brahim tells me. That afternoon I am ragingly thirsty. My mouth burns and dries. I know that the water is safe and that the bad effects will probably be limited to diarrhoea, but I am going to have to get used to the psychological effect. No matter how much you drink, the salt signals going up to the brain make you think you need more. I spend a lot of time trying to reconcile myself to the new normal. It's important not to get too dramatic or miserable about anything when there are weeks ahead.

Later, Addi comes bounding past carrying the purple basin full of rising dough, a sack and the kettle. 'Come on, we are going to make *aghroum* Ait Atta, the bread of the tribe of Atta, *aghroum* Sahgro, the bread of Saghro.' We cross down into the little oued where Ychou has already made lots of preparations. He had gathered hand-sized flat stones and arranged them in a circle in the sand. On top and underneath, he had set a fire of brushwood and the stones were now burning hot.

He and Addi brush off the coals with a stick and break off a couple of branches of leaves from the tammayt bush and sweep off the ash. Addi uses the sack to beat as much of the remaining ash off the flat stones as possible. It is time for a last-minute knead and Addi folds over the dough and plunges his fists into it for a couple of minutes. You can see the dough falling in on itself and then puffing up again, almost like it's breathing. 'Water, Zahra, water!' My job is to sprinkle his hands and add tiny drops into the mixture. Satisfied, he plops the plump round of dough on top of the stones and presses it down, jumping back when he gets too hot and then going in again. 'Zahra, water!' I sprinkle. When he's happy that it's just flat enough, Ychou covers it with more embers and sets some more brushwood alight. Ychou then pours on a bag of pebbles he has collected, spreading them evenly until there is no dough visible. He piles on the lit brushwood. We sit round feeding the fire and letting the bread cook in its stones for about twenty minutes. Brahim arrives with the tea and gets the pot going.

The men decide the bread has cooked long enough. They scrape off the brushwood and the pebbles and Addi, with his Teflon hands, goes in and grabs the blackened loaf. He throws it from hand to hand and then onto a cloth on the ground where he uses a knife to scrape the charcoal off the top and prise out the stones that are sticking to the underneath. He takes the cloth and thwacks the bread on both sides till the worst of the black disappears. Brahim pours the tea and we sit around eating big chunks of stone-cooked bread – crisp and hot on the outside, soft and warm on the inside. Hamish looks on from the shelter of the acacia trees – those irresistible eyes – and we take him some bread to enjoy too.

Brahim has cut a new walking stick from one of the trees and is whittling it. He and Addi debate whether it's better to use a knife or the fire. By evening, the stick is perfectly smooth and they both show it off. Ychou asks me if I would like to see pictures of his family, which of course I do. His wife has traditional tattoos under her bottom lip but she has raised five very modern daughters. The oldest is studying biology at university and the youngest came top of her year for the entire region. Ychou is full of pride at their achievements. All of the men have one overriding desire for their children regardless of gender: education.

'Zahra, come out, hurry.' I scramble out of the tent and there are two women dressed in *milfahs*. It's the mother of the young man who had popped in to visit us earlier and her daughter-in-law.

Me: 'Peace be upon you. How are you? How is your health?'

The women: 'Upon you be peace, we are fine, everything is well. How are you? Are you well?'

Me: 'Thanks be to God. Will you come in and drink soup with us? What are your names?'

The women: 'No, no. Thank you. May God give you health. Our names are Fatima and Zahra.'

Me: 'Zahra? I am Zahra too.'

Zahra, the daughter-in-law, and I laugh and embrace fondly. She is a woman in her thirties, rounded and lively. It transpires she is a Tashlaheet speaker so we do all the greetings again in Tashlaheet to her great delight. Addi brings out soup and bread and she drinks it, although Fatima only eats the bread. They come to my tent and inspect everything carefully, exclaiming that the sleeping bag looks very flimsy and not warm enough for desert nights.

Zahra says, 'Please come and stay with us tonight, Zahra. We have everything warm and you can be with me. We don't live so far away and my husband can bring you back.' I daringly try a joke reply in Tashlaheet about coming if I hear wolves in the oued, which is met with blank incomprehension, but I soldier on and after a couple of goes, Zahra laughs and hugs me. It is tricky navigating jokes in a language you don't know very well but I am pleased I tried. The women leave us and the men settle in to get all the gossip. 'She got a whiff of her homeland and came. She is Schluh from Zagora,' says Brahim. Ychou tells me, 'Zahra drank the soup; it is from her home. The mother didn't. Sahrawis just take milk, bread, tea, meat and *goufiyya*. They don't even really like our tea. It is too weak for them.'

In the morning, Zahra arrives laden with gifts, just as the dawn is breaking. She has brought camel's milk which is still warm, two loaves of bread – 'I baked that one myself but the other one is from the shop', henna, some perfume and an apricot tie-dyed *milfah*. She shows me how to tie it and I put it on over all my other clothes so I resemble a giant peach. She gives me good advice. 'Don't buy camel milk in the market in Layoune; they mix it with all sorts. This bottle I brought you, my husband got it straight from the camel this morning and then I walked over immediately so it is good.' Addi comes out with a big bag of return presents including macaroni, tea and sugar. 'No, I can't take it. You poor things have got so far to go,' she says, but Addi presses it on her and I add a little bracelet for her personally. I leave in a shower of kisses.

The plain is flat and very calm in the morning light and a bit further on we meet Zahra's husband and his brother. They tell us that this whole area is settled by one extended family who came here from Marrakech in 1928. It is a very friendly plain. 'Where there are no tourists it is like this,' says Brahim. 'People just want to help you.'

This is borne out by a young man called Hassan who walks out to meet us and take us for tea. His encampment is a scene straight from *Mad Max*. The tent is a white square with a pointed roof, like a knight's pavilion, and in front of it is a low wall made of brushwood. This acts like an informal cupboard with branches for shelving and thorns for hooks. Household objects are hanging and scattered everywhere. I spy a bidot, an iron griddle pan, a jellaba and some other clothes, a useful sack and what looks like a red plastic rose. There is a covered area and an enclosure further to the right for the animals, also formed out of wood. A black iron cauldron is bubbling over embers. Inside, the tent is light and pretty, sewn from different lengths of coloured material, old *milfahs* I think.

Hassan's mum, Aaliya, dressed in a white *milfah* covered in brown and blue flowers, is sitting cross-legged on the floor beside a fluffy white Dr No cat with pink ears, who rushes over to our shoes when we take them off and kneads at them, purring. Presumably they smell delicious to a cat. When I tell Hassan the story of finding Mr Cat near the hot well in the desert, he laughs. 'Yes, he is well known. Everyone who visits that place brings him some meat.' No wonder he disappeared off before we left.

Hassan busies himself making tea over charcoal and we are offered a big bowl of fresh camel's milk. Brahim and I drink deeply, while the two nomads – Addi and Ychou – shudder inwardly and refuse smilingly. Aaliya is my age and lives in the tent with Hassan, visiting her other children in Layoune, but happiest here in the desert with her cat and her spotless tent. It's so peaceful and enjoyable, I can understand exactly what she means. It is all about living in the moment and appreciating what you have: shade from the sun, hot tea and silence. I could stay all day but we have to get on. As we are leaving, Aaliya presents me with a set of prayer beads and each of us with a stick to clean our teeth with. Hers are beautifully white and strong and I look meaningfully at Brahim and Addi.

Hassan says he will drive ahead and see us at the mosque and shrine of Murabbi al Rabih, who Aaliya says was her grandfather, although I wonder if I have caught that correctly and he isn't a great- or a great-great-grandfather. The shrine was destroyed in the great flood of 2016, which Hassan tells us swept through the oued crushing everything in its path. Forty of his camels were killed.

When we get there, Hassan is up in the minaret waving at us. The shrine itself lost most of its walls in the flood and was left as one room intact with an intricately patterned dome. Inside is the coffin of the sheikh. 'He is the best *sayyid* [holy man] in Morocco,' Hassan tells us, and Brahim and I reflect on the fact that every community thinks their *zawiya* is the best.

We are frog-marching along the piste so that we can get to Layoune on schedule and I am fed up. 'This is just exercise, walking fast along the piste. I won't have anything to write about. It's not exploring,' I moan. For the most part, we have been crossing the wilderness, using the sun to navigate or sometimes following old nomad paths, but occasionally to make up time, or because it is the only way, we have to follow a dirt road. I never enjoy these sections as much, although they are easier on the legs than broken stones, and on the camels' feet if one of them is injured. There is much less chance of spotting a plant, insect or animal and we always pick up the pace, which is hard going. Everyone just ignores my sulkiness and it wears off. I'm lying hotly in LPF after lunch when Brahim arrives at the door. 'Get up, Zahra, and put on your nice clothes. We have been invited by the Qaid. We have to walk to a place called Dshira and bivouac in his oasis, so hurry up, we are packing up.' I am dismayed. Packing up and walking after we have bivouacked? It is my worst nightmare. When I see Brahim putting the flags on the camels I wonder if I'll be allowed to ride if we are doing a detour, but I get a withering look. I dig my trousers and shirt out of my bag; they are crumpled but clean. They're both raspberry-coloured so match my complexion.

We walk for an hour. Brahim says, 'Everything is good,' which is his go-to response when things are tough and drives me crazy.

Me: 'No, it isn't. Some things are better and some things are worse. You say that but you don't mean it.'

Brahim: 'Everything is good.'

Me: 'Agh. No. It would be better if we weren't walking, but were having casse croute at the bivouac and resting.'

Brahim: 'But if you accept that everything is good, it makes it easier. We don't have a choice so we may as well think that this is good. If we think it is bad, it will be bad.'

At that point we realise that we have to go slightly back on ourselves and then climb a steepish hill on a tarmac road. There is no oasis in sight as we trudge up the hill into the sinking sun, just a barren expanse with a few low-lying houses, and everyone feels demoralised. Then everything changes. We come over the top and waiting for us is a group of about twenty men, some in army uniform and some in smart jackets, filming us on their phones and smiling broadly. We are greeted and introduced to everyone and it seems that all the dignitaries of Dshira have come out to meet us. The Qaid is a tall, broad, energetic man and immediately asks if we need hay for the camels, thereby winning the hearts of

Addi and Brahim. We are guided through some gates and in front of us, hidden by the dip and the walls, is a perfect palm oasis. The temperature drops to cool and birdsong fills the air. This has turned from a nightmare to a dream.

We unload and put up the tents with lots of willing helpers and rapid questions. One raffish chap asks me if there is room for two in LPF and his friend says, 'Look out, he's already got three wives.' The Qaid is very taken with my solar lamp. While we are setting up, our hosts erect a tent of their own. It is a ceremonial one with carpets on the floor and woven walls showing mosques and Islamic designs. Red and gold plush chairs have been set out along the back and two sides, and a Moroccan flag flies beside an enormous picture of the King, which stands in the entrance. An upright, older man in a grey jellaba speaks to me in perfect English. 'I haven't spoken this language in twenty years, but it has come back to me.'

We are brought into the reception tent and fresh juices and posh pastries are handed round with bottles of cold water. I am beginning to feel extremely well disposed to these kind people. I explain what I am doing and get lots of good advice. 'Make sure you get everyone's tribal name and write it down.' 'Come back and spend some time with a family getting to know all the traditions and history, especially from the older generation.' The men and the Qaid talk directions and check the next stage of the route. After about half an hour, the Qaid gets up. 'We will leave you to rest and recover now. We've arranged for meat to be brought and water and everything you need. We want you to relax and be comfortable. You are very welcome here.' With that, all the dignitaries get up and after saying very warm farewells, leave us to it with just the Sheikh and one of the soldiers.

Addi and Ychou start building a fire from palm fronds and

preparing the meat. Our wonderful hosts have brought us a whole goat, enough bread for about forty people, bottles of cold Coke and stacks of water. The Sheikh then offers us showers in his house and we gather up our soap and towels and pile into his car. Dshira is a small community with one main road, flanked by impressive solar streetlights, and houses on both sides. The shower has unending hot water and I scrub all the filth off and wash my hair gratefully.

When we get back to the fire, the *titliwin* are underway and Addi is wielding a small axe to chop bits off the goat. He is thoroughly enjoying himself. We lounge on the rugs and cushions and the Sheikh puts the teapot on the coals – not entrusting the tea to us. Addi passes round the skewers and the stars shine brightly above. We eat and chat and just sit in companionable silence. A white kitten arrives and eats her body weight in meat. We stay till long after our usual bedtime, enjoying the feast and the company and the cool of the oasis. Finally, I have to give in to exhaustion and am settling myself in LPF when a small, white face appears at the doorway. The kitten has followed me and spends that night curled up on my chest, purring like crazy.

The next morning, our hosts bring us another feast for breakfast and then load us up with water and bread for our journey and we leave with their generous farewells ringing in our ears. We are all overcome by their hospitality and the way they had thought so much about what we needed and wanted, from the very first moment with the hay for the camels, to the last when they brought us supplies for our onward journey. 'Everything is good,' says Brahim. 'I told you so.'

Riddle answer: sand in a hole.

11

Christmas in the Sands

Layoune – the grand dunes

20 December 2019

We do a quick refuelling stop in Layoune, the main city in the area, and also pick up our new team member, Lhou Ounasser. Layoune is quiet and calm and has a very African vibe about it. The women are butterflies in their colourful tied-dyed *milfahs* and the men stroll elegantly around in their sky-blue *boubous* – long, open-sleeved robes covered in gold embroidery. In the main square, families are taking photos and being bullied by their children into buying balloons from the seller who stands in the centre with a bunch of multi-coloured globes. The suq is full of shops that sell only perfume and tea, the two staples of Sahrawi hospitality. After we have shopped, we stop off at a juice stall by the side of the main road going out of the city and order avocado shakes as the sun goes down.

A cacophony of horns and revving engines approaches us. It is a Sahrawi wedding party. There are four horsemen at the front with two jeeps directly behind them, almost with their bonnets under their tails. Three of the horses are black and one is white. They are all caparisoned in blue and gold with tassels and richly tooled leather. Three of the men are wearing blue *boubous*, but one is in the white and black of a sheikh with a white *chech*. They are all carrying hunting rifles lifted aloft and holding the reins in just one hand. Behind the jeeps is a phalanx of cars with lights at full blast, carrying the wedding party, all pressing heavily on their horns. The jeeps stop and let the horses prance and cavort about 20 metres ahead, then they rev the engines full throttle and scream towards the horsemen. They slam on the brakes to stop just behind them and I can actually smell the burning rubber of the tyres. They do this over and over again and my nerves are shattered. I can't imagine how the horses stand it, but they do.

Lhou is our new companion and has come to take the place of Ychou. He is Jean-Pierre's oldest friend in Morocco. He is in his sixties with a close-shaven head of grey and laughter lines furrowing his face. He immediately makes himself useful around camp with the camels and the tents and even tries to take over my dishwashing duties.

At lunch, I spot a watermelon in a blue bag beside the mess tent and go to bring it over. I open the bag and stick my hand in, only to feel hair and an eyeball. Surprise! It is a goat's head. It's a leftover from our feast and that afternoon the men cook it. They scrape off all the hair, tie the head tightly into a plastic bag and then boil it for hours in the big *gameela*. We are dining round the campfire and I am hoping that I will be able to get away with not eating it in the darkness and just filling up with bread. However, Addi, in typical nomad style, wants to make sure I share in the delicacy. When he sees my face, he takes pity on me and peels bits of the cheek off for me. They are gelatinous but do taste good. Lhou tucks in with gusto.

We leave Layoune and its phosphate factories behind and

walk into the dunes. Whereas Erg Chebbi and Chigaga further north cover a relatively enclosed area, this range of dunes stretches right down to the south. Dune walking is exhausting and I am soon labouring hard to keep pace with the camels, whose hovercraft pads allow them to just float over the sand that I am sinking into with every step. It's not just me, though. 'Zahra, my legs have got a headache,' Addi says at lunch. On the whole, Brahim steers our tribe round the bottom edges to save our energy and we snake along in caravan. A whirring sound alerts us to a forest of wind turbines whose modernity contrasts with the ancient sands and our old-fashioned caravan. They do look magnificent outlined between the gold and the blue of the sky.

We've left all the variety and colour of Sakiya al Hamra behind us and now we are surrounded by vastness. It is time to focus on the details. This is one of the great benefits of walking. You have time to look closely at the land you are moving over. Seeing all the small things busily going about their lives in the vast emptiness of the sands gives me a sense of connectedness to the planet. And, when you look, there is a richness hidden in the desert.

I'm learning all the different animal, bird and insect tracks, or at least trying to. A jerboa has its four feet but also traces of its fluffy pompon tail. A lizard is mainly a tail trail with its claws on either side. A hedgehog is rather delicate and a snake is one long sliver. We find footprints from the desert fox, but fortunately they are old so I am not forced into a mad dash over the dunes again. But the prize of them all is finding hyena tracks, which are extremely rare.

We are in a sandy patch in a meeting place of different dunes when we see them. There is a series of them in the soft sand. A clear one shows the pad of the paw, which looks like a smudged heart, with the imprints of the claws inside it. There appear to be two different types – larger ones and smaller ones, so we speculate that there are cubs. Actually working out what they are for me takes some time. Brahim keeps saying 'iffiss' and describing a predator, but it brings me no further as I list all the words I know for the different predators in Arabic and in Tashlaheet – feeling a bit proud of myself that I know quite so many. Brahim just keeps saying 'iffiss' louder. Finally, I get an inkling. 'Does it sound like Addi when he laughs?' I ask, and I've cracked it.

The species found in this area is the striped hyena. There are only 10,000 of them left in the world so I pray fervently that it was a family that made the tracks and that those cubs grow up. The striped hyena is small and mainly scavenges for food although, in this kind of desert environment, it must be hunting for small prey – mice, lizards – as well as feeding off dead camels and other carcasses.

I'm getting to know Lhou. 'I am a *fellah*, a peasant farmer, Zahra,' he tells me. *Fellah* is quite a hard word to translate, as 'peasant' sounds pejorative but gives the broadest sense. He has a substantial smallholding which he calls his 'jardin' – garden, where he grows all the subsistence crops for the house, like potatoes and onions and fodder, but also cash crops of dates and cumin. He recently bought in solar panels to operate his well and irrigation system and is paying off the credit with the bank. One of his grown-up sons works the smallholding with him, as does his wife. 'I have a very good wife; she works very hard every day.' He has done long expeditions with JP and has lots of fireside stories to tell and he loves it in the evening after supper when we share riddles, guessing hard at all the answers and chuckling happily when I find the answer to one of his.

Riddle: you slice the liver and put the salt in the cracks. Then when the liver is cooked you take out the salt and eat it but you leave the liver. What is it?

(Answer at end of chapter.)

We have the dunes to our left and a wide sunken valley to our right, called a *sabkha*. The sense of space is infinite and the dunes are silvery and rippling and somehow look cool under the sun. We find traces of the past lives that have been spent here. We come across a series of flint tools: knives for cutting and arrow heads. We count eleven. They range from a definite knife to broader, spoon-like shapes – the spearheads that Professor Mouloud had mentioned. There are also long pointed needles. They are all recognisable from the pictures we saw at the rock-carving centre in Smara. This area must have been inhabited for some time for so many tools to have been left, but there is no obvious source of water and it is impossible to imagine the dunes supporting human life. We try out one of the stone knives on a piece of twine and it cuts through it easily. I am absolutely thrilled by this – by using something that our ancestors created so many centuries ago. It ties me to the past in a visceral way.

Walking on, I think my eyes are tricking me. I can see shimmering ahead that looks like water, but I assume it is a mirage. It isn't. In a hollow is a pool of clear water about 10 metres by 10 metres. It is like stumbling on a magic pool. We are surrounded by pure sand – how did it get here? 'It is probably a place where the water collects when there are rains and it stays, year after year,' Brahim tells me and that seems to answer the question about why we found so many tools in one place.

Not only is it water, but it is pure, sweet rainwater good enough for Sahrawi tea. The men take the halters off the

171

camels and they drink deeply. I drink too and it is delicious. Just as I am finishing a big mouthful, I look up to see Alasdair in the middle of it having a really long wee. Regardless, we fill up our water containers. Then, we all get our feet in. It is cold. I plunge my heat-swollen hands in up to mid-arm and can almost see the puffiness going down. I think about going and lying down right in the middle with all my clothes on, but we still have a way to go to bivouac and the pleasure of the moment would be paid for by stomping along in wet clothes. I learn two new Tashlaheet words: *ifurd*, which means a lake/place of water which is usually empty but fills up with rain, like Lake Iriqui; and *amda*, which means a lake/place of water with water actually in it. This is an *amda*.

It is Christmas tomorrow. On our Christmas Eve walk I tell the men all about our Christmas customs in Britain and they immediately chime in with what they have to contribute in celebration. Brahim says that he will tell the story of Issa, Jesus, in the prayers and Lhou and Addi say they will eat porridge with me in the morning in honour of the feast – 'No milk, though, Zahra,' from Addi.

Our camping spot is in the shelter of the great dunes. There are a few scrubby plants for the camels to graze on and they go off in search of amrad trees as soon as they are released. 'Do you want décor? I'll put the door of the tent directly in front of this garden,' Brahim tells me. The garden is one small shrub about 10cm high with reddish berries on it, which feels almost Christmassy.

At lunch, I say that in the evening I will need one sock from each of them.

Addi: 'Is it OK if they are dirty?'

Lhou: 'What if they are old and have holes in them?'

Brahim: 'Why only one?'

Addi: 'One each?'

Lhou: 'Will we get them back?'

Brahim: 'Lhou only has one pair!'

That afternoon everyone is busy scrubbing with lots of soap and a rationed mug of water each in the sandcastle buckets and the tents are festooned with single socks in varying states of repair.

I explain Santa Claus with my own embellishments. 'In our tradition, there is a very great jinn called Santa Claus. He is big and fat with a long white beard and he wears a red jellaba and red *babouches*. He has six strong camels who can fly like the wind and his job is to visit all the children of the world to help them celebrate Issa's birthday. All year, he and his army of minor jinns work hard in their hidden workshops in the icy north to make toys and gifts. Then, on this night, he loads his camels with the gifts and flies to every corner to seek out good people. We have to hang one sock each on the *giton* and if you have been good all year, the great jinn, Santa, will come and fill it with something nice. If you have been bad it will stay empty.' A general discussion ensues as to the meaning of 'good' and what the criteria are.

I have taken the precaution of bringing four clothes pegs and after supper we all troop outside and hang our stockings on the guy rope, each one of us intoning, '*Bismillah*, in the Name of God.' I say goodnight and warn them all very severely, 'Oh, Men, it is very important that you stay in the tent all night. You must not go outside. If you hear movement in the night, do not fear, it is jinn Santa. But you cannot see him or he will turn you into a camel and take you back to the icy north. Be warned, stay inside.'

Of course I have brought supplies, and I sort everything out in LPF. I have carried, or rather Hamish has, a family tin of Quality Street. I divide it exactly into four piles and then add a hundred dirham note to the men's. When I hear snoring from the *giton*, I sneak out into the night and immediately fall over a tent peg and yelp loudly. I freeze but the snoring continues and I keep going on tiptoes and fill the stockings.

The next morning after prayers there is a yell from Addi. 'Zahra – look! Jinn Santa has been – the socks are full.' The men are all waiting eagerly in a line in front of their stockings and at my say-so unpeg them and duck into the tent where tea and porridge are waiting. They empty them out on the floor in front of them and are gratifyingly delighted with the sweets and the note. 'But, Zahra, why don't you have any money?' Brahim asks me suspiciously. 'I heard a very big jinn in the night. Santa shouts out like a woman, Zahra,' Addi adds slyly.

It's a strange day because I am thinking so much of my family at home. I spend the afternoon sewing Quality Street wrappers onto a twig to act as our Christmas tree and dreaming of turkey. Our lunch is actually cold, leftover macaroni, which isn't really the same. My mum, with kind foresight, had bought little boxes of Edinburgh rock for each of the men and wrapped them in tartan paper and I had my presents from the suq in Smara, which I piled up under the Christmas twig in the *giton*.

They are opened after supper. The Edinburgh rock disappears in a flash with appreciative crunching and the tartan paper is carefully folded and kept. The men are all touched that my mum has thought of them. 'Farida is a good woman.' Lhou and Addi put on their *chechs* and demand to be told how smart they look. 'Very beautiful,' exclaims Addi as he admires his head wrapped in 4 metres of glorious tie-dye in vibrant reds, yellows and pinks. Alasdair joins in the celebration by sticking his head right into the *giton* in search of snacks. It's Christmas so we give him some bread as a treat.

The dunes are treating us to the most magnificent sunrises and sunsets. Our camps are always in the lee of them which provides shelter from the wind. We have seen no humans but will come across a stone-age tool or an old sardine can to show that these places have been constantly used to camp through the ages. In the evenings, all four of us usually go up to the top of the dunes to watch the sun sink before prayer. I take my chair up so I can write and we sit together, toes in the sand. The colours are like waves rolling across the sky towards the sand of the dunes. The blue is wiped away by yellow, then orange, lavender and pink deepening into soft crimson as the sun disappears. The men run down to pray and I gather up my chair and charge down after them. I discover a new marvel. The dunes have a voice which is roused by me running down them. They sing with every step, a kind of deep rumbling that is earth- rather than manmade and reminds me of the vibrating sound of a didgeridoo playing. I wonder if they are grumbling at me for disturbing their sleep.

Apart from water, our daily obsession is meteorites. Meteorites are the gold at the end of the rainbow, the equivalent of winning the lottery, and the men always have one eye to the ground. Addi picks up a stone and throws it to Brahim. 'What do you think?' 'No.' 'Close?' 'Maybe thirty per cent'. It is a part of modern nomad culture to search for them and the men are hopeful that they will find some on our journey. 'The thing is, Zahra, in famous places for meteorites like Tissint and Tata, everyone has looked and all of the meteorites have been found, but here there are no people so we still have a chance,' reasons Brahim. Tissint is where in 2011 a meteorite from Mars landed, shattering in all directions to the benefit of many. It's one of only five rocks from the Red Planet ever to be found on Earth and actually carried traces of Martian soil. Fragments sold for a thousand dollars a gram and the Tissint meteorite entered into get-rich-quick folk-lore. More space rocks have been found in Morocco metre for metre than any other country.

The nomads have become experts in spotting them and very often will carry a magnet to help detect whether the stone is just another stone burned black by the sun or is a meteorite with a fusion crust formed by a journey millions of kilometres through the burning atmosphere of space.

Meteorites are divided into three basic groups: irons, stones and stony irons, and all contain a significant amount of extra-terrestrial iron and nickel, hence why the nomads carry magnets. The stone meteorites will stick to a magnet but the iron and stony iron ones will stick so strongly that it is actually hard to prise them off. Another sign that you have picked up a meteorite, not just a stone, is weight. Because of the amount of iron in them, a meteorite is much heavier than a normal stone. A tennis-ball-sized meteorite could weigh around 2.5 kilos.

We had spent the very beginning of our journey work-ing out how we would divide our spoils should we find something.

BB: 'We are a team. If we find anything, we should divide it evenly. Then, we all benefit.'

Addi: 'No way, if I find anything, I am keeping it all for myself. I will be rich.'

Brahim: 'I think we should have a sliding scale. If one of us finds something up to a certain value then we keep it, but if it is worth more than that then we can share it.'

I was with BB but am not sure if that wasn't partly

motivated by the knowledge that the chances of me finding anything ahead of the men, who constantly scoured the land beneath our feet with their sharp eyes, was pretty well zero.

The sand has taken on a 3D effect and the herring bones appear to be shifting, making me feel dizzy. I am trying to film it as a *watta* (Land Rover) rolls up with a father and son inside. It is a classic: the old blue colour with an open back and a roof rack. It is covered in dents and bashes and the paintwork has been scraped off in parts but, of course, no rust because the air is so dry. The back is packed to the gunnels with supplies for their camp, including a fine-looking white chicken who is poking her head curiously out of the netting.

We exchange our greetings and the father, Mohammed, tells us there are wells 'around', which sounds a bit vague to me and more difficult when you are on foot than when you are in a Land Rover. He gives detailed directions to the nearest one, Bir Abbas (which turns out to be a few days' away), to Brahim and Lhou. Salih, the son, and Addi, who are about the same age, nip round the side of the Land Rover and put their heads together in intense discussion. Salih is somewhat of an expert in meteorites and he has a special kit with a knife, a magnet and a magnifying glass which he's demonstrating to Addi, whose eyes gleam with covetousness. He shows us two small fragments he had picked up. Each one is the size of an olive. One is darker while the other is browner. They both stick to the magnet. While Brahim is jotting directions in his notebook, Salih is Bluetoothing pictures to Addi's phone showing surfaces of stones. Addi redoubles his scouring of the earth.

We only have two bidots of water left and that is too low for safety, so Brahim decides to head us away from the dunes and towards the sea for a spell. He has seen a speck of white far in the distance.

Me: 'Where are we going?'

Brahim: 'We are heading towards the ocean.'

Me: 'We are running out of water. What are we going to do?'

Brahim: 'Well, we are in the hands of God. You remember a few days ago we found the amda – the little lake – when we needed water? Today, if God wills it, we will find nomads and they will be able to give us some water.'

Me: 'Do you know for sure there are nomads over there?'

Brahim: 'Everything will happen according to God. We trust in Him. I saw something over there; maybe it is a tent, maybe it is a well. We are going that way and we know that nomads are in the area.'

Brahim's voice is calm as always.

This water stress is with us throughout the expedition. It always weighs at the back of my mind. Will we find water? Will it be sweet? Will there be enough for the camels? Of course, we had planned the route carefully with JP and we knew that you could expect to find nomads in certain areas to give us water, but the very nature of a nomadic life means we didn't know exactly where. However, I have complete confidence in Brahim, as I know he would never let anything happen to us. Also, we could always walk two or three days to a road or alternatively to military outposts on the beach. I have read the statistics and know them intellectually. 'With the existing climate change scenario, by 2030, water scarcity in some arid and semi-arid places will displace between 24 million and 700 million people,' according to the UN, but that is a very different thing from actually experiencing water scarcity day after day. I was doing this journey voluntarily and it was a joyous thing, but the lack of water was a looming threat. For the herdspeople who live it, it is an ever-present disaster that threatens their existence.

After a couple more hours of walking, the white flash reveals itself as two square tents. There is a man sitting to the right but, unusually, it is a woman who comes out and ushers us in for tea. She is called Maymouna and she explains that the man is a Saudi called Abdullah from Riad and that he is here with a Saudi hunting group. Abdullah comes forward and sits down with us for tea. He tells us that there are fifteen of them camped about 20 kilometres away and that he is here for three months. He then shows me a very gruesome video of a hawk chasing down and killing an ahbar bird. Two other ladies join us as we wait for tea. 'Sahrawi tea takes forever,' Brahim whispers. 'You need an hour just for one tiny glass.' The ladies use the time to quiz me with the standard questions.

'Do you have a *watta*? No? Why not!'

'Do you ride the camels? No? Why not? It is a very long way to walk!'

The nomads are able to spare us two bidots of good water and we carry on – Abdullah passes us later in his fancy 4x4 with a cheerful wave.

The ahbar is the Houbara bustard which is native to North Africa. It is a small to mid-sized bustard and has a light brown body with a white underbelly. It mainly runs along the ground like a grouse.

It's a conservation success story. Until 2004 its numbers were declining but now they are increasing. This is largely due to the intervention of the Gulf States who have been breeding the birds in captivity and releasing them into the wild, in order to then hunt them.

When you see pictures of the bustard conservation projects in Morocco, it shows the ambitious scale of them. There are rows and rows of breeding sheds and large facilities for research and development. The men tell me that the conservation programmes lease vast areas of the desert to release the buzzards into and protect them with rangers. Hunting is controlled and taken very seriously. The hunters arrive with their guns and their falcons and spend weeks chasing down their prey. They are supported by local Moroccans.

'But, Zahra, there is a secret,' Brahim tells me. 'When they kill the bird, they open its stomach and take out something that is hidden there. They give the meat to the Moroccans but we are never allowed to see the thing that is inside the bird.'

'That's right,' chimes in Lhou. 'We have a lot of ahbar in our area near Zagora, big ones, chicks, everything. We think that the ahbar eat a mineral which turns into a precious stone in their belly and this is what the Arabs are searching for.' I am intrigued by this Amazigh story but will settle happily for just seeing a live bird.

In fact, I put seeing an ahbar up into the top four team aims of the expedition. Brahim wants to get us there safely, Addi wants to find a meteorite, Lhou wants to persuade Addi into an appropriate marriage, and I want to see a Houbara buzzard.

Addi is feeling fed up.

'Zahra, this place is no good.'

'Why, Addi? What's the problem?'

'No water, no signal, no oats [for the camels], no vegetables [for us] – nothing!'

But Addi's life is about to get much better. We have been heading for the well at Bir Abbas, which we know is big enough to water the camels as well as fill up all our containers. When we get there, the trough is crowded with mothers and their young camels cavorting on bendy legs, watched by a tribe of wide-winged storks. The guardian comes out to get the pump going and three women with two children pull me into their tent. The tent is spacious and ordered with a large, intricately patterned, maroon, Persian-style rug on the floor. An old man is lying on cushions to one side. The matriarch starts brewing the tea and we are served goat's milk and dates with a creamy butter on the side – the idea is to scoop the butter up with the date and the combination is extremely rich and delicious. One of the two sisters has a little boy who plays around our feet and the other sister, Rabab, dressed in a bright orange *milfah*, busies herself taking selfies. As is customary, she sprays my chest with perfume to cool me down (and disguise the smell of Hamish) and then goes to the corner where there is a pile of blankets neatly folded on a wicker box and pulls out a grey and white *milfah* which she drapes on me.

I am really enjoying my girl time and being in the cool and off my feet when the men arrive – my three, the guardian and his son. Addi is uncharacteristically silent but the rest of us exchange news on what we have seen, our camels, their herds, the lack of water, hopes for rain and, of course, directions to the next water supply. The old man revives with tea and recites some classical Arabic poetry to us. He congratulates us on our exploration, saying, 'An orphan is not someone who has lost their father and mother but someone who has not experienced anything.' Time passes too quickly and we get up to continue. Rabab runs out of the tent and comes back holding a watch in a little box, which she insists I take along with the *milfah*.

We are barely out of camp when Addi loops his camels onto Brahim's and nobbles me.

Addi: 'Zahra, show me the photos of the tent, of the girl.'

Me: 'Which girl?'

Addi: 'Zahra, there was only one girl, the other one had a baby.'

Me: 'Rabab? Wearing the orange *milfah*?'

Addi's eyes do something I've only previously seen in cartoons. They spiral and pop and love hearts spill out. 'Rabab,' he sighs. I obligingly get up the pictures on my iPhone.

'Isn't she beautiful?' Addi exclaims. 'And she can read and write. I want to marry her. Do you think she would marry me? I hope so. Do you think Lalla Ito would like her?' I am not sure about this, but I reckon that Lalla Ito would rather Addi marry someone from closer to home who is used to the harsh conditions of the mountains.

Lhou chimes in. 'Addi. What do you know of this girl? She is a Sahrawi. She cannot even bake bread. Yes, she is beautiful and nice, but do you think that is what marriage is about? Can she herd flocks? Can she work in the garden? She is from the desert. Here the life is easier. The women can stay in the tent and look after the children. They don't have to go out to the mountains. In Saghro she will be outside all day and she isn't used to it. She is fat – do you think she would be able to walk far with the goats? What about her family – they will be so far away from her. This will be very hard.'

Addi makes a valiant defence: 'She can learn to bake bread and I can leave her in our house in Nqob. She can raise the children – because she can read, she can help them with their schooling. I want a woman like this, beautiful and educated.'

That night, I make a big cultural error. Rabab texts me and asks me to send her all the photos that I took. I do that and include one of Addi in his Christmas *chech* looking very dashing, but when Brahim sees me doing it he is horrified.

'No, Zahra. If her brothers or her father see that picture they might come after us. It is very dangerous. A woman's honour is sacred and they will think that Addi is playing with her. You have done a very bad thing.' I spend the night awake worrying at every noise that it is the family coming to beat us, but all is well.

For the rest of the expedition, Addi begs me daily to look at Rabab's photo. He also asks me to send it to him, but now I know better.

Politics and religion may be left best undiscussed, but living in Morocco I have got well used to being tackled on both. 'Are you a Muslim?' is something I am almost always asked within minutes of meeting someone new and when I say that no, I am a Christian, the follow-up is invariably, 'But why? You are so nice. You must become a Muslim; Islam is the true religion. You must convert.' Sometimes it jars but I never take offence. In our culture, it would be unthinkable to say these things, but it is the intention that is important. People are not trying to insult me or belittle me; they are just spontaneously reacting and encouraging me to do something that they believe in absolutely and that they believe would be good for me. Politics is more dangerous, though. I want to know how the people who live in this region feel and what they think about the situation. I get glimpses as we meet Sahrawis on our journey, not usually by asking but just by listening.

Khadija is a woman of about my age who lives at the Well of Cold Water, Hassi al Ma' Bard. When we stop, she gives me tea as the men water the camels and sprays me so thoroughly with perfume that when we go on our way Addi demands that I walk downwind of him. When I tell her we are heading for Guerguerat, she asks, 'That is far away on the border. Do you think it is Moroccan or Polisario?' I parry,

'Khadija, my sister, what do you think? That is more important than my opinion. I am only a foreigner.' 'It is Moroccan,' she tells me firmly.

New Year's Day is cold, the coldest day so far, and getting dressed is a dance of taking my night clothes off and putting my day clothes on inside my warm sleeping bag. A couple of days before, the sand in my ears had itched me so much that I had poked a big needle in to try to clear it out. I'd pierced the skin and got an ear infection for my stupidity. It had got worse and the whole right side of my face is clogged, so I decide it is time to break out the antibiotics. The men have lit a fire to heat up their socks. '*Asougwas Amayno!* Happy New Year!' We all greet each other and embrace to welcome the new year. I sit by the fire eating my porridge and watching the orange sunrise fade to blue.

I do the dishes and go to bring in Hector. I untie his hobble and swish him lightly on his back legs to get him moving towards camp. He knows I am a soft touch and stops at every prickly thorn bush to grab a quick mouthful of extra breakfast. We set off at 8.17. No matter what time we wake up or how fast or slow we pack, we are always on the road within five minutes of that each way.

'It is New Year's Day and today we are going to drink camel's milk,' announces Brahim. Lhou and I nod enthusiastically and Addi makes a 'yeuch' face. An hour into our walk, we come up to a neat, square white tent with a pointed roof which is obviously inhabited. There are about twenty goats close by and a big water container. 'Zahra, get up here, you are the key, go first,' Lhou tells me. The men stay at a safe distance away, around 50 metres, with the camels. With no men visible, they would not come into a tent where there are women they don't know. That is why I am the key, because I can approach freely.

Khadija arrives and greets me with surprise and then beaming hospitality. 'Come in, come in. Drink tea with me. Have you eaten? Would you like some *goufiyya*?' I thank her and drink deeply, then ask if I can take some to the men outside. Brahim and Lhou say, '*Bismillah*,' and take long draughts. I persuade Addi into a sip which he promptly spits out. 'Not good, Zahra!' he says and looks at me accusingly.

I go back into the tent, where a black and white kitten is lapping at a dish, and sit down for some tea, which is being brewed over hot charcoal. 'Perfume, get the perfume,' Khadija tells her daughter. My last proper wash was well over ten days ago. I drink my tea and take three glasses out for the men, then as I am going back in to say goodbye, I hear Lhou yelling urgently, 'Zahra, get out here!' I duck out quickly and see a tall, well-built man with a flourishing moustache bearing down on us. He is running fast and brandishing a large stick threateningly. He looks extremely fierce and furiously angry. It's Khadija's husband and he is not happy about these strange blokes near his wife. Just then, he spots me and the tension is diffused. He puts down the stick and greetings are exchanged. 'I'm glad you came out quickly and that we stayed back away from the tent,' says Brahim to me as we leave, 'he was big and that stick looked strong!'

We had stopped for our elevenses – my favourite part of every day – when up drives a *watta*. A short, stocky man climbs out, with the hood of his jellaba firmly pulled up over his *chech* to keep the wind out. We say our hellos and then ask him to join us for a snack, 'No, no, I have everything in the *watta*,' he says, but he accepts some orange when pressed. He crouches down. 'Where is she from? Spain? France?' he asks the men. 'She's from Scotland, Injleez,' replies Brahim. 'Yes, I'm from Scotland,' I chime in. Realising that I speak Arabic, he looks at me sternly. 'And which country are you in now?' he asks. This is a very tricky political question and one that has to be answered with some delicacy. I think fast. 'I am in the Sahara,' I say truthfully and neutrally. 'May I ask which country you are from?' 'I am from the Western Sahara, the Western Sahara in the west of Africa,' he says firmly.

The wind strengthens and starts to whip up the sand. It hovers between hot and cold. 'Why don't you put on your jacket, Zahra? You will get cold,' says Brahim. I say no as I am still warm from walking and he asks again. 'I think I am OK, thank you, Brahim.' Five minutes later, he stops the camels and brings me my jacket. I had not given the right answer.

Actually, I am soon glad of it as the temperature drops in the face of the wind. Up ahead, we see our friend's *watta*. He is standing by his *shiqawa* – the enormous plastic stores for water which allow the nomads to live here. He beckons us over. 'Come and fill your containers,' he says. 'Take as much as you like, fill everything and let the camels drink.' This is a really generous offer as water is such a precious commodity and so hard to get. His stern manner has given way to kindness and he goes to get a bowl from his *watta* so we can ladle water into the bidots more easily. The camels hadn't drunk for five days and cram their heads down into the trench. 'My name is Mohammed Raha,' he tells me. 'Don't forget. Write that in your phone. Take a picture of me and tell your people about the Sahrawis.'

Head down, I trudge into the wind. 'Look, Zahra, look. The camels are coming,' shouts Brahim. It is a magical moment. Appearing out of nowhere, through the misty veil of the sandstorm, I can see dozens of them running towards the trough. They must have seen or heard the *watta* and are coming down to be watered. There are dark honey-coloured ones, pure white, and piebald, all different sizes. Some are galloping, others are racing each other in little spurts and the larger, older ones at the back are walking at a measured pace. Soon, I can't see the water trench for bodies.

Now, the wind is gale force and directly in our faces. Sand stings any part of me that isn't covered. There is no point in speaking because nothing can be heard above the howling. My *chech* is wrapped tightly round my nose and mouth. It is wet from my breath and from the endless river of snot coming out of my nose. I feel like I am being smothered and lift it up. Immediately, the desert blows into my mouth. Sand coats my teeth and chokes in my throat. I pull the *chech* back up and walk on. This is one of the really tough things about this stage. Sandstorms are mentally and physically very hard to deal with. I imagine that if you suffered from claustrophobia, you would panic, as the world shrinks down to nothing.

Then, Addi yells across, 'Zahra, Zahra, for you.' He has found a solitary yellow flower, rather like a dandelion, and has picked it for me. I am still in the hell of the sandstorm but my heart has lightened with his thoughtfulness. 'The wind is tiring for all of us, even the camels. It plays with your head,' shouts Brahim. I feel better for knowing I am not suffering alone. The thing is, though, on this kind of adventure, you have to keep going. You have to keep walking no matter how you feel or what the circumstances are. There is no real room for misery or anger as you have no choice but to accept whatever nature throws at you. It is an endless, excruciating lesson in patience. It is also where you mine the depths of companionship and come to rely on each other to make it through.

We slide down into a sunken bowl where some scrubby

thorn bushes are growing and there is some shelter. Our 20km are done and it is time to set up camp. We crowd into the mess tent and go about cutting up the vegetables for lunch: a salad of cucumber, onion, black olives, green peppers and raisins with sardines in tomato sauce, bread and hot, sweet, life-saving tea. I have brought eye drops in for the men after a day in a sandstorm and when I go to administer them, they all fling themselves flat on their backs ready for the medicine and hold their eyelids open with varying degrees of success. 'You're my mum, thank you, Zahra,' says Addi.

EXPLORING NOTHINGNESS

From west and south of the grand dunes – Argoub

3 January 2020

Brahim is quiet but his eyes – which are the only part I can see of him – are filled with disquiet. We are down to a couple of litres of water. Two days ago we gave our bidots to the park ranger and muqaddim who had come to visit us in camp in their *watta*. They said they would fill them and bring them back to the bivouac in the morning. We hadn't seen them since. Our morning is spent mainly in silence as we force our way through the screaming gale. Sand blasts any tiny strip of uncovered flesh and pushes us back as we try to move forward. Then, in the distance, we see a speck of white travelling fast, kicking up dust. It swerves off course and comes towards us and I assume it is the authorities with our water. 'It's not them,' says Brahim. 'Different coloured *watta*.' We stop the camels and a nomad leaps out. He is called Mohamed and we shout greetings at each other over the gusting wind. He asks how we are for water and tells us he has a *sagwa* nearby and can give us some.

We follow behind him to where it is hidden in the dip – a

giant, white plastic sack which can hold 60 tonnes of water and which is replenished by trucks coming in from Boujdour, where he lives, around 50km away. He is a herdsman but lives in the town and just comes in every two days or so to check on his camels and water them. He knows where Scotland is and even that it's part of the UK and has just had an election. He has to pay for his water but won't accept any money from us and kindly allows us to fill up the smaller holders we have left. Just as we are finishing, a second *watta* turns up with the authorities and our bidots. 'We drove around all last night looking for you. Where were you camped? We were so worried when we couldn't find you. Thanks be to God that you are here,' they say. They have also brought us four freshly baked baguettes.

'Zahra, do you know the story of Suleiman and the ant?' Brahim asks me as we walk on, reflecting on our water gains. 'King Suleiman [Solomon] the Wise was walking in his garden when he came across a fat, healthy ant. God had blessed him with the ability to speak to all creatures and so he stopped to talk to her because in Islam ants are very clever. Camels are deemed to be the most perfect of animals but ants are also high up. "Greetings, O Honoured Ant," said Suleiman. "Tell me: you are so fat and healthy, how many oats do you eat in a year?" The ant thought carefully, "O Prophet Suleiman, to keep in good condition like this, I eat about three bags of oats a year." King Suleiman built the ant a beautiful enclosure with sand hills and bushes for shade and plenty of space to make a house and left her with three big bags of the finest oats. After a year he came back and he was very shocked. The ant was skinny and there were one and a half bags of oats left. "Why did you tell me you ate three bags and yet you have only eaten one and a half?" "O Lord

Suleiman, I eat three when I am free because then God is providing and God always provides. But here, I saved half because you could forget about me and leave me for two years and then what would I do?"

'You see, Zahra, we are worried about water but God has given us ample water. If I keep the bidots with me and we meet with nomads, then we can fill them and have enough, but if I give the bidots into the hands of others, then that can be a problem. God provides all things.'

The wind is debilitating. We are walking fast and hard and our food is low again. We spend the whole day debating whether we might have to ration sardines at lunch to half a tin each. Addi is violently against it, while prudent Lhou is arguing for it. Our gas is also low so we don't want to use it for bread and Addi and Lhou bake in the sand instead. There are no stones here but the concept is broadly the same. Lhou walks far to find a dead tree and drags back an enormous branch. A patch of sand is dug out and once the wood has burned down to embers in it, they are scraped to the side, the round of dough is put in and then covered with fresh sand and the embers on top. Lhou is the fire master in camp and he feeds the wood on top. As I watch, the dough under the sand starts to rise and a little volcano-shaped mountain emerges. It's magic. When it is ready, the bread is dug out of the sand and beaten to get rid of any grains. To my amazement, it isn't at all gritty. The sand hasn't stuck. I like it even more than the stone bread as it is a bit softer and denser on the inside.

Now, we have no water for washing ourselves. Addi's feet – which are famed for their scent – are the exception. 'Brahim ordered me to wash them with soap,' he tells me. For the washing up, the men don't trust me and measure out

191

tiny amounts for me to use. Lhou does the tea glasses – water only, no soap.

There are lots of female camels around so our boys are constantly bubbling and roaring. One follows us closely for half an hour until Lhou has to go and chase her away or she will be too far from her herd. We come across a mother crying for her baby. The melancholy sound haunts us all and we search for it. We find her fresh tracks with the little one so we know they were together not too long ago and hope that they find each other. We can't stop, though. The pace is relentless but with supplies so low, we have to move on quickly. A new bird appears which is shaped like a swift and is black on top, but flashes white underneath, and a hare springs ahead of us out of some bushes and dashes across our path. We find a perfect dead owl, preserved in the dry air.

There are still some amrad trees and we always head to them to bivouac. I find two perfect white arrowheads in one camp – proof that this has long been a safe haven in this brutal landscape. The grazing is meagre and the camels are constantly trying to find snacks in camp, snuffling up every discarded onion skin and gulping down my soapy meagre ration of washing up water if I leave the bucket for an instant. If we have any leftover pasta, I take it out to them and feed them. Hamish likes it if I feed him with a spoon. The camels have even started drinking any extra soup straight from the *gameela*, bending their nostrils down to it first with mighty suspicion and then putting their noses right in and bringing them out with a loud whoosh and a spray of turmeric.

For 200 miles, we have been heading towards the hot springs at Jirifiyya where there will be water for everything: us, the camels and washing. Brahim has been navigating using the sun and the wind, which are both constant, as well as directions from the nomads we meet. At night, he checks where our red dot has got to on downloaded Google maps. On the morning we are due to arrive, we wake up in a thick mist and no wind. Brahim leads us surely across the featureless landscape. Then, out of the mist appears a strip of trees. He has found it: a small patch of green maybe 1 kilometre by 500 metres in an enormous sea of sand. It is an astounding feat of navigation and he is justifiably triumphant. 'No need for GPS, Zahra.' Lorries are pounding up and down, carrying tar to tarmac the piste and create a new road, as we emerge from the desert. There is an empty hut on the lip of a ridge which looks down onto the first green we have seen since Dshira.

As soon as the tents are up, the men take the camels down to the troughs to water them and then let them loose to eat to their hearts' content. There is a whole network of pipes and channels and what looks like a swimming pool with steam coming off the hot water and a big notice that reads, 'Do not swim.' Addi has gone for a 'shower' and explodes into LPF. 'Zahra, quick, give me some of that perfume the nomads gave you. Spray me.' I do as I am told and then get my shampoo and soap and towel and walk up with Brahim to a shack in the woods beside a source pumping hot water into the channels. I take the biggest bucket and a sandcastle one. Five times, I hand that big bucket out to Brahim, who is doing his washing outside, to fill, until I am white and wrinkled all over. Now, I understand why Addi needed the perfume. I stink of rotten eggs from the sulphuric water, but I feel amazing and at least 3 kilos lighter after scraping off layers of dirt and dead skin and rinsing sand out of my hair and ears and eyes and every orifice.

I'm walking around barefoot enjoying the soggy grass in the bottom of the hollow below our tents when Addi calls out, 'Zahra, come. This donkey is hurt.' A sad little creature is standing there with a rope hobble that has cut so deeply into his leg that it has almost severed his hoof. Addi and I go up to camp and come back with the first-aid kit and Brahim. The men gently cut the rope out from the flesh while I hold the donkey's head. He shivers but stands still and lets them free him. I think that someone must have left him tethered and he eventually had to pull his rope to get food and water until it cut right to the bone.

Addi throws away the severed rope and then Brahim douses the wound in betadine (antiseptic) and smears in copious amounts of antibiotic cream. Addi wraps a gauze bandage round and round, tying it off at the end. The donkey stands good as gold through it all; he understands we are trying to help. At the end, we let him loose and he hobbles to the trough to drink. He has plenty to graze on and to drink. In the evening I go down to check on him and see that a herd of wild donkeys have come in from the desert to the water, so he has company too.

We are about 30km away from the nearest shop and we need to reprovision. A young Sahrawi is collecting some water from the springs and gets talking to Brahim. He offers us a lift to the shop and back and we hop into his car. He lives in Dakhla and is taking a camping trip into the desert to explore for a few days. He is so open and friendly that I gain confidence and ask him about what it is like for him, as a young man who was born before the conflict started, to live in this disputed territory. He tells us that his life is very good. He has been to college and he has a job. He lives with his family and is hoping to get married. I ask him if there were a referendum how he would vote. 'For independence,' he says without hesitation. When I ask him why, he says it

Armed with hunting rifles, the four horsemen lead the wedding party in Layoune.

Once we left Layoune, we were walking in the dunes. While the camels can almost hover over the sand, for the rest of us the going was much tougher.

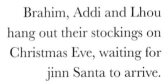

Brahim, Addi and Lhou hang out their stockings on Christmas Eve, waiting for jinn Santa to arrive.

Taking a moment's rest on the long, featureless walk.

For the final part of our expedition, landmines were a constant source of concern.

As we neared the end of our journey at Guerguerat, we crossed an arched rock bridge created by years of erosion.

The Atlas Expedition

21 August–27 October 2020

By the time we began the third leg of our journey, the world had changed and strict Covid rules meant we had to wear masks as we set off – even the camels had been affected by lockdown.

After some of our camps in the Sahara, this was a beautiful location to stop at early in our trip.

The fast-flowing River Za is not easy for the camels to cross, but the coolness of the water was a great relief in the heat of the sun.

The Beni Hilal people are Arabs, and very distinct from other Moroccans. (Left) A small, low metal screen separates the kitchen area from the living area, while (right) that evening we were offered a whole spatchcocked sheep for dinner.

(Left) Lachlan is treated after developing blisters on his pad, which can be a very serious problem for a camel. (Right) A rare desert monitor lizard – scientists aren't sure if their bite is poisonous, but as it was about 1.5 metres long, I wasn't going to find out.

My favourite sort of landscape.

Walking past Lake Isli, the deepest lake in Morocco, which occupies a special place in Amazigh legend.

As we entered dinosaur footprint territory, this cave had a little grotto outside it, filled with plastic hairbrushes left by women hoping to conceive.

A line of dinosaur footprints – fourteen of them – clearly visible in the rock.

With our journey nearly complete, this Amazigh village was stunningly situated.

Top: Brahim, Addi, BB. Bottom: Ali, Lhou, JP.

Me and Hamish.

is not because of the current situation, which is good, but because of the past when his grandparents were oppressed and their lands and flocks taken and members of his extended family were killed.

I'm starting to struggle with the physicality of the trip. It's hot and the wind just doesn't stop. We are walking fast for five hours and I don't want to drink because I can't afford to stop and pee and then have to run to catch up. I am thirsty and dehydrated. Mentally, 'I don't want to do this anymore' is starting to creep in but that is a thought I mustn't entertain. The desert is constantly challenging. Its beauty comes at a high price and I marvel at the nomads who make their life here.

That life is not easy and sometimes it becomes untenable. The effects of the drought are becoming more and more visible. We are passing herds of camels, and sometimes sheep, grazing on the scrub that is left, but it is not rich. In the distance, we see a group of large lorries stopped in the middle of the wilderness. When we get there, it is a nomad family. They are loading all their sheep and camels onto the six lorries and are heading east towards Guelmim. They have relatives there who have told them that the grazing is better. It is the modern nomad way, using vehicles to transport them the long distances to the potential of a sustainable life.

We are en route to Bir Anzarane. It is the next place with food and water and every morning we chant – 'Where are we going?' 'Bir Anzarane, by the Grace of God.' With less and less on the outside, we are focusing inwards and trying to find our amusement where we can. Everything takes a long time, which is a good thing because we have lots of empty space to fill. Addi finds a hollow metal bar on the walk and he and Lhou plot to make a flute. This takes a whole day at camp.

They get one of the iron tent pegs and hammer holes in the tube at regular intervals. Then, they squish the far end so that the air is compressed. When it is done, Brahim and I sit back ready for our evening's music recital. Lhou has first go and, to our amazement, actually coaxes a kind of tune from it. Addi takes up the instrument for his turn and gives it a good blow; nothing. He puffs again, going bright red; nothing. A third mighty effort and a tiny peep comes out. 'I am the champion!' proclaims Lhou. 'The old beats the young.'

With all the female camels around, we have to bivouac somewhere that we can tie up the camels at night. 'Otherwise I will be sitting here all night with their cords in one hand and a stick in another,' says Brahim bitterly. Ideally we would camp far from any nomads, so that the boys wouldn't have to spend their afternoons bound to the trees with their little heads bobbing up like meercats every time a lady camel passes, but amrad trees are in short supply so we bivouac near a nomad encampment and share the grove.

At lunchtime a tall, dark-skinned youth appears, shyly ducking his head into the tent and asking for a light for his cigarette. He is called Mohamed and is from Mauritania. He tells us that he has been here with the herd belonging to the nomads for a year and is earning 3,000 MAD a month (£250). I ask him if he is lonely and if he gets to talk to his family or go home. He says he gets to talk to the family sometimes in the Land Rover because they have a signal there. He is so reserved that he refuses to come into the tent but hovers at the door until we use our joint pressure of hospitality to force him inside.

He drinks some tea and we give him a plate of sardines and salad and bread for lunch, which he nibbles at. Brahim and Lhou quiz him about which part of Mauritania he is from as they have walked some of it. Mohamed is overjoyed when they work out that they have actually been to his town. He says he hopes to go home sometime in the next year. After he has gone back to the camels, the men explain that it is very common for the nomads in this area to go to Mauritania to hire young men as herdsman. 'It is hard work looking after the camels and they are rich. They have the animals, maybe two to three hundred, and they have their wives and families in the cities like Layoune and Boujdour. They come out in their *watta* every few days to check on things and to bring supplies and water to the herdsman. And he is happy too. 3,000 MAD is a lot of money, and in Mauritania it is a fortune. He can help his family and maybe when he goes home he can start a small business,' Brahim tells me.

We are packing up the camp in the morning when suddenly all the men drop what they are doing and run at full speed to the edge of the grove. It is Hector Saghro on the rampage. He had spotted an attractive white-faced *talrumt* (female camel) and her calf on the outskirts of the camp. While we were busying ourselves with taking down the tents, he seized his opportunity and crept surreptitiously through the trees until he was right beside her. Some serious speed-flirting had obviously taken place because, by the time the men saw what was happening, Hector was nibbling lovingly at her neck and she was sinking down to couch, ready for some action. Poor Hector, just as he was about to achieve his heart's desire, he was grabbed by all three men and dragged off. The hussy was chased away and Hector was led bubbling and frothing back into camp. 'I would have let him do the deed,' Brahim tells me. 'But the other camels had seen him and were galloping up. It would have been a mass rape.'

We haven't left the grove of thwarted love far behind

when we came across a baby camel so newly born that it is still partially covered in its umbilical sack. It is couched and its legs look far too big and bendy for its body. The mother is nowhere to be seen and it's crying for her. I don't want to leave, but the men say that she will be close by and has just gone to graze. She will soon return to feed the baby. With all these female pheromones in the air, Hector and Hamish are in a permanent sexual daze. They are trying to spread their legs to pee and flick as they walk which produces an odd stiff-legged gait and they are frothing so much that Brahim looks like he has been to a foam party in Ibiza.

Exhaustion is ever-present and our last day into Bir Anzarane strains the team's spirits. It is further than we think and we follow a piste which takes us in the wrong direction. We have to double back for a time and are all silent and despondent. Then, there is a flash of white and a desert fox dashes out of its burrow almost under the camels' feet and speeds off into the distance. Everyone is shouting at once, 'Zahra, did you see it?' 'A fox, a fox, at last.' I had been longing, ever since the Draa, to catch sight of one of the little creatures and I was overwhelmed with excitement. It streaked past us, so I had no chance to take a picture, but I had seen it really clearly and everyone was happy for me. 'This is a blessing from God. It is the reason that we took the wrong path and came this way,' says Brahim.

Because we have been chanting Bir Anzarane like a mantra for days, my expectations are very high and inevitably I am disappointed when we finally get there. It is a cluster of small buildings and a service station on the side of a road. There is a big mobile phone mast. We set up camp on a cleared space filled with litter: plastic bottles, juice boxes and sardine cans. It is dirty and uninviting. We're all tired, though, and it is not too far from the well and the shop at the service station so we can get food for ourselves and the camels.

We're setting up when an official jeep arrives carrying Colonel Jamal and his junior officer, Adel. Both of them speak good English and are serving with the Moroccan forces in the area. They offer to give the men a lift to fill up from the well and then to go to the service station and bring them back with the heavy supplies. Lhou takes the camels to water and Brahim sorts out the water and food. Addi and I have a nice glass of tea. When they come back, Colonel Jamal has brought me a tin of Sahrawi tea in a lovely brown tin with a camel on it as a gift and we brew up again. Lhou, a tea expert, proclaims that it is of the first quality.

The next day, we have all finally had enough and we walk for just an hour to leave the outskirts of Bir Anzarane and put up camp so that we can rest. Hamish is especially pleased. Every day for a few weeks now, when we get to camp and unload him, he has been stretching out full length on his side and putting his head on one of the green saddlebags as a pillow to have a little post-walk snooze.

Respite over, we set out reprovisioned. An owl scoots off not far from us and the men tell me that in the Amazigh tradition if an owl comes to a house, that house will soon empty of people. The owl is an ill omen. I have an owl nesting in the walnut trees beside my home in Imlil, so hope it is just a folk tale. Addi finds a solar panel and dusts it off to take with us.

'It's like finding 500 MAD,' he says excitedly.

'Addi, you have to put it back,' Lhou says. 'Look, it is in a pile of nomads' things. They will come back for it. You can't keep it.'

'Yes, I can, it was just lying there. All the stuff left is rubbish. They are not coming back for it, they've abandoned it.' Lhou and Addi argue the rights and wrongs for two more days.

On the Draa Expedition, Brahim and Addi had always slept outside. They would form a three-walled enclosure by stacking the saddles and saddlebags up, then lay out rugs in the middle and Brahim's sleeping mat on top. Addi didn't have one. They would sleep in their sleeping bags and use the camel blankets, if needed, to keep them warm. However, the strength of the Saharan wind had driven them inside and all three of them were cuddled together every night in the mess tent. One morning, as we warmed our feet up by the campfire before putting our boots on, Lhou had a tale to tell.

'Zahra, I was sleeping very soundly last night.'

'Yes, you were snoring very loudly,' interjected Addi.

'When,' continued Lhou with dignity, 'I felt something.'

'Where?' I asked.

'In my trousers,' said Lhou.

'Oh dear,' I said apprehensively.

'I jumped up like this and started hitting my leg. There was something running up and down it.'

'Danger!' chortled Addi. '*Khatar!*'

'I ran out of the tent, and jumped and danced and then it fell out of my trouser leg. It was a mouse.'

'Thanks be to God for a safe delivery,' declared Brahim.

'Yes, it could have been fatal,' agreed Lhou.

He accompanied his story with a full re-enactment of slapping, jumping and wriggling which had me, Brahim and Addi rolling around in tears by the end of it. Then, he solemnly took me into the tent and lifted up the edge where his head had been, to show me where the naughty mouse burrowed in.

I had thought that I had seen, and understood, empty, but

that stretch from Bir Anzarane to the coast redefines nothingness for me.

It follows the route of the old Paris–Dakar rally and is
relentlessly flat. I feel like I am walking on top of the world
and that I could fall off it if we get to the end. Sometimes I
feel dizzy, as though my feet might fly off the earth and into
space; other times my legs are so heavy that I think I will
sink into the sand. The curve of the horizon is clearly visible.
There is nothing to attach yourself to visually: no trees, no
rocks, no dunes. It is just the flat, golden earth and the blue
sky. The nothingness drives you inside yourself. I walk in a
kind of fugue state, focusing on putting one foot in front of
the other. I block any thoughts of the future out of my head.
If I think about how long we still have to go that day, that
week, for the rest of the expedition, I will become totally
demoralised. It is the ultimate lesson on how to live in the
present – even though the present is very tough.

Whereas before we would get excited about seeing a hare
or an owl, now it's a tree. 'Look, there's one, Zahra, take a
picture,' says Addi.

The wind does not stop during the day. It howls in our
ears. Brahim teaches me how to judge direction by seeing the
way the sand has piled up around a stone or plant, even if no
wind is currently blowing. On a good day, the sand is settled
and doesn't blow into our faces, scouring any uncovered skin.
The wind is the single, hardest thing to bear. Everything is
hard but the wind gets into your head and won't leave any
part of you in peace. The tents are our refuge, but even in
there the wind beats the sides, keeping up its deafening din.
It's hot too, especially as we are brewing up tea at lunchtime.
If it drops at night, and we have been lucky enough to scav-
enge some wood or dried shrubs, we eat outside around the

campfire, riddling and looking up at the Saharan stars. 'That's the Shepherd's Star,' says Lhou.

But there is a glory in it, this test of body and soul. 'This is a real adventure, Zahra,' Brahim says to me.

Bivouacking is hard. Often, there isn't even the stump of an acacia and I look back on past camps where we had one or even two as a veritable Black Forest. After four and a half hours, we stop at a slight dent in the land, which is the best shelter we can find. There are some of the black, heather-like plants that the camels can eat, so they wander off after we have unloaded. My energy levels are so low that the only task I undertake that day apart from doing my notes and the usual camp chores is to brush my hair. It hasn't seen water since Jirifiyya, so that is slightly harder than it sounds, but unimpressive, nevertheless.

Talk in the *giton* is about women and babies. 'If the mother dies, the cushion is outside the door. If the father dies, the cushion is on the mother's knee,' the men tell me. I am not at all clear what they mean, but they explain that if a mother dies and the father marries again the new wife won't love his children. She will be neglectful or even cruel to them and always favour her own above them. However, if the father dies, the mother will always prioritise the children. This leads on to a story told to me with great earnestness by Lhou but backed up by the other two, so it seems to be an urban legend of some kind.

A taxi driver picks up a woman who has obviously been to the market and is carrying heavy bags. He drops her at the corner she asks for and she heads off. He carries on but hears a strange noise coming from the back. He looks behind him and there, in a bag, is a baby crying. The woman has long gone and so the man, being a good Muslim, takes the baby back home to his wife and tells her what has happened. She flies into a towering rage, thinking that he has been having an affair and is now trying to foist his love child onto her. Her family, the neighbours and the imam are called in and they all berate the taxi driver. Driven to despair, he agrees to pay the money for a DNA test and goes to the doctor. He and his wife go to the surgery for the results. 'There is good news: you are definitely not the father,' confirms the doctor. 'But there is also bad news: you are infertile and always have been, so the five children you have with your wife do not belong to you.'

The men's perspective on this has nothing to do with the children or any affection the taxi driver might feel towards them; it is all outrage that he was exploited and had spent years working night and day to feed other men's children.

We shift direction and the wind shifts with us. It is at our backs now, which is much better, but it has also gathered strength. I have to push backwards to stay upright and the gusts make me stumble and trip. I keep my mouth shut, my jaw clenched, my *chech* up to my nose, sunglasses over my eyes and my cap jammed low. We see a couple of clumps of trees, but then it is back to nothing. The strength of the wind whips up the sand and we can see it coming in. By mid-morning, we are walking through a full sandstorm. I am covered in a fine film of it. My teeth, my hair, the rims of my eyes, inside my nose and ears, my hands. It has infiltrated my clothes, sneaking in to nestle in the crevices of my knees and elbows. I retreat into LPF, but I have to open the window or I will stifle in the heat. We have put it up so that it is sheltered from the wind but the sand finds its way in and covers my bags and mattress and notebooks in fine layers. It is like spies or flies, sneaking and buzzing and causing maximum discomfort.

Lhou and Addi have been walking together and talking about Addi's plans to find a wife. He has got to the age where it is expected and he seems to be torn between delight at the idea and horror at losing his freedom. He is also heavily aware that he has to fulfil the expectations of his parents. Marriage is not just about the individual; it is about the whole family. The new wife has to be happy to be integrated and also has to find a welcome from her husband's clan. Lhou has been married for forty years and has grown-up children and some grand-children. He has strong opinions on who Addi should choose.

'Addi, it is best for you if you accept the wife that your mother and father choose for you. It is time for you to settle down. You need a wife who understands the mountains and understands the life there. You have to have a wife who can help Lalla Ito with the goats and the sheep. You need some-one who can work hard. Too many women today are not used to work. They will work for a week and then stop. Or they will ask you for a quad to go to work in the garden and not accept a donkey. Your life as a nomad is hard; you need a strong wife.'

Addi is not convinced, though. He has a few girls that he is chatting to on WhatsApp and is not ready to commit yet. Lhou is outraged.

'Addi, you are like a fox in the sheep. Foxes don't actu-ally harm the flock because they come in and say, "I'll have that one. No, I won't, it's too fat. That one – no, it's too thin. Maybe that one – no, it has brown hair." They end up with nothing. Then the wolf comes in, grabs a sheep, drags it off and feasts all night. You must stop being a fox and become a wolf.'

Addi listens hard and looks as though he is weakening. Lhou presses on.

'Look, give me *tissint nifsi* and I will find you a bride that will make you and your family happy.' I have to stop them to find out what *tissint nifsi* is and it transpires it is a little salt and the meaning is 'grease my palm'. Lhou is willing to settle for a couple of hundred dirhams.

Addi starts listing his requirements. 'She has to be a good shape and pretty and have a good temper. She must be well educated so she can look after the children and teach them properly. I like girls from the town.'

It's too much for Lhou. 'Addi, you are possessed by a jinn; it is driving you mad with all these ideas of different women. We have to remove it from you. I am going to perform an exorcism to chase out these jinn.'

At the bivouac, after lunch, as Brahim and I are drinking copious amounts of tea, Lhou prepares to do the exorcism. He ties Addi's hands together with green twine and recites the Quran over them, holding them in his own. He pulls each of Addi's fingers as though he is trying to crack them, still reciting verses. Then he gets to the left thumb and pulls it really hard. 'One thumb is enough, Zahra. The jinn is now gone and Addi will be able to make a choice between all these girls. Thanks be to God.' He is half laughing and half serious. Addi has both giggled and looked alarmed all the way through. We all chime in, 'Thanks be to God.'

After the emptiness, the land starts to dip and curve, warping the flatness, and there are actual small clumps of trees. Tents appear on the horizon and we count seven in all. A pretty young woman in a delicate *milfah* emerges from one and invites me in. She speaks perfect English and takes my hand in her soft ones. She tells me she lives in Dakhla but that they have come out to visit her grandfather, who still lives in his tent with a small herd. 'I've been here for five days now

205

and I want to go home. Look, I am going really brown – it's awful.' She shows me her hands and wrists which are caramel coloured and I tell her, honestly, that she is beautiful. She tells me she learnt her English by watching films and TV, but that she also speaks Italian and Spanish. What a contrast between her and her grandfather, who cannot even read and who is very happy to live his life, as his forebears have, in the solitude of the wilderness with his animals. In a relatively small amount of time, life for this community has transformed.

The landscape continues to change as we move towards the coast. The flat of the plains is broken up by small, pointed hills. There are some areas that look like the American national parks with their colourful gorges. I am given a lesson in different types of hill. *Ifarda* is a long oblong hill with cliffs; *tafarda* is a small pointy hill that also has cliffs; *tawrirt* is a smaller round hill with no cliffs.

We are heading towards Argoub and as the small cluster of buildings appears we are rewarded with a water tower – a chateau – and a trough. The camels drink thirstily, it is a long time since they last had a proper water stop.

We come to the top of it and everything is transformed. The air cools, the wind changes direction and ahead of us lies the vast, swelling sea. We have swapped one kind of emptiness for another and now we are on the last leg of our journey, turning directly south through the militarised zone, to Guerguerat.

13

LANDMINES AND QUICKSAND

Argoub – Guerguerat

22 January 2020

The wind is now firmly at our backs and we are on a narrow strip sandwiched between the Atlantic and the main tarmac road that links sub-Saharan Africa with Morocco and then goes on to Spain and Europe. Lorries hammer past us, making the ground shake. We stick to the beach where we can, enjoying the sound of the waves and the fresh, salty smell. There are shells and stones to be collected and lots of seagulls wheeling ahead of us in shock when they spot the camels. Hector has taken over from Hamish as most frothy camel; Hamish's naughtiness seems to be waning so perhaps his peak heat period is over.

Brahim hates it if we have to do a stretch near the tarmac.

'Are you afraid?' I ask.

'Yes. Absolutely. These camels are one hundred per cent possessed by Satan. They wait till a car is right there and then they dive straight in front of it. May God keep us safe.'

Having the sea right next to us means I can finally try to address the problem of my bags and mat all stinking of camel pee, which has plagued me for so long. I empty everything out and fill a bucket with salt water and bleach then scrub fiercely. The bleach fumes are infinitely preferable.

We pass a crumbling old gate called Puerto Rica and are joined by a friendly black and tan dog. He is fascinated by the camels and wants to be as close to them as he can be, which is a risky venture. He is obviously a young dog, healthy and very friendly to humans. He sticks close and after a couple of hours, as we leave the cliffs and walk further away from any people or places for him to eat and drink, I start to worry. 'Don't worry, Zahra, he is like the wind. He comes and goes as he pleases,' says Brahim. We have had good signal and Addi has lots of news from home.

'Zahra, four camels have been born. One white, one black, one a chestnut colour like Hector and one I don't know. My brother is staying at the house with his new baby and eating lots of *titliwin*. Lalla Ito says you should get married and have two children. It is snowing in the hills now. Soon it will be spring and there will be lots of pasture and lots of milk from the goats. That is all the news from the *bled*, the country.'

There are fisherman's shacks and tents beaded along the cliffs. They look poor and there are no women or children. Long ropes have been anchored at intervals onto firm rocks at the top of the cliffs so that the men can easily climb up and down to the water.

I've called the dog Azwo, the wind, and he has stayed with us. We are feeding him on bread soaked in sardine oil and I am giving him half my lunch sardines. He is a very good dog and just wants to play and be loved. There is a real problem, though. The men are kind to him and make sure he has enough water but, in their culture, dogs are dirty and danger-ous. It is probably the equivalent of my walking with someone who introduced their giant pet cockroach into camp. They tell me that if a dog comes into the house then the angels can't enter and order me not to let Azwo into the tents, or anywhere near the washing up. Another problem is that if the dog licks them, they have to perform *wdou* again. Brahim keeps blaming me for the dog, even though I had done nothing to encourage him.

Oblivious, Azwo trots along happily with his tongue out, at the very front of the caravan. Addi plays with him, throwing a plastic bottle which he fetches back, unfazed by the distances we are going. Azwo shows his love for me by enthusiastic jumping up and attempted licking of my entire face which I strongly, and unsuccessfully, discourage. He is absolutely desperate to get into Le Petit Fromage with me, but I know that the men would hate that so I keep the zip down. He contents himself with snuggling against me through the canvas, back to back, and in the morning, the minute he hears the zip going up, he rushes round and the first thing I feel is a wet nose.

We come to a place called Umlili. It is a brand-new village built using Moroccan government aid to give affordable housing to the Sahrawis and it is completely empty. We walk the camels down the middle of the well-laid-out streets. It is as if we have strayed into a post-apocalyptic universe. The doors are open. The houses are nice – with sitting rooms, kitchens, bedrooms, a bathroom and a yard. There is water and electricity. There are archways and fretwork but there are no people. The wind plays lazily in and out of the hallways. There is a mosque with cracked windows which lies silent even as the time for prayers sounds on Addi's mobile. All of us want to get out of there and we march on. At the edge of the town we see the first signs of life: builders. They are building yet more houses.

A day later, we find a well. It is in a clump of bushes and short trees and the camels drink up while we fill all our water containers. I am nosing around when I come across three 50kg bags of white flour spilt across the ground. I call to the men and they come to look. The flour is completely spoiled so we can't use any of it. The men are horrified by the waste. 'The government gives subsidised flour, petrol, sugar to the people in this area. And here it is thrown away on the ground. Spoilt. None of us could afford to throw away food like that. In the mountains, people are really poor, we eat the stick [life treats us very harshly]. No family would throw away a 50kg bag of flour. We eat the stick.'

It is a pretty spot and there is shade, so we leave the camels to graze and eat our elevenses, then load up the camels with the water. We have filled every container and the water is heavy so we make sure it is evenly distributed. The stronger camels like Hamish, Hunter, Callum and Alasdair take a bit more.

Ahead of us is a *sabkha* extending for about 10km and 2km across. A *sabkha* is a kind of sunken bowl which is at, or below, sea level. The sand can be soft and usually we go around them for that reason. In this case, though, we decide to save ourselves hours of walking and cut across. The camels are now heavily laden with water and we don't want to make them work more than necessary. The sand is reasonably pale, not the deep red that signifies danger, and it feels solid underfoot.

We are walking in our usual formation, Lhou and Addi in front leading Callum, Alasdair and Sausage, and Brahim and I slightly behind with Hunter, Hamish and Hector. It is still early, around 11 a.m., and the wind has dropped so my heart is light.

'This sand feels good underfoot,' I say to Brahim.

'Yes, it seems to have got a bit harder,' he replies.

Then came that second. That second when your tyre blows on the motorway; the doctor looks up from the test results; the phone rings at 3.24 a.m. The second which shatters normal.

From nowhere, Addi screams out, 'Lhou, Lhou, come and help me.' I look over. Callum is up to his chest in sand, plunging and rearing, his eyes wide in panic.

Quicksand!

Behind him, Alasdair has gone down too, dragging Sausage in his wake. Their mouth halters, which are tied around the bottom of their jaws and then connected to the forward camel with a rope, mean they have no escape without ripping half their own faces off.

Brahim immediately turns his three camels round and starts walking them quickly back to safety.

Addi is shouting directions at Lhou, while trying to pull Callum up and out. There is a huge bond of trust between Addi and Callum and I can see the camel giving everything to him. Lhou has got to Alasdair's head, but poor Sausage at the back is grunting and wallowing alone.

'Zahra,' yells Addi. 'Come here, come and take Callum.' By now he has got Callum out. I rush up and grab his halter and stand as calmly and quietly as I can while Lhou struggles to bring Alasdair up and Addi runs to Sausage, still mired at the back. Sausage is the gentlest of the boys and I hold my breath as Addi coaxes him out. The six of us, three humans and three camels, huddle together, all panting for breath and high on adrenaline. Then we take off after Brahim, who is now 50 metres ahead, moving to the edge and safety.

In slow motion we watch as first Hunter and then Hamish sink screamingly down in front of us. Lhou is leading the three, so Addi and I sprint towards Brahim's stricken team. Hunter is down deep and Brahim has somehow pulled his luggage off, Hamish is thrashing around, but Hector is only in to his knees and Addi yanks him out, thrusts his halter into my hand and dashes to Brahim's aid. I walk as quickly and lightly as I can back towards the others. Addi gets behind Hunter, pushing him up as Brahim pulls and gets him out, Hamish follows and the two are led over to the rest of us.

Trembling and still shocked, all six camels stand quietly by me while the men go to retrieve the baggage, lugging over the weighty water carriers and bags. They load Hunter up again and we set off in single file, moving steadily in our old footsteps towards the far bank. None of us speak as we test out the sand and take in how close we had come to disaster.

'We were so near. If they had gone down any further, we would have lost them. We have escaped a great danger. Thanks be to God,' says Brahim. 'Thanks be to God,' we all echo.

We walk cautiously but at pace, trying to follow our old footsteps. I am trembling from the adrenaline and we are all still physically on high alert. The minutes pass and eventually we get to the safe sand of the *sabkha*'s edge and can relax. Our adventure has cost us a day, but that is a cheap price to pay when we could have paid a much higher one and lost our camels.

We all feel a surge of relief, and with that come the words. We relive every moment of what's happened, telling the story from our own viewpoint. Then, the men bring out their other near-escape stories and we walk on regaling each other with our tales of disaster averted. God is thanked many times. 'We will never try to walk across a *sabkha* again, unless we see tracks from the tyres of a *watta*,' Brahim says. 'If the tracks are there it means the sand can carry a lot of weight but otherwise it is too dangerous. God was watching us and protecting us this time. We need to celebrate; tonight we will have a party: the Eid al Sabkha.'

Our options for a party are rather limited but we do our best with pasta and sardines and I have a secret surprise. I have been hoarding one small bottle of Coke in my bag. I wrap it in a damp towel to cool it down and then at dinner I whip it out. 'Party!' exclaims Addi, and quickly cleans the tea glasses and pours out exact measures for each of us. We toast each other and sprawl out on the rugs to really savour it. No connoisseur of fine wines could drink as tenderly as we do and nothing could ever taste as good as that Coke. That night, there is another blessing. It rains a little and we have to put the plastic sheets over the tents. The camels lick up the rainwater that has gathered in the creases of the sheets and we decant some for our tea later – we are becoming Sahrawis.

We pass through an area of dazzling white sand, a total contrast to the golds and beiges of the rest of the trip. The sky is sharp blue with swirls of white clouds. It is our last day with Azwo. We pass a military post and the soldiers come running out. The posts are spaced about 2km apart all along the coast and usually are a corrugated and concrete shack which houses two men. All Moroccan soldiers do a stint of six years in the desert and many of them are recruited from the mountains. The military is a good job and pays relatively well, so is an obvious path for boys from poor families. The soldiers are reprovisioned with water by army trucks and will always share some with us. They are also keen for company and, if they are Tashlaheet speakers, even more happy to meet the crew.

At this checkpoint, the more senior man takes a shine to

Azwo and asks us about him. When we explain that he just joined us, he asks if he can have him and promises to feed and water him well. Most of the checkpoints have dogs but this one doesn't. He seems to be good with him and it is a solution for us. The end of the trip will come and our other alternative is to drive him back to where he started following us, Puerto Rica, and leave him there. Addi unties a halter and puts it round Azwo's neck who goes willingly inside with the soldier. I am really sad to see him go but I know it is actually better. 'He will have a good life, Zahra. The soldiers will feed him sardines and bread and he can guard them and also he is free. He can always leave. He is the wind,' says Brahim. Part of me still hopes he will break out and find us later and for a couple of days I am always looking back over my shoulder. 'It is like a death,' says Brahim. 'He was with us and now he is gone.'

We bivouac a few hundred metres from the sea, opposite a group of fishermen's tents. The road is not too far away, so Addi goes off with a couple of bidots to beg some water. The camels have a small copse to graze in which is covered in camomile plants. As their pads crush the yellow flowers, the smell floods the camp.

A man from the tents sees we have water and comes over to ask for a bidot, which we give him. He is called Mostapha and he invites us over to his tent, where he is living with his two sons, aged nineteen and twenty-three. They are not – as I had thought – fishermen but are there to harvest the seaweed which chokes the shoreline. They have been here for nearly three months. They spend all day in the water. They have wetsuits and a mask and fins and they dive down, cut the seaweed and then cram it into a large net they have on the surface. When the net is full, they drag it back to shore and lay the seaweed out to dry. They then go back into the water and keep cutting. They sell the dried seaweed by the sack to an intermediary in Boujdour or Dakhla who sells it on to Spain. They get 10 MAD (80 pence) per kilo.

Their tent is sparsely furnished but neat and clean. Three sleeping mats are spread out and they have a camping gas stove for cooking. Mostapha's wife lives in Boujdour with his two daughters and he and the boys will stay here until the seaweed is gone. They are full of cheer even though their work is excruciatingly hard and the boys are excited for the evening because their football team, Real Madrid, is playing. There is hardly any signal so they have to go outside the tent, stand on a nearby hillock with an arm stretched up holding the phone to hear the match – but that doesn't detract from their enjoyment of it. They tell me that their dream is to go and live in Europe and work there. 'Ask anyone. They will all tell you the same. It is the dream of all our youth.'

I want to tell them that life in Europe may not be the fun they think it is. Then I consider that they are spending eight hours a day submerged in salt water just to earn the most basic living, and I realise that my perspective is totally skewed. Mostapha quizzes me on Arabic and is delighted when I can recite some Quran. 'You must learn as much as you can from the imam, Brahim,' he tells me sternly. I talk with the men about the desire to go to Europe. 'It's money. That's the problem for us Moroccans. We want to work hard. We do work hard. But look at Mostapha and his sons, look at the results. Nothing.'

Addi has rolled up his trousers to wash his feet and is sharing my Kew Gardens lavender soap sent to me by my brother, Robbie, and sister-in-law, Catriona, for Christmas and opened in great delight in LPF. Addi is very partial to it – 'It smells so good, Zahra, and it is soft.' I notice that he has a number of burns on his legs, like cigarette burns.

'Addi, what are those?'

'They are medicine.'

'What do you mean?'

'When you have problems in your health, you know like when your skin becomes very red and itchy, then you burn the skin in two places with *kibrit*, sulphur.'

'Doesn't it hurt?'

'Yes, it hurts very badly but it is only for a short time and then the pain is gone and the sickness is gone. We don't have so much medicine, so this is what we do. It works.'

We have a sardine emergency. We have run out and we are still far away from our next – and last – provisioning stop, Bir Gunduz. Addi searches frantically through all the secret food stashes and finally comes up with two tins. This is a disaster. There are very grim faces all round. It is going to be rice and pasta till our next reprovision. It isn't our lowest culinary point, though; that was the porridge.

The men always laugh at me eating porridge: 'Oats are for camels, Zahra.' However, there comes the day when that is our only option. 'You make it,' Addi commands. 'You understand it. And don't put any milk in, because I can't eat milk.' I dutifully make porridge in true Scottish fashion with salt and water, but lay out sugar in a dish for those who might want it – we have a little of the posh, ground stuff left. Most of our sugar is in cones about 300cm high, which you bash with stones to get chunks off to put in the tea. Addi comes up to inspect my work and hmms. Before I can stop him, he grabs the olive oil used for breakfast and pours it in. The porridge turns slightly green. I ladle it out onto the plates and we all tuck in. It is disgusting. I add milk and sugar, which alleviates it slightly. Oily porridge may give you calories but it will not give you pleasure. Addi and I plough through ours, but Brahim and Lhou love it. They smack their lips, proclaim it delicious and go in for second helpings.

Two wild-eyed, wild-haired nomads roar up in a *watta* and we all stop to chat and to ask where the nearest water is. They offer to take Brahim to a well which they say is a couple of kilometres away and to fill up our bidots. To my surprise he refuses and says we have to go on and we part ways. It transpires that they were demanding 1,200 MAD (£100). There may be an argument for paying something small for water if the nomads have to pay for it, as our friend Mohamed did, although he wouldn't accept our money – but in many places it is freely supplied by the government or by rural associations – but that price is extortionate. They are relying on the fact that we need it. What is more, this water actually comes from a well which is free for everyone to use.

Brahim and Lhou disappear off mid-afternoon when the sun is high. Then, they dash back into camp full of glee. 'Ha!' says Lhou. 'The camels have drunk.' Tea is poured and the story comes out. Brahim and Lhou took the camels up to where the men had told them the well was, behind a dune. Brahim recites the tale:

'We sneaked up. The motor for the well was running and there were some houses next to it. We told the camels to be quiet and then, softly softly, we took off their halters and urged them to drink. We filled up the bidots and all the time we were worried that the men would come out and beat us. They must have been asleep; thanks be to God. Maybe they ate a big lunch. Then we crept away around the other side and walked back as fast as we could. God provides.' I have a mental image of Hamish tiptoeing around the trough.

Our next visitor is a very nice Sahrawi called Mohamed who gives us six loaves of bread and takes tea with us. But he leaves us unnerved. 'Where is your machine?' he asks. 'What machine?' we chorus. 'You know, the one for detecting landmines. This area is all mined and you need to have the machine so that you can find them. Look there.' We all dutifully turn round and see a pile of twisted old metal. 'That is a jeep that was blown up in 2001. Yesterday, someone was killed when his *watta* hit one. May God have mercy on him. It was a mine for cars not for people.' I don't know how seriously to take this. We are in a militarised zone, but there are also camels grazing everywhere. We don't have a mine detector. We all discuss it but come to no conclusion.

The sardine emergency is mentioned quite frequently.

Bir Gunduz is just in sight on the horizon. The wind is now shifting direction and the piles of sand on the plants are at different angles. What look like mini skyscrapers are emerging out of the heat haze. It is our first town for a long time and we all start doing the mental shift from nothingness to people and buildings and, of course, litter. There is general excitement at the thought of having sardines again for lunch. Finding a campsite is, as always near habitation, a bit difficult. We want to be near water but we can't be too close to the town for the camels. We settle on a little decline where there is grazing on thorny bushes. It is a heat trap, but it works for the animals and to my eyes is rather pretty, although I suspect this is only in contrast to the nothingness we have come through. I think if anyone was transported there from Scotland they would consider it a hell-blasted hole of barren grimness. We set up camp and Addi runs to the petrol station at the edge of town to buy sardines and treats. He chooses sardines with the hottest chillies I have ever tasted and by the end of lunch we are all sweating copiously.

A plump, cheery chap called Mohamed arrives to welcome us with a full delegation of gendarmes, qaids and muqaddims. We are all introduced and he says to me, 'I know who you are, Zahra.' Teasingly, I ask him, 'So, what is my birth name?' 'Alice Morrison and you come from Scotland and you live in Imlil,' he chirrups happily. He has been following our progress on social media and delights in all the pictures from the route.

The skyscrapers of Bir Gunduz are blocks of flats set back from dusty roads. It is clearly planned rather than organic. There is very little traffic and kids play football in the streets. Women flit in and out in their tie-dyed *milfahs* in the peaches and browns of the Sahara. There are a few small shops and a well for water. It is a fully functioning town rather than an outpost like Bir Anzarane. There is a park and a school, some pharmacies and lots of mechanics' shops for car repairs. There is even a hotel which has palm trees and a garden in the foyer. We go in, but Addi and I are too shy to stay. We are too filthy. We are invited into the muqaddim's house for a shower and to use his washing machine – I don't think he understands just how dirty our clothes are. When he is all clean, Addi goes off for a wander. 'You know where he has been, don't you, all dressed up?' Lhou asks me back in camp. 'He's been in search of women.' Addi smirks. 'Yes, but I didn't find any.'

The town has an odd feel to it. When Brahim and I go in to reprovision from the vegetable shop and the grocer's next door we find that both are Amazigh. They tell us that 70 per cent of people are from dakhil, the interior, and are here for work; only 30 per cent are Sahrawis. We buy all our goods and a *watta* carries them to the roadside opposite the camp so we can carry them in.

That night, the official delegation arrives back at camp bearing gifts. We have all the rugs spread out and it has mercifully cooled down. Our campfire is burning so that the embers will be ready for Sahrawi tea. We are overwhelmed, once again, by generosity. Our guests/hosts have brought everything with them. Teapot and fancy glasses on a tray with top-grade tealeaves, sugar and even their own water. They also have a big dish of savoury rice, called *marro*, which is a traditional Sahrawi dish. All the men are Sahrawis and work for the government. They tell me they are happy to do so and that they are treated well. The qaid is particularly interested in history and recounts the complex politics of the region since the Spanish left in the '70s. He is very even-handed, blaming neither one side nor the other but hoping for a solution that can allow things to progress. He also quizzes me closely about Brexit and asks me why Britain has taken such a step. Again, we are warned about landmines and to take advice where to walk. Meanwhile, Hafidh has been making the tea. He is a big character.

Hafidh: 'Zahra, say *la illaha illa Allah*, there is no God but God. Say it. Say it and you'll go to heaven.'

I have no problem saying these words, and have my own interpretation of them, but being forced into something in this way goes against my nature.

Me: 'Hafidh, I have my religion and you have yours.'

Hafidh: 'How old are you?'

Me: 'I am fifty-six. How old are you?'

Hafidh: 'I am fifty-two.'

Then he turns to Brahim.

Hafidh: 'Does she have any children?'

Brahim: 'No.'

Back to me.

Hafidh: 'Why don't you have children?'

Me: 'How many do you have?'

Hafidh: 'Three.'

Me: 'Three? That's not enough. You better hurry and have more.'

The group laugh at that and Hafidh goes on to talk about how his wife is too old and how he is going to take a second wife. The qaid intervenes, 'It is not right to be talking about women in this casual way.' I feel relieved and grateful to him and the conversation turns general again. It is very companionable. I listen to the men talking and add in little bits and enjoy the night sky and the food. At the end of the meal, as we are beginning to tidy up, Brahim starts to sing the prayers. He starts off with a part of Surat Al Baqara, the chapter of the cow. 'We believe in the prophets who God sent to us' and then goes on to a prayer:

'God lead us on the righteous path with those who walk it.

And give us health as you have to others.

And bless us with what you have given us.

And distance evil from us.

For you are the judge and cannot be judged.

God raises up who he will and brings down who he will.

Praise be to God.'

Hafidh has tears running down his face and at the end of the prayer kisses Brahim again and again on the forehead, exclaiming at the beauty of his voice. I immediately forgive him for his baiting of me.

After the guests have gone, we sit around for a bit longer enjoying the night air and drinking a cold bottle of Schweppes that they brought us. Suddenly, Brahim jumps up. 'Where are the sardines?' He bought dozens of tins at the petrol station but they are nowhere to be found. 'I must have left them behind.' We all rummage through everything again but have to admit defeat and go to bed with sardines on our mind.

We leave the kindness of Bir Gunduz a little late as we need to collect our forgotten sardines from the petrol station. The shopkeeper laughs at us: 'I didn't know if you were coming back.' And then we continue on, sticking close to the road where we have been told there are no mines. 'Do not stray more than four metres from the tarmac,' the qaid told us. The sea is not far to our right.

It's cold in the mornings and I eat breakfast wrapped in camel blankets. Hector and Hamish are constantly fighting for dominance. 'Camels and humans are the same. When they are hungry they are calm, but when you give them oats, their sugar rises. Then, they have energy and they start fighting. Just like humans, once you have the necessities of food and water then the energy is used for sex and battle. Satan is always circling,' opines Brahim. To tamp them down, they get extra loads to carry.

We are bumbling along when suddenly Addi's three, Callum, Alasdair and Sausage, start bucking and rearing and pulling away. They are as skittish as mares in spring. '*Bismillah ar Rahman ar Raheem!* In the name of God, the Compassionate, the Merciful,' says Brahim quickly four times. 'It's the *junoon*, jinns. They have left Addi and now they have got into the camels.' 'That's because of Lhou,' says Addi. 'It's his fault. He keeps going on about *junoon* being in me because I can't choose a girl to marry and now we have attracted them!'

We've been told to stick close to the tarmac because of the landmines, but Brahim wants to head for a piste closer to the sea which he has seen from Google Maps. That piste will take us almost directly to Guerguerat. We leave the side of the road and head seawards. If not on piste or tarmac, we have been told to stick on rock or hard-packed sand but both of those run out and we are on the softer sand as we move, what feels like very slowly, towards the safety of the piste. I tell Brahim I am worried and he becomes exasperated. 'If there are mines then they are everywhere and what are we to do? Even if we focus on the tarmac or the piste, we have to bivouac off them and then the camels go to graze and we follow them. We have no choice. I don't think there are mines everywhere. If there were, this place would be completely forbidden to us. How could they say, "There are mines everywhere but go and walk anyway"? And, Zahra, you know the time and manner of our death is written by God. It is not for us. We are all in his hands.'

I feel slightly comforted but that feeling flees when, as we reach the piste and walk along it, we spot landmines that have been dug up and placed at the side. They look like camping gas cylinders.

Addi spots something. 'Look, Zahra.' He picks up a handful of round animal droppings the size of peas and starts to scan the horizon. 'Gazelles. There are lots of them, look at the ground. As many as a herd of sheep.' Then we spot them. There is a whole herd right over towards the sea. My eyes are not as good as the men's, but I see them running and as I watch I spot four quite clearly. It's a huge boost. '*Yawm azeem*, a Great Day!' I say. 'Are you happy, Zahra?' Addi asks me. 'Yes, very happy, now there is only the *abhar* left to see.' '*Qareeb*, it's close,' says Brahim. But since he has been saying *qareeb* since I first heard of the *ahbar*'s existence, I am unconvinced. The gazelles have actually profited by the lack of people and must be getting water from somewhere, perhaps as a result of the military outposts? To see a herd is something extraordinary: a counterbalance to the endless of acres of drought.

I'm always looking for little tidbits to give to Hamish. It is cold and I have my pink bobble and wool jellaba on as I scour the camp for bits of extra carrot. Hamish sees me and walks up. Then, he closes his teeth round my head. I leap out from under his jaws in time so he grazes my face but no skin is broken. 'That camel has the devil in him. I told you so,' says Brahim helpfully. I hope that it is because he mistook my hat for a juicy piece of fruit but I fear it may just be that Hamish is a bad boy.

We are into the last week of the expedition. I have one afternoon when I actually feel physically comfortable. Nothing hurts. It's not too hot or cold. There is no wind and I can lie outside on my sleeping mat propped up on bags and blankets, shaded by the tent. I luxuriate in it.

Mindful of safety, we always ask the nearest military post about safe spots for camping and on this day they direct us around a corner. A sheltered bay appears, kilometres long with bright white sand and calm waters. Hundreds of sea-gulls, 'sea goats' as Addi calls them, sit at the edge of the sea. The bay is filled with boats of all shapes and sizes. There are blue fishing boats of the kind you see in Essaouira all down the coast, larger vessels and one Senegalese pirogue painted in blues and yellows with a proud, carved prow. At one end of the bay is a small fort right on the promontory and the soldiers tell us that all the boats have been intercepted either for carrying contraband goods, including drugs and people, or for fishing without a permit. The crews have fled or been arrested and their boats are here in limbo. The Senegalese pirogue was taken for illegal lobster hunting. I walk up the hill behind them and find a small wheelie case sitting forlornly in the grass, now empty of its contents.

The story of the boats is sad, but they themselves are graceful and sit like swans on the beach. We use them as anchors for the tents and a place to hang our clothes. One is called Aicha, another Arminia, their names written on the prows. Others have incantations inscribed – *Allahu Akbar*, God is the Most Great; *Inchallah*, if God wills it. The pirogue is magnificent. It is solid wood and every inch is painted with symbols, swirling waves and even faces. One is of a cool guy wearing dark glasses that could easily have come off a wall in the New York underground.

A thought strikes me. 'Brahim, can camels swim?' 'Yes, as long as they have remembered their swimsuits.' Boom boom. He is very pleased with his joke.

The water is so calm that Addi and I persuade Lhou and Brahim to come in. Lhou is game but Brahim is deeply suspicious. 'The sea is dangerous. I am from the mountains and the desert. Not the water.' All four of us walk to the edge of the sea and me, Addi and Lhou plunge in. It is calm as glass.

Brahim: 'It's cold.'

Me: 'Nonsense. We are in the Sahara.'

Brahim: 'I don't have a slip [pants/trunks].'

Me: 'I have one I can lend you.'

Brahim, wading in grimacing: 'Agh! My eggs!' (I think you can guess what eggs are.)

Me, Addi and Lhou all laugh like hyenas. Addi sinks under the surface and has to be dragged up choking.

Brahim, still grimacing: 'They've left, gone on holiday.'

We are now hugging the sea and the scenery is spectacular. Swooping cliffs dive into water that shifts from clear turquoise to a blue that is almost black. White waves dance their crests towards deserted golden and white beaches. The water has worn away fantastic caves and statues into the rocks. We cross an arched rock bridge with sea on both sides. It has been created by millions of years of erosion. The surface rocks are punctured with geysers which spurt up unexpectedly, showering us with salt and cool water from the ocean beneath. The wind has given way to sea breezes and we march to the rhythm of the waves.

Our last push to Guerguerat begins in the dead of night. We want to get to the border for dawn. It is pitch black when we wake and breakfast and then pack up. We walk without head torches as the men can see so well in the dark. I can't, so hang on to Brahim and try to pick my feet up so as not to stumble. There is no wind and all is still apart from the occasional barking of dogs who sense us as we pass. The stars are bright above and I look out for the ones I know: the North Star and the Shepherd's Star.

Just before dawn, we stop and I take hold of all the camels as the men lay out a rug and join together in the final prayer of our journey. Brahim calls out our thanks for safety and an expedition completed. The pinks of the sky start to emerge and ahead of us we see an outline of buildings.

At the end of the Draa Expedition I had had time to get used to the thought of it finishing. The first presage of it had been the sea breezes and then, as we had got closer to the coast, the land had changed. This time, even though I knew of course that it was coming, it was somehow a shock, an abrupt termination of the journey. I was ready to finish and I was more than ready to get out of the landmined area and leave that constant danger behind, but I wasn't really ready to leave the vastness of the Sahara. That emptiness right at the extreme of nature had cleansed my mind and soul somehow. I didn't want the noise of modern life to start up again; I'd been happy in the sands.

But everything ends. We walk round the buildings and we are there. No fanfare, no sea to splash into, just a concrete and wire-gated wall with flags flying above it. Behind us stretches a line of 200 cars and lorries, their drivers sleeping or just starting to rouse and brew tea. They are waiting to cross over into Mauritania on this busy trade route. We find a space to gather in between the trucks and Lhou, Addi, Brahim and I line up with our arms around each other. Hunter, Hamish, Hector, Callum, Alasdair and Sausage are behind us. The cameras click and we hug and smile. It has been tough but magnificent. We have come through safely and in harmony, our little expedition family knit together over the miles of nothingness. 'This was a real adventure,' says Brahim once more.

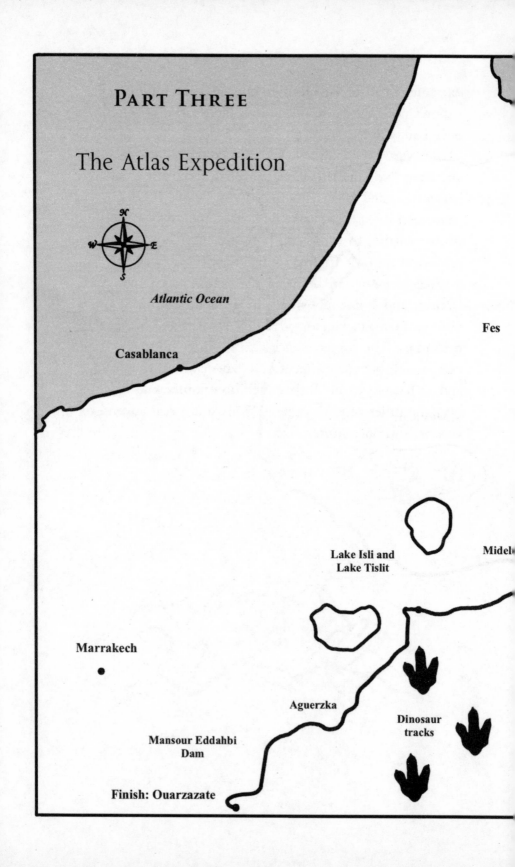

PART THREE

The Atlas Expedition

Atlantic Ocean

Casablanca

Fes

Lake Isli and
Lake Tislit

Midel

Marrakech

Aguerzka

Dinosaur
tracks

Mansour Eddahbi
Dam

Finish: Ouarzazate

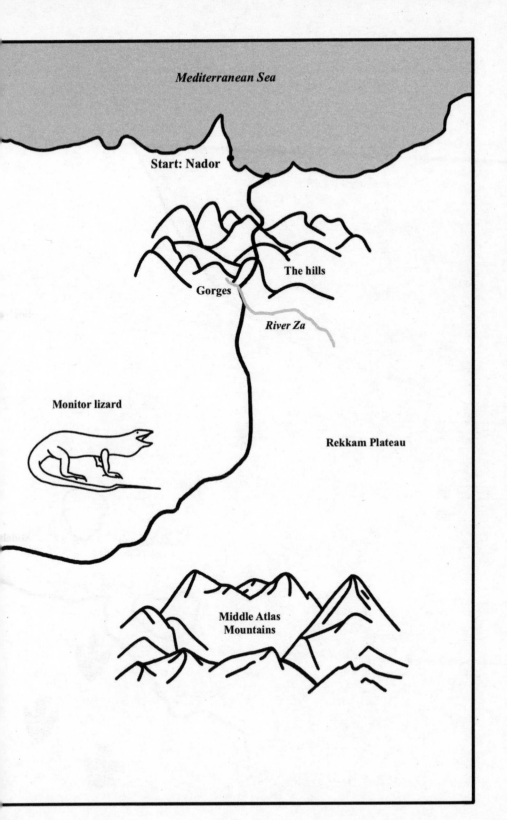

14

FROM CORONA TO THE COAST

Nador – the Za River

21 August 2020

Who could have predicted when we said goodbye to each other at Guerguerat on the Mauritanian border that the final leg of our cross-Morocco expedition would be undertaken under the shadow of a worldwide pandemic?

I was back in the UK doing press and interviews about the Sahara Expedition in March 2020 when we heard news about Covid. At first it seemed like something far away in China, but then Italy fell and we started to talk about it being present. I flew back to Morocco on 14 March. On the plane, I was one of only five people wearing a mask and the couple beside me had left their three kids at home to go on a holiday. I wondered if I was being too cautious. At the airport, our temperatures were taken, which, at that time, felt very odd. As I switched to my Moroccan SIM, an email popped up from the British Embassy, for whom I am a Warden, which means I am a point of liaison and help for Brits at times of emergency: 'Morocco is shutting its borders tomorrow. Please help get all British citizens to the airports.' Suddenly, this was an emergency.

I arrived home in Imlil to an ecstatic welcome from Squeaky the Cat. The next morning, I called a meeting of the women in the family compound and we stood socially distanced in our yard. I wondered what they knew. It transpired that they knew everything I did and more; Moroccan state broadcasters had been doing a great job on information, and they were way ahead of the UK. 'You need to stay distant from us for two weeks,' Nezha said. It was horrible. I felt like a leper when little Othman ran towards me shouting, 'Alice, Alice,' with his arms wide ready for an aeroplane swing and his mum grabbed him back. Morocco moved into full lockdown four days later.

Lockdown was very strict. We were not allowed to leave the house at all except for necessary shopping, and for that each household was given one permission slip from the local authorities. Farmers and shepherds were permitted to continue work. I was caged and the village below me was silent, as if dead. I watched the shepherds herding the goats in the oued, dutifully wearing their face masks even though we were in the middle of the mountains and there was no one around.

Being locked in the house was torture for me and I watched my Western friends posting about their long runs and hikes outside with bitter envy. But, I did have something of great value. I was isolating with my neighbours in our family compound and so – once my quarantine was over – I was never alone. We are four houses plus mine carved out of the mountain and enclosed by a gated wall. The cow lives under my bedroom, which makes summer a bit smelly, and I can pick walnuts off the trees from my terrace when they ripen in the autumn.

We kept each other sane and comforted and during

Ramadan, which I observe even though I am not a Muslim because I live in a tight-knit community and I want to share everything, I ate at Fatima's house in the back kitchen with the women every night. The love and friendship I am given so freely in my adopted homeland became even more precious as we all worried about the virus. We had no cases, but we all listened to the news and were infected by the all-pervasive fear of what would happen to us, our livelihoods, and our families in other cities and countries.

The government's speedy and cautious response saved many lives and the numbers in Morocco stayed low. Eventually we were let out, and on 21 June I left my house and got to hike up into the hills. All the fitness and stamina I had won so hard in the Sahara was gone, but I have never appreciated a walk so much as I did that first day going up to the pass of Tizi Mizik, which lies behind my home at around 2,300m.

Immediately, Jean-Pierre and I started working towards the third leg of the trip from Nador on the northern Mediterranean coast down to Ouarzazate and the Mansour Eddahbi dam, where the whole expedition had started. We knew that we would have to set off by the end of August at the latest or the weather would trap us in the Atlas Mountains. Snow can fall any time from late October and camels don't like snow. The downside to this is that August is the hottest month and as we began we were likely to face temperatures as high as the early forties centigrade. This would be a real challenge, hotter than the Sahara when we'd crossed it.

We had to get permissions for the trip. Understandably, the various regional offices, the gendarmerie and local authorities were all cautious about letting a foreign woman cross the mountains during a pandemic. There was no ban on movement around Morocco, particularly to these wild areas, but government had a lot to do and I was seen as an unnecessary annoyance. I had a lot of sympathy with this view, but I also knew that the expedition was even more important at this time. I would be able to document how the coronavirus was affecting the most remote of communities as we passed through the mountains and plains of the far north and east, before skirting the foothills of the High Atlas and turning towards the west.

JP spent hours in local offices, sending off dossiers, and finally, with some help from the Ministries of the Interior and Tourism, was given the go-ahead. This was a testament to JP's hard work, his unquenchable enthusiasm and the contacts and respect he had built with half a century of experience in expeditions across the country. I took a test and we all stocked up on masks. Addi and I in Nqob and Imlil respectively had had no cases of virus in our area at all. Ali and Brahim had been sheltering with their families in Ouarzazate, where cases were minimal, and the rules on mask-wearing were strict and back home in Ait Bougemez there was also no Covid. We were as confident as anyone really could be that we didn't have the virus.

Usually when I set off on an expedition, even if I am not feeling as well-trained and fit as I should be, I am mentally charged and ready for the challenge ahead. Expeditions require a strong mental effort. It's as if you take a deep breath at the start and then release it at the very end when you have achieved your goal. This time felt very different. There were so many factors out of our control. The last few weeks had been spent in a pelter of worry about whether we would actually be allowed to set off and even as I was packing my kit I was thinking, *We are going to be stopped. They aren't going to let us go.*

But they do, and on Friday 21 August we strike camp, load up the camels and head south away from the sea.

We leave Moulay Ali Sherif on the cliffs near the outskirts of Nador at 7.45, all dutifully wearing our masks. The sea means the humidity is sky high and every movement causes sweat. A feeling almost of unbelief envelops all of us as Brahim says, '*Bismillah*, in the Name of God,' and we take our first footsteps on the journey. We are all smiling and JP is capering about like a lamb. He warns us, though, that the King has said that if people don't start obeying social-distancing and mask-wearing instructions and the coronavirus numbers keep rising then another general lockdown will be imposed in two weeks. If this happens, we will be stopped in our tracks. My stomach plummets, but I drag my mind back to the present. I'm walking now; that has to be enough.

Ali Ahalfi, who was with us on the Draa, is back and will be staying for the whole expedition, and we also have three new camels: Farquhar, Lachlan and Struan. My brother, Robbie, suggested Farquhar as a name 'because you can call him a silly Farquhar'. Struan means a stream and I translate Struan for the men as *Al oued aamir bilmaa*, 'the riverbed filled with water'. Farquhar is big and white and strong and has the sweetest temperament. This is in strong contrast to my favourite, Hamish, who is with us again and came running over when I called his name as I arrived at camp. Whether that was for me, or for the whole orange I was holding out to him, we shall see. We also have Hector Saghro and Sausage with us from the old crew.

All the camels, with the exception of Farquhar, are thin and not in their usual good condition. They have spent lock-down in the south, free grazing, but the ongoing drought has meant that vegetation is sparse. There have been no tourists since March so they have not been walking and fed oats as they normally would be on trips. I can see Hamish's ribs and his hump is almost non-existent. His neck is attenuated and his eyes stand out big in his face. This is the first indication of how coronavirus has affected livestock in the country.

Poor Struan has a nightmare on that first day. When we load him, he isn't strong enough to stand up from his couched position. He tries but nothing happens, except some recalcitrant roaring. We unload virtually everything from his back and redistribute it to the others so that he can get up.

We start through a low-lying mud village in the midst of pomegranate and olive trees. The pomegranates are almost ready to eat; another month or so to go. The fields are well-tended but empty and there is wild lavender underfoot, throwing its scent up at us. We have a bonanza day for wildlife: a fox, a hare and an owl all before casse croute and, rather bizarrely, peacocks afterwards. The giant prongs of the aloe plants frame the Rif Mountains we are heading towards. With every step, our energy rises. We are all so happy to be out and free and doing our jobs instead of sitting at home.

Sweat is pouring off me as the temperature rises to 40°C. My face is bright red and my hands hurt from the sun. I wrap them under my *chech*. The camels' flanks and necks have darkened with sweat too and, as we leave the plain for the hills, they start to struggle. Hamish is audibly puffing. The sun is pounding down and the road winds up with no place possible to camp. Struan keeps stopping. Ali and Addi take everything off him and Ali leads him while Addi goes behind to encourage him. Brahim leads the other five and I walk up and down the line urging them on as they flag.

The hills are not outrageously steep, we go up about 500 metres in total that day, but it is crucifyingly hot and the animals are laden and not used to walking because of the fallow months of Covid. By now, we are stopping to rest every two to three minutes. What a contrast to the beginning of the Sahara Expedition, when we went hard and fast from the beginning. All my sympathy is with our camels, but there is a part of me that is relieved. This time I am not the least fit member of the caravan, and the pace means I am not tired or aching in the way I was then.

Struan has given up. He couches with finality at the side of the road. 'Zahra, the riverbed full of water should be called the riverbed empty of water,' Brahim tells me. We leave him there to rest and, as soon as we can, turn off on a narrow goat's path on our right to go down the mountain and find a bivouac place. We get to a piece of flat land with a ruined house on it and unpack. The sun is beating down and my head is an anvil. When I go inside the *giton* to help make the salad, I feel like it might actually explode with the heat. I watch Ali boil the water for the tea with increasing desperation. More than anything I want to snatch the pot out of his hand, pour myself a glass and just gulp it down. However, etiquette prevails and we dish out the salad and the bread and say, '*Bismillah,*' and then, at last, the tea is poured and in my hand. It lasts about three and a half seconds. I scald my tongue, but in the general heat haze don't even feel it. It is a five-glass lunch. I don't really want to eat anything, just drink tea, but I force down the sardines. Expeditions are long affairs and keeping healthy is paramount.

Brahim goes back to collect Struan and the rest of us settle down in whatever pieces of shade we can find to hide from the sun and rest. I fill up my 500ml tin mug with water from one of our bottles that is as hot as if it has come out of a hot-water tap, add two electrolytes and gulp it down. A flock of sheep arrives from over the horizon and surrounds the camels noisily. It is accompanied by the shepherd, Ismail, who has a round, smiling face and is wearing a smart checked shirt. Addi springs into action making tea and bringing out a plate of biscuits.

Ismail has a queen of a dog with him. She is pure black and the nearest species I can think of to her is a greyhound, but she is actually the image of Anubis, the Egyptian dog god who you see carved on pillars and tombs or painted on the walls of temples. Unlike many shepherding dogs she is friendly and deigns to come and have her ears pulled, arching her back like a cat and sitting by my chair. She is so regal that I feel honoured. Ismail is proud of her and tells me she is pure bred and from the region. He says that this year they had quite good spring rainfall in the north, unlike the south, even though to my eyes it seems arid. He admires the camels, who are standing around looking shellshocked as if to say, 'This isn't the seaside holiday I thought I'd signed up to. I'm going to sue Tripadvisor.' Ismail leaves, taking his flock and his elegant dog with him and the men go to pray.

It has finally cooled off enough for me to go inside LPF when I hear a commotion and peek out in time to catch Hamish galloping past me at the speed of light. The men are giving out the oats and it is dinner time for hungry camels. That night, proof that Hamish does love me. At 3 a.m. I wake to the sound of padding and couching. He has come right up to my tent and spends the rest of the night ruminating noisily – obviously those oats were good – and I enjoy the companionship.

'Zahra, quick come and look.' Addi is squeezed beside a rock face, pointing. I crouch beside him and there in a shallow cave is a mother tortoise and her babies, snoozing in the cool, dusky interior. They are wise because the breeze outside is hairdryer hot. Struan has recovered a bit and we start off downhill which is good for everyone.

We are walking through a pomegranate orchard when a truck on the road turns in and comes speeding towards us, putting on the brakes hard at the last minute and blocking our route. An angry man jumps out and starts shouting at us before his feet even touch the ground. 'What are you doing here? Where are you going? Why aren't you on the road? You have no right to be here.' Just as he is reaching the peak of his fury, Hamish, with impeccable timing, reaches down and grabs a big mouthful of grass from between the trees. 'And your camels are eating my crops. Just turn round, turn round and get out!' Brahim, who had been making soothing noises throughout the diatribe, obviously decides that there is no point in arguing and starts to edge the camels round, which is not easy in the confined space of the path.

I decide to try a bit of *salaam alaykum* diplomacy and politely greet the man. He does a double take and I *salaam alaykum* again and praise his crop of pomegranates. I apologise for taking the path and say I am sorry we have made him angry. Politely, I mention that if we keep going on, the road is much closer than if we go back. To my amazement, he agrees. 'OK. OK. For the sake of your face, my sister, you can continue, but this is not your land.' 'Wow, these Rifis are stern,' whispers Addi as we quickly exit.

We pass through some small settlements of deserted, but rather grand, red-brick houses. 'They are all built by Moroccan expatriates,' Ali tells me. 'They work in Spain but they want a house in the *bled*, the old country. So, they build and then they come back for Ramadan and Eid, or in the summer. They don't want to live here.'

Our conversation basically consists of complaining about the heat in various different languages.

JP: '*Il fait chaud.*'

Addi (Tashlaheet): '*Lhma al hal.*'

Brahim (Arabic): 'I never sweat and I am sweating. I am hot from the inside. It is different from the Sahara; there it is hot on the outside.'

Ali (Arabic): '*Skhoun al hal.*'

Me: 'I am like a shower. Every time I drink it comes straight out of my skin – *whoosh.*'

After five minutes, we say it all again.

The land is rich with red earth and plentiful water. We are surrounded by fruit trees and even spot some bananas. There are many small farming settlements and we pass a number of people. Some are friendly and some are not. 'Some northerners think that we people from the south are a bit backward,' Ali tells me. There is also Covid to contend with. We always have our masks at the ready and take our cue from the people who approach us. If they come with hands outstretched to shake and big smiles then we respond. If they are more cautious, we respect that.

We are talking about Covid and its effects on tourism. Brahim sums it up: 'What does the mouse understand? If you only have one hole, God will be sure to block it up and then you will be caught and eaten by the fox. You have to have more than one thing to rely on. It's a problem for Morocco and us. If we only have tourism then when it goes – like now – we are in trouble.'

Our path is along the edges of the Rif Mountains and winds up and down through the conifers. There is water for the camels to drink at least once a day, and they do as they are losing so much through sweat. A fat turtle is startled by their big muzzles in a green reservoir and looks at them, with his eyes popping, before he dives deep. Not much further on, we come to what looks like a wild dog lying dead by the road. 'It is an *ushun*, Zahra, a wolf,' Addi tells me, and now I can put a form to the voices I heard howling in Sakiya al Hamra.

The hedgerows are filled with barbary figs, or prickly pears. In Tashlaheet they are called *tazart taroumit*. I'm pondering the fact that in English we say Barbary (coming from Berber) and in Tashlaheet they say *taroumit* (coming from Roman) when I hear a yell. 'Zahra, look out for the thorns!' It's too late. I have blundered into the undergrowth and tiny thorns have covered my leggings and jellaba. They are as fine as hairs but they prick and aggravate and I have a long afternoon ahead trying to pick hundreds of them out of my clothes and skin.

We camp on the far side of a village and it is not long before a stream of visitors starts to arrive. First the children, who adore the camels. 'I like the black one [Hamish].' 'The white one is so beautiful [Farquhar].' 'This one is very sad.' This was Struan, who had just flaked out after the hills, and had his neck stretched right out in front of him with his head resting on the ground in an attitude of despair. A young cow grazing near us came up to investigate him. She seemed astounded with what she was seeing and kept approaching and then backing away. Finally, summoning all her courage, she went right up to him and sniffed his tail. He swished and twitched and she leapt backwards, stiff-legged in alarm.

'Zahra, come here, Addi wants to have a party,' Ali says and, intrigued, I leave the cow and go round to where the men are sitting, grinning, on the rug under a carob tree. They are fanned out in a circle with a fragrantly roasted chicken on a platter in the middle and a pile of warm, fresh bread. 'A present from the village,' says Ali. 'They want to invite us to eat with them, but they are a little worried about Corona so they have brought us this gift.' The chicken lasts about five minutes as we tuck in ravenously and then throw the bones far from the camp in case of more wolves. For dessert we nibble on carob pods from the tree. Carob is a rich crop fetching 60 MAD (£5) per 100g in the suq at Ouarzazate and the farmers in this region have started growing it as a cash crop. Traditionally, it has been used for medicine and is said to be very good at stopping diarrhoea, which is the exact opposite of what I have been told at home.

Hamish is up and about and keeps wandering down to our left to a clump of trees. Every time he does, Addi leaps up and dashes after him to chase him away. When I ask him why he is preventing poor Hamish from enjoying some shade he says, 'Zahra, they are almond trees. The nuts are ripe. The camels love them, but if they eat them then the farmer will be angry and he gave us a chicken.'

We leave the village for a sea of plenty. The palette is still browns with the dark green of the pines, but now there are fig trees bursting with purple fruit and the lighter foliage of the almond trees. The fields are stripped of their wheat and barley and the short-cut stalks glint golden.

Three women are harvesting figs in the next field and they come out when they see me and ask for camel milk, which is very healthy and something we are asked for all the time. 'They are all boys,' Brahim says apologetically. The older of the women says she wants it for her daughter who has what looks like scoliosis and is also covered in birthmarks. 'We have sent her to the doctor but it is no good. Do you have any medicine?' I dig out some paracetamol and tell her to take one and drink at least one whole glass of water with it if the pain gets bad. I am always conflicted when the women ask me for medicine because I have no medical training and I don't know if they have any allergies, but the girl is in pain and I know that a severe reaction is very rare.

Because they have asked for camel milk, I cut off some camel hair, which is another thing we are often asked for, and give it to the woman. 'What is this for?' she asks me in surprise. I realise I have made a mistake in assuming she wants it but then she says, 'Ahha, good microbes, thank you.' She is a very active mother. 'I have a son,' she tells me. 'He is a really good boy. Can you help him? Can you help him get to Spain? Can you help him to get work?' I explain that I am from the UK and, although I have disappointed her both in terms of camel milk and employment, we part as friends and she presses a bag of fresh figs on me.

Addi has had to revise his opinion of the people of the region being harsh as we are made welcome everywhere and showered with gifts of fresh bread, figs and almonds. It isn't possible to get sick of fresh figs because they are so delicious, but we do give the squashed ones to the camels, who accept them graciously. These farmers have been little affected by the economic knock-on of the virus as their almonds, figs and grain are all for the local market. Brahim buys oats for the camels who are starting to get stronger. 'These local oats are the best,' he tells me. 'The other ones from China or the USA just go straight through them. When you look at their dung, you see whole oats in there. They haven't been digested.'

The hills have flattened out to be more like the Borders than the Highlands, much to the relief of the camels, and we pass many flocks of sheep and goats. Our movements are being monitored by the local authorities and we are visited by the qaid in green fatigues who checks our documents and talks through our route for the next few days. He tells us that he doesn't normally wear a uniform, but they were issued with them because of the pandemic. He has been on call twenty-four hours a day since it started five months ago and says it's exhausting. He advises us to camp nearby on a flattish plot of land where we can get water from the house, which is up a steep slope.

As we are unloading, I see movement in the house and I am dispatched up with a couple of bidots to ask for water. A graceful young woman called Bouchra welcomes me in through her wide courtyard and into the kitchen which sits off it. Her mother-in-law is playing on the floor with Bouchra's daughter, Salwa, who is two. I sit on the floor and Salwa and I form an instant connection. She gurgles and toddles over and we play peekaboo and I get lots of kisses. 'She never goes to anyone like that,' beams her granny, and all walls come tumbling down.

For the rest of the day, I am up and down to the house. Bouchra is obviously desperate for company and tells me something of her life. Her parents are divorced, which was very hard for her mother who she is close to and who lives not too far away. She has a younger brother, who arrives on his bicycle to visit after school, and her husband works in construction so is away most of the day. I meet him later and he is kind and clearly in love with his gentle wife and daughter. Bouchra works hard in the kitchen and prepares a giant dish of lamb with chips and fresh bread and tea for the men and me for lunch, which I carry down to them. As a young woman, she cannot fraternise with men outside the family.

For supper, she cooks for us again with ribs and more fresh bread and tea and little cakes for afterwards. The abundant hospitality doesn't stop there. After we have eaten, she offers me a shower, and clears away a space in her back room, bring-ing in full buckets of hot water. She is so thoughtful for my every comfort that she supplies me with soap, shampoo, a comb and then one of her own jellabas to change into after-wards. The most touching thing is that, after she has piled everything else up, she produces a pair of clean knickers. 'It is nice to have a clean slip after you shower, Zahra,' she tells me delicately. I spend all evening in the courtyard, cooing at baby Salwa, and resting my back against the cool clay wall chatting to the women and enjoying being in a home.

The heat is still intense. I feel slightly unwell all the time. I am sure my organs are cooking inside my body. I swear I can sense my liver hardening and turning grey. My throat and my chest are raw from panting in hot air and my ankles, feet and hands are all swollen. My belly too – from all the water. My lips are cracked and burnt and I have a strip of sunburn just under them which has peeled off, leaving a sore red line. I stink. I'm hot, everything is hot, and I can't cool down.

We are heading for the River Za, Oued Za, which we need to walk up and then traverse to continue our journey. Our road is down a dry mountainside with patches of wild fennel growing tall and skinny, dotted with small yellow flowers. I break off stalks to chew and freshen my mouth. We turn a corner and see a ribbon of green ahead with water shim-mering through it. We have arrived. Even from a distance, I can feel the drop in temperature and start to dream of an afternoon camped in the shade of the plentiful trees on the banks of the river.

Then, at about half a kilometre from the water, on a stony layby right next to the currently abandoned school, Brahim stops the camels and starts unloading. We go and look through the windows at the school. There are '50s-style pictures of men doing the various professions – doctor, lawyer, farmer – all round the walls and the teacher's white lab jacket hangs sadly on his or her chair. The small wooden desks and chairs are all covered in a light film of dust. Ali and Brahim are angry, reflecting on the cost of Covid to children's learning. 'Education is the thing that will move Morocco forward; it is the most important thing. It is why we work,' says Ali.

Addi, Brahim, the camels and I set off down to the river. Ali stays behind to guard the camp and also to entertain the two men who have arrived with their five taxi donkeys. These are to ferry visitors from the road, across the river and to the hamlets beyond. Fig trees are canopied with grape vines – all hanging with luscious fruit – but the camels ignore them for a bush with lilac fringes of flowers which is covered with silver white butterflies. It's a tamarisk. The butterflies flee as the boys approach and they have good reason. Hamish tears straight in and within five minutes the bush is bare. Clearly, tamarisk is a camel delicacy.

Our three characters become apparent in the way we tackle the Za River. Addi strips down to his Calvin Kleins – well, the equivalent – dumps all his stuff on a pile in the beach and dives into the river, spluttering and shaking like a seal and careering down with the current. Then, he surfaces and scrubs himself thoroughly in between, whooping and trying to splash me and Brahim, occasionally making a dash to the shore if one of the camels looks like he might invade the orchard.

I am hampered by the dictates of modesty and I go in with my top and leggings so as not to give the men a heart attack. I decide to turn this into a virtue by pioneering a new approach to clothes' washing. I rub Tide all over myself outside and inside my clothes and then wade in up to my neck and scrub it off with one hand while holding onto a big rock with the other. It is a genius plan, foiled only by me getting dragged away by the strength of the water and landing in a big patch of mud and weed which turns everything I am wearing poo-brown. I give up and just go ahead with shampooing and soaping. My scalp feels like it belongs to my skull again. I stay in till I am wrinkled and squeaky and then come out, change in the trees into a jellaba and start scrubbing my clothes on the rocks the old-fashioned way.

Brahim fills up his big bucket with water and stays at the shore clad in a T-shirt and shorts, which reach past his knees, washing each item of clothing carefully and hanging it up to dry on the thorn bushes. When he has finished he daringly strips off his T-shirt (the long shorts stay on) and wades in up to his neck where he bobs gracefully. Then, his worst nightmare happens. A gaggle of women and children come clattering down the hill while he is semi-naked by his reckoning. 'Zahra, I have to stay in the water till they pass. *Hachouma* – shame.'

The group of women are all wearing their very best clothes and the taxi donkeys are with them laden with suitcases. A fat ram is tied behind. 'It's a wedding,' says Addi. 'They've got everything ready – new clothes, presents and a sheep. Maybe we will be invited.' Brahim stays cowering upriver. The women start to cross the fast-flowing stream, shrieking as the water clutches at their legs. There is a very elderly grandmother who leans heavily on her stick in serious danger of getting swept away by the current. The donkey driver ignores her and instead leaps to the aid of the prettiest girl in the group, who is dressed head to toe in peach, and piggy-backs her to the other side. Brahim is faced with a dreadful quandary: does he stay modestly submerged or does he go to help a struggling grandmother? He rises to the occasion and, bare-chested, surges from the waves to help the *hajja*, gently shepherding her across and coming back several times to ferry toddlers and urge on the ram.

Ahead of us is a full day of walking the camels upriver. The gorge comes down steeply on either side leaving a wide strip of vegetation in the centre with the river running straight through it. It is like the Garden of Eden. Fruit trees of every kind, smothered in bees and butterflies feasting, give shade to farmed patches where the scarlet of peppers or tomatoes pop out from the rich green. Most people live up on the hills and come down to tend their gardens but we find one family encamped in a tent and a tree whose thick trunk and low branches act as a second home.

Getting the camels through is not going to be easy. The river runs fast and deep and underfoot the stones are sharp. I wear my strongest shoes and take a sturdy stick. The men take extra care with the loads, balancing them precisely, and Brahim's starting '*Bismillah*, in the Name of God' is even more heartfelt than usual.

We wade in. Farquhar is as placid as ever and walks calmly, but Hamish is not happy. He looks at the water and decides it is a hard no from him. The message is clear: 'Walk in that wet stuff with no idea what is underneath? I am not a fool. No way.' Brahim patiently zigzags him and eventually he reluctantly enters. Our progress is slow. We have to constantly readjust. We can't take the risk of the camels slipping and avoid muddy patches wherever possible. I am enjoying it hugely, ploughing through the water up to my thighs, but for Brahim, Addi and Ali the responsibility of getting the boys through it without accident is a serious one. When we can, we come out and lead them through the gardens, but most of our morning is spent in the water. Hector does very well until we come across a herd of cows also crossing. The combination of bovine intruders and knee-high water does not appeal to him. To my sadness, and everyone else's intense relief, we finally come to a path on the right which brings us out of the gorge up onto the hills. In the distance we can hear the women singing and the rhythmic beat of the wedding drums as we head south and away from the paradise of the Za.

15

THE REKKAM PLATEAU

The River Za – Beni Tadjite

1 September 2020

My Tashlaheet is coming along and every day I try to learn new words, which involves me working out what something means and then using it endlessly with my other words to make sentences. Today it is tall and short, heavy and light.

Me: 'Zahra is tall.'

Addi: 'No, Zahra is short.'

Brahim: 'And heavy. Zahra is heavy.'

Addi: 'Yes, she is fat.'

Me: 'Oi! Don't call me fat.'

Brahim: 'Well, what can we call you then? Can we call you *sahih* [fat and healthy], like a camel?'

Me: 'No! Do not compare me to a camel. *Zahra oogh tigi talrumt* ['Zahra is not a female camel' was one of the first phrases I learnt].'

Addi: 'But Zahra, camels are good.'

Brahim: 'And you are *sahih*.'

Me: 'Addi, a word of counsel while you are looking for a bride. Do not take any advice from Brahim about talking to women. Brahim, it amazes me that you are married with five and a half children. God must really have helped you on that one.'

I think my masterful put-down has silenced Brahim, but five minutes later he sees a warning sign on the road. It is a picture of a cow in a red circle.

Brahim: 'Look, it's Zahra!'

I resort to violence.

We have entered the flat lands of the Rekkam Plateau which extends from the Middle Atlas to the Algerian border. It lies at 1,000–1,400 metres of altitude and is about 100km long so will take us around five days. For the camels, it is a welcome break and something they know well – a long, flat, sand and hard-packed earth section. It is very like the Sahara stretch which took us along the route of the Paris–Dakar rally. I soon get into the rhythm of nothingness again.

At regular intervals we see nomad encampments. They all follow a similar format. There is a large black goat's hair tent, a concrete building at the side with solar panels, an enclosure for the animals and a big Ford truck, often red, at the side. If the family is lucky, or rich enough to drill, they may have a well within the enclosure. If not, it won't be far and they can transport the water with the truck. The flocks comprise both sheep and goats and most of the homes have one fabulously beautiful horse tethered nearby. 'They are for weddings and celebrations,' Ali tells me. I wonder if this is a result of their Arab heritage.

The people of this area are very distinct. They are Arabs and call themselves the Beni Hilal, 'the people of the crescent'. They trace their ancestry to the army of Muslims who came over from the Arabian Peninsula in the waves of Islamic conquest that swept over North Africa from the 7th century. They speak Arabic, which I find easy to understand as it is closer to Middle Eastern Arabic, but it is different from the Hassaniyya of the south. There have been no cases of Covid here and we are welcomed and greeted with handshakes and embraces wherever we go. 'We must follow their lead,' Brahim tells me.

Our first introduction is a girl called Nadia in a turquoise jellaba who runs out from her home and intercepts us. The men have told me firmly that on no account are we to stop for tea. Nadia looks up at them with glowing brown eyes. 'Excuse me, but I have been sent by my mother and father to bring you for tea.' Ali and Brahim are powerless to resist and abandon their principles, immediately turning towards her tent. Her mother and sisters make us very welcome and while the men sit outside with the father, we chat in the kitchen.

They are very lively and free. Nadia brings her pet goat to show me and bottle-feeds it some milk. Then she does cartwheels while I munch on the flaky bread that is typical of the region. Her mum, Fatooma, gives me a clean mint-green jellaba as a present and I immediately take off mine and stuff it in my bag, delighted to have something that doesn't smell of Hamish and is a pretty colour. I fish out the little brace-lets I have brought to give as a return gift. We take tea out to the men and the father approaches me to shake my hand. They tell us that there is no Covid here and that they have managed to survive because they have two family members in Spain who have been sending over money which 'secures the homestead'. We water the camels at their well and then after lots of selfies take our leave. 'These people are very good, very generous; they understand hospitality,' Ali says. 'Yes, Zahra, and the father thought you might make a good second wife,' Addi chimes in.

The ground is dry but there are patches of abundant herbs.

We go through a whole section of thyme which spices the air as it is crushed and then a section of harmala, Syrian rue. Ali tells me that the animals don't eat it but the nomads use it for lots of different medicinal purposes including getting rid of lice and worms. When I research it later I find that it contains beta-carbolines which have effects similar to the medicines used to treat Alzheimer's.

We see a splash of green in a declivity ahead and decide to camp there. As we approach, a contingent of black goats gallops towards us. The goats' herder, a slim girl in red who I later find out is called Hanan, heads them off by expertly throwing stones past them and then to the side to bring them back to the main flock. About 500m away is a nomad encampment. When we start pitching, a couple of men and boys walk over to watch. They are fascinated by everything and willing hands hold the tent pegs and offer to hammer. Their verdict on LPF is: 'It's nice, but hot.' We end up with six guests for lunch and it is a bit like the loaves and the fishes. The highlight is when I show them how to feed the camels with the leftover lemon rind and Sausage takes the pieces from them with gentle lips.

We're invited to tea and set off at 4 p.m. to the camp. We are met by a delegation of men led by a fine-looking Arab in a brown robe and white *chech*. I am taken off to the tent where the women are and the men go to the concrete house, the salon. You have to bend to get into the tent, but once inside you can stand up straight. Outside it is black but inside it is roofed with plaited straw mats and old hessian sacking. The sacks are held up by sticks of wood of varying lengths and girths which act like a forest of tent poles. The floor is pressed earth and is obviously swept very regularly.

I am sat down by the front entrance on a rug with a cushion

and brought some tea. To my right is the kitchen area. Two women are squatting comfortably on the ground and one is kneading dough. A metal screen about half a metre high shields the fire in the kitchen from the sitting area. The fire uses branches gathered from the oued and there is also a gas-fired oven for bread, which the women will make fresh every day. An ancient black kettle is on to boil and an equally black heavy iron griddle also rests on the fire. One of the women places a perfect round of dough on it to produce the flaky bread. All the other kitchen utensils are piled up neatly behind. The sleeping mats and blankets are folded and stacked up where I am sitting in the middle of the tent.

Further over, there is a cloth cradle attached by ropes to the top of the tent and Hanan's four-month-old baby daughter is being rocked in it by her grandmother. On my left, there are three lambs: twins and a frail newborn. The twins' mother comes to the outside of the tent and calls for them and they run out to meet her. Two cats prowl in and out. The women tell me that it does get cold at night but there is no snow and that if it rains they have a big plastic sheet to put over the whole tent. They bring over the fresh bread served with butter from their goats with honey from the market. The women tell me that a few years ago some foreigners had passed this way and ply me with questions:

Are you married? Why not? What are you for?

Are the men your relatives? Where are they from? Are they married? How do you know them? Do you pay them? How much do you pay them?

How far do you walk every day? Do you get tired?

Can you get milk from the camels?

Do you know how to make bread properly? Do you know how to knead the dough?

Are your parents alive? Do you have brothers and sisters?

How does it work with the tents? Where do you sleep? Where do the men sleep? Do they ever come into your tent?

I stay for about an hour and a half and then excuse myself to go and write as we are invited back for dinner.

The camels have actually wandered off to graze as there are things that they like to eat in the oued – tammayt bushes. It's the first time they have really gone far afield since we started this leg and I hope it means they are feeling stronger. Until now, they have tended to stick around camp waiting for their morning and afternoon oats. They have been gaining in bulk and are starting to look healthier.

A couple of hours later, we all head back to our hosts. 'You go to the women, Zahra,' says Brahim, and I feel a stupid surge of resentment at being relegated to the kitchen. In fact, it is an honour to get to spend time with the women and children and understand a little of how they live. I feel privileged because it is something that male explorers just can't do.

The tent is baking hot when I duck in. The reason is clear. A big pile of embers is glowing in the kitchen area and a whole spatchcocked sheep is spitted on one long branch of wood. Two men – one at each end – are slowly rotating it by hand over the embers to cook it through. Dinner. One of the sons of the house, Mohammed, is eating an early supper and he sits down to talk to me. He tells me that his tribe is the Ibn Guil and that they originate from Yemen.

Two women I haven't met before come in and start asking me about my religion. I tell them I am a Christian but that I respect Islam greatly. If I were to say I was an agnostic it would have no meaning for people and I am baptised and did go to church when I was at school. They ask me if I pray and fast and I say that our prayers are different, we don't have a schedule or set words in the same way, and that I do fast for Ramadan out of respect for my neighbours. I can see that they don't approve and that I am failing to meet their standards of what a good woman should be. Mohammed rescues me: 'We are all people of the book. Christianity is not far from Islam.' He finishes supper and goes to the corner to pray and I am summoned to the salon, where the men are, to show my papers to the gendarme, sheikh and muqaddim who have arrived in the meantime.

The salon is a long, narrow room with the usual carpets on the floor and cushions against the wall. There are low tables in the middle. It is stuffed full of men. It's rather intimidating but I decide to go for it so say a cheerful 'Salaam alaykum', which is resoundingly returned. The lieutenant of the gendarmes is very pleased with my Arabic and congratulates us all on our trip, laughing a bit as I say I want to find dinosaurs. After he leaves with all the other dignitaries, everyone relaxes and I go to sit down beside our host, the hajj. He takes a liking to me, which I reciprocate, and twinkles his eyes.

The men pick up their conversation which, to my vast amusement, is all about directions. It seems that you can be in a totally different continent but that people will behave in exactly the same way and that, in our gender-fluid times, the men will still cluster in a corner at a party and discuss the equivalent of heavy traffic on the M1. Ali and Addi are sitting opposite me and Addi's head keeps dropping as he nods off. Ali's eyes are sliding shut over his eyelids. Usually by this time we have eaten, washed up and I am falling asleep to the gentle sound of snoring.

Our hosts bring in bowls of excellent soup. It is the goat equivalent of oxtail, rich and meaty, and we all eat up. The hajj and I are getting on great guns and I am constantly supplied with morsels of bread and have my water glass topped up with cool water. 'Our water from the well is excellent,' he tells me.

Then, the door opens wide and, with gasps of appreciation from all of us, the roasted sheep is brought in on a platter. The men all move in close to the low tables and settle themselves for proper eating. '*Bismillah*,' and we are off. Well, *they* are off. Our fingers are our knives and forks and my fingers are not up to the task. The meat is burning hot, the fat-crisped skin is still sizzling from the embers, and when I try to pinch off a piece I can't hold it. *Hajj* to the rescue. He instructs his eldest son to tear pieces off for me, laughing gently. The meat is as succulent as you imagine. The crackling is perfect and juicy and the mutton is sweet. Silence reigns as everyone concentrates. I look over at Addi, Ali and Brahim and they are all trenchering with absolute focus. That whole sheep lasts about ten minutes and by the end there is only a small pile of bones left. Addi cracks all the big ones with his fine teeth, sucking out the marrow. I made my way through a couple of ribs which were salty and crunched easily.

After we have finished, one of the younger sons brings round a kettle of warm water and pours it over our hands into a bowl so that we can wash and we sit comfortably.

Into the silence, Brahim raises his voice and starts to sing a prayer. His voice fills every part of the room. The men sit up straight, pull their jellaba hoods over their heads and open their hands with the palms facing upwards. There is the sound of running feet and the young men, who weren't at the feast, come in and sit down. Brahim's face is transformed. He is a conduit for something greater than himself. The men are rapt. Some watch him, some join in when they recognise the words of the verses and some look inwards. The music of

Brahim's voice swells. It is lifted up by the power of the words and the palpable faith of the gathering. Then, he brings the prayers to a close.

Our hosts thank him. They have provided us with a feast, but they value Brahim's contribution far more highly. As we walk back under the stars he tells me, 'A party is just a party. You eat and talk and that is it. But a prayer puts a khatim, a seal, on it. It finishes it and also ensures that it ends properly with good feelings and intentions regardless of what came before.'

I'm given a lesson in the different types of butter by Brahim. 'You take the milk from the goat or cow and churn it in the *tigwit*.' A *tigwit* is a sausage-shaped container about two-thirds of a metre long and a third of a metre high which is suspended from the ceiling by a rope at each end and which the women push to and fro so that the milk can churn. 'It forms into a hard lump, which you take out. That is butter. What is left is the *lben*, buttermilk, if you leave that for a while and it curdles, you can then boil it and that becomes *tishlilt*, curds.' We had been given curds by a woman called Jumia who was diabetic and missed sugar. She showed me how to eat a spoon of curds and then drink my tea through it and said it helped with her cravings. It was rather like drinking bitter tea through cottage cheese.

Hamish greets me with a spray of saliva and as I wipe it off I realise that it is pink and flecked with blood. In a panic, I go and get Addi. 'It's a *tidi*, Zahra,' he tells me. 'They get it when they drink water from the pools.' I have no idea what this could be and so Addi goes into a convoluted mime of something grabbing on to my skin and then getting bigger and bigger and the penny drops. It is a leech. Hamish has picked up a leech from one of the waterholes and it is stuck right under his tongue where it attaches to the bottom of his mouth. The men tell me that, if left there, leeches can actually kill a camel so we have to get it out. All morning, Hamish bleeds from his mouth and we try to avoid being spattered.

In the bivouac, after lunch, the men set up their makeshift clinic. This is a dangerous procedure for Hamish but also for the men. Hamish is a biter and they need to get right into his mouth and under his tongue. Hamish is led in and comes quietly, innocent of what he is about to be subjected to. When he is couched, they tie his back legs, a rope round each thigh and under his knees, and then do his forelegs in the same way. This is so he can't kick out and injure anyone or himself. Then, Brahim puts his halter on and bends his head right round towards his back legs where it is immovably wedged against the back of his belly. Ali brings one of the iron tent poles and pushes it crosswise into his mouth, over his tongue and behind his long incisors to keep his mouth open. It can't be wood because he could bite through it.

By now, Hamish is roaring and bellowing. He is tightly pinioned but is still trying to thrash about. It is hard to watch but that leech has to come out and it is the only way. Addi goes in with a red and white kitchen cloth wrapped over his hand and tries to grab the leech from under his tongue. Hamish goes crazy and Brahim and Ali have to brace to stop him freeing his mouth. Addi gets a stick, wraps the cloth around it and tries to knock the leech out that way. For seven minutes, he and Hamish battle each other. Blood and saliva spray everywhere and Hamish's cries are heartrending. Addi sees that the leech has loosened and reaches in for a final grab with his hand wrapped in the cloth. Triumph, he gets purchase on the leech, pulls it out and holds it up for us to see.

It is about the length of half my index finger and a third of the width. The leech wriggles, fighting for its own life, but we kill it. We can't risk it getting to another animal. Ali and Brahim free Hamish and he trots off to the far edge of camp where he gets his head down and starts grazing. It's a relief as I can see there is no permanent damage done.

It's not the end of camel clinic, though. Struan and Lachlan, our weakest pair, have developed foot problems. The lack of work over the summer left their feet soft and they have both developed blisters. The men had cauterised them with animal fat but they weren't healing properly and we were worried about Lachlan in particular, whose pad was separating from the flesh of his upper foot. That is a very serious problem and if it continued to get worse would mean he had to be pulled from the expedition. Brahim explained to me that he needed to grow a new pad, like a new toenail, underneath. Every day we treated the wounds with antiseptic and antibiotic cream and put a pad and a dressing over them. My pink kinetic physiotherapy tape, meant for supporting tired or injured muscles and ligaments, was then wrapped firmly around the top of the camel's foot, under the foot, over the dressing and back up, but it wore out quite fast. It usually lasted about a morning and then had to be renewed.

We needed a solution to protect the dressings over the sores on the soles of their feet that wouldn't come off. The men are never at a loss for long and when we found a square of thick rubber on the road, they had a bright idea. Brahim and Addi got together to fashion this into two shoes – one each for Lachlan and Struan. They cut out a rough pad-shape from a piece of old rug and from the rubber. Then, Brahim sewed the two together with thick twine. The pad was foot-sized but the carpet was bigger so that it could come up and over the pad. The biggest logistical problem was how to keep the shoe on the camel's foot. We tried all sorts of things over the days. We started off with the green twine which is a camp staple: wrapping it up over the shoe and under the foot, but it wore out quickly as it got grated along the ground. What we needed was something that didn't get stepped on and worn out. Brahim came up with a kind of suspender system which entailed long pieces of twine being threaded through the top of the shoe through the rug edges and then being tied above the camels' knee so that it didn't just slide down, or, if it did, could be easily hoisted up again.

Skirting the Middle Atlas, it was noticeable how much poorer the countryside and the people were. We got our first requests for money and it looked like it was much needed. We had left the Arabs of the Rekkam and were back with Tashlaheet speakers.

We also saw our first camels, being herded in a valley.

Brahim: 'Oh no! That's it, everything is gone. No more bread, no more honey, no more milk. They've got camels, so we are not special anymore. If they have got *chechs* too, we are really done for.'

Ali: 'Yes, but we've still got a *gawriyyaa*, foreign woman.'

Addi: 'Hmm, I am not sure she is enough.'

A new plant has appeared on the plains. It is shaped rather like a brain coral and sometimes has little purple flowers on it. When I ask Ali for the name he says it is called 'the cauliflower that wears the *chech*'. We are near a spot named the Red Heart and the people here are very wary of us. Brahim says they are always suspicious of outsiders in this region but now Covid has made it worse. He says they might think we are treasure hunters.

In Morocco, treasure hunters are greatly feared. In rural

areas, it was quite customary for ordinary people to bury coin or jewellery to keep it safe. It is believed that once it was buried the jinn would then guard it and consider it theirs. Treasure hunters trawl the countryside looking for hidden caches and if they find one, when they dig it up, they allegedly have to offer a blood sacrifice to appease the jinn. This could be a number of things, from blood from your own palm to an offering of a black cockerel. But the old tale is that it could also mean sacrificing a child if the haul was particularly big, and so children are told that they might be snatched by treasure hunters.

We camp up about a kilometre from a small cluster of houses and are at first told to leave by one of the men, but Ali argues well and we get to stay. We need water. Addi and I tie the empties onto Hamish, put on our masks and walk up to the hamlet. When we get there, all the children run away into their houses. Addi wants to leave, saying that we have to avoid them, but I am determined to get some help with the water. I tell him to stay back with Hamish and I go a bit closer so I can speak to the woman who is standing with her daughter near the door of their house.

I shout greetings and ask if they have a well. 'Everyone has run away because they are afraid of you. We don't have a well here but there is one nearby,' she shouts back. I ask her if someone could show us the way and, while she is thinking about it, her husband arrives. He makes us welcome, brings us cold water to drink immediately and leads Addi and Hamish off to the well. He also invites us for dinner that night, which we accept gratefully even though we have already cooked our soup and meat. 'We can eat the soup for breakfast and the meat will keep till tomorrow,' says Ali.

It's dark and raining very slightly as we walk back from

dinner with our hosts. Addi runs on ahead. 'He's definitely going off to call one of his girlfriends,' I say.

I'm eating my porridge the next morning when I notice that there is a commotion round the mess tent. Voices are raised and Ali and Brahim seem to be telling Addi off. Addi is laughing but also looking shamefaced and shuffling around guiltily. Brahim heads over to me and tells me the sorry tale.

'Zahra, something has happened. Addi has done something very bad.' I can't gauge whether he is being serious or not because his expression keeps changing from stern to slightly smiling. 'Do you remember last night when we walked back from dinner, Addi ran ahead? You thought it was because he was full of jinns and wanted to phone a girlfriend, but that wasn't the reason. He came back early to eat meat from the casserole pot.'

By this time, Ali has joined us. 'Yes, Zahra, I have proof. Look what I found this morning outside the tent.' Ali holds up three small meat bones. He is also semi-laughing but adds, 'This is very wrong. No one should eat unless we all eat. It is shameful to take meat for yourself in this way. Addi has done something very wrong.'

I call over, 'Addi, is this true, did you really eat some meat from the pot?'

Addi ducks his head. 'I was still really hungry after supper with our neighbours. I didn't want to eat too much of their chicken because they were poor so when I came back I had two small pieces of meat. Forgive me.'

That day is dominated by Addi's transgression. We eat the rest of the meat at lunch and Addi forgoes his share, but after a long discussion, Ali and Brahim decide that reparation must be made. They tell Addi that, at the next suq, he has to buy a whole chicken with his own money and then cook it for us.

He agrees to the terms and begs them to stop talking about it now that he is going to pay a penalty. They agree and almost stick to their end of the bargain, only mentioning it every hour or so over the next two days.

Brahim: 'Casserole for lunch today.'

Ali: 'Only if there is any meat left.'

Addi: 'Zahra, I only took a tiny bit – the size of my fingernail.'

Ali: 'I found three bones.'

'If Addi doesn't get meat for three days, I get worried,' says Ali. 'I can't sleep well. What if I drop off and then when I wake up in the morning, I have a hand missing or a bite out of my leg?'

The weather is changing and the sky is throwing out herds of black clouds. There is a low rumble of thunder. We all rush for the plastic sheets to put over the canvas tents to keep them dry. The wind is blowing so hard that we can't hear each other and the sheets are thumping around like stampeding horses. I am told to stand on one end of the sheet while the men anchor them. They do this by putting stones about the size of a Pizza Express doughball inside the plastic and then tying a length of twine round the outside so it is firmly anchored. Then they tie the other end round the tent pegs. It's ingenious, but I am not paying enough attention and fail to notice one just next to me, which flaps violently and then thwacks me brutally on the side of the head. There is a nasty crunch and I wobble a bit but there is too much going on to worry. I grab the twine, wrap it round a peg and help as much as I can. I'm left with a lump and a bruise and no sympathy when I tell my story. 'Pay attention!' says Ali.

We cross into green, agricultural lands, fed by the water off the hills and follow Oued n Izm – the River of the Lion.

There are little shops in a village and Addi slopes off to make good on his promise and endure his punishment.

He buys the fattest chicken I have ever seen; it is more like a turkey. He cooks it for us in our biggest pot with coriander, garlic and lemon. He has not skimped, even buying two large bottles of Coca-Cola. We all eat until we are absolutely full and only bones are left. Bellies bloated; we agree that Addi has done a very good job of making up for his transgression. Then, there is a confession.

Ali: 'Zahra, do you remember when you and Brahim climbed up the mountain in the Draa where you found Mohamed's leaf.'

Me: 'Yes, and then we came back down and cooked the goat.'

Ali: 'We did. But what you don't know is that Addi and I ate some of that goat before you and Brahim got back.'

Hilarity ensues.

16

TOWARDS HEAVEN'S FINGER

Bni Tadjite – Tabanast

16 September 2020

We are in my favourite type of landscape. A long, rolling plain unfolds ahead, dotted with oueds and crevasses where water collects for drinking and bathing. Mountains frame the journey, shimmering ahead of us in the heat, or to the sides. The sky dominates everything and is a constant play of light and colour. From the softest of greys to a harsh, violent blue, it changes throughout the day. The clouds show off, floating in white candy-floss puffs or blackening with a storm, threatening rain. Sunrise is soft, all pastels and lemony yellows. At night the sky is black, untroubled by human lights, spotted with slivers of stars or a glowing moon.

After the confinement of lockdown, my pilgrim soul blossoms in the space and freedom. Walking day after day to the rhythm of the camels feeds something deep within me and I revel in the emptiness and scale of the planet. It is the simplest thing, walking, one of the earliest things we did as humans, and infinitely satisfying as we tick off the kilometres, slowly progressing.

We pass into a narrower section where the mountains roll down and stop at a well where a stunning young woman is drawing water for her flock with her father. She helps us with the buckets for the camels. She is wearing a tiered maxi skirt which is covered in spangles that throw off glitterball lights in the sun, a red and black top and a tie-dyed headscarf wound high like a turban. Jangling bracelets clink up and down her arms as she pulls up the bucket. The men are all rendered totally silent, but when I tease Addi afterwards he says, 'Yes, she may have been beautiful, but she was not a girl; she was a woman.'

We come across a series of necropolises, conical mounds of stones. It would be a nice place to rest. There are lots of azugwar trees which provide a brown kernel or nut which tastes sweet and is sold in the markets. It is very good for poor kidney function apparently and we gather some for Brahim, who has kidney stones. When we get home, he says he will take them to the spice shop to be ground and will mix the powder with water to drink.

Suddenly, Addi leaps up in the air and simultaneously backwards. 'Danger, Zahra.' He bars my way with his arm. 'Can you see it?' We all pile to a halt and there in front of us to our left, almost completely camouflaged, is a giant lizard. It has puffed itself up to its fullest extent and is hissing aggressively. The men call it an *akka* and to me it looks like a monitor lizard. It is about a metre and a half long from nose to tail and is perfectly camouflaged with a beige and white mottled body and diagonal stripes in a darker brown. Its throat is engorged and its body is a leaf shape – broader at the bottom. Its front feet are just like hands and its back legs are longer and folded up underneath it. It has a powerful tail. When I Google it later, it turns out it is a *Varanus griseus griseus*, a rare desert monitor. Scientists are not sure whether they have poison glands or not, but you don't want to be bitten in any case because of the bacteria in their mouths. The females are more delicate and prettier, so ours was definitely a male. They are really good swimmers and live off fish as well as mice and eggs. Although that seems unlikely in this environment, there are pools around, so perhaps there are fish too.

I am sure it is more scared of us than we are of it and we carefully guide the camels in a wide circle to avoid it. When we pass on and I look back, it has deflated itself but is still hanging close to a small bush for camouflage.

The place names have become very descriptive. We head for Heaven's Finger, which is a long sliver of rock pointing straight into the sky and guides us for several days past the Heart of the Cow, a mountain shaped for its name. This part of the country is inhabited by Ait Sbaa, 'the tribe of the lion', and they are somewhat fierce with us. We pass a shepherd who shoos us off his patch: 'There is not enough water or grazing here.' He obviously thinks that either the camels will eat too much or that we are just the vanguard for a group of nomads and there are more with all their flocks behind us. When we go to stop in the lee of a hill, the muqaddim from the local village comes out to warn us that there is a plant in this area that will kill the camels if they eat it and tells us we should move on. It looks like a smaller, brighter alogo and attracts swarms of very small white butterflies. Ali and Brahim suspect that he may be telling us that to discourage us from camping near the village, but they don't want to take the risk and we move on.

Ever since the Rif, we have been grappling with one of Addi's riddles.

'It is good if it goes into something small, but not good if it goes into something big. What is it?'

The three of us have been using all our joint brain power trying to find the answer. Under riddle rules, you are allowed to ask questions and to make as many guesses as you can. After supper, I do a quick summary of what we have learnt so far, 'So, Addi. It's *halal*, it's got a soul but it hasn't got a soul. It's got horns. It is big like a camel but it fits best into a small place. You can buy it in the suq but it is rare.' 'Yes,' says Addi, 'and Hamish has seen it.' Ali and Brahim and I ponder this new information and start running through the names of every animal that we know, as that seems the most likely answer.

'A sheep.'

'No.'

'A goat.'

'No.'

'A billy goat.'

'No.'

'An elephant.'

Addi: 'An elephant isn't *halal*.'

Me: 'Maybe it is. What do you think, Brahim?'

Brahim: 'No, an elephant isn't *halal*.'

'A *mouflon*. What is a *mouflon* in Tashlaheet?'

'It's an *ani*.'

'No. It is not an *ani*.'

Addi is delighted with himself. 'Baa, do you say Baa? Say Baa!' Baa is the way you give up on a riddle.

Brahim and Ali in unison: 'We will never say Baa. Baa is not in our vocabulary. There is no Baa.'

Personally, I would be up for a Baa as I really want to know the answer. But I can't Baa alone – I would shame the whole of Scotland. I plead for special favours, 'Addi, help Zahra, just whisper in my ear, I won't tell the others.'

Addi is even more delighted with himself. 'I will help you all. It has small eyes.'

We are walking on the plain when Addi comes up. 'Zahra, my eyes are sore.' I look at them and they are red, but we are only about twenty minutes from stopping. I tell him I have some medicine in my big bag and if he can wait till we bivouac I will get it out there. Two minutes later, he stops and cries out. He is in real pain. We lay him down and pour lots of water from the water bottles into his eyes to rinse them. We carry on walking but in another 100 metres we have to stop again. Addi can't go on. His eyes are swollen shut and burning. I want to unpack and get my eyedrops out, but Brahim says it is better to get to camp. We lift Addi up on Lachlan and he ties his *chech* over his eyes and hangs onto the pommel.

We camp up as soon as possible and put him down on a mattress between two of the saddlebags to shade him. I dig out what I have in the first-aid kit: hand sanitiser, eye drops and ibuprofen. I want to get whatever he has on his hands off them, soothe his eyes as much as possible and give him a bit of pain relief. The eyedrops are probably the most effective thing, but the whole ritual of cleaning his hands and wiping his face, putting in the eyedrops and finally giving him a painkiller soothes him. It is comforting to be taken care of. About ten minutes later, he is feeling much better and tells us that he had seen two pretty flowers and picked them for me. Then, he rubbed his eyes and immediately they started to burn. They must have had a corrosive sap. 'Addi nearly died,' he says solemnly.

We have left a section of pure white sand for an area that is covered with the cauliflowers that wear the *chech*. Some are like perfect miniature trees, a trunk with a lollipop just as you used to draw as a toddler. Others have red flowers on them.

'They are like the sequins on the headscarf of an Amazigh girl,' says Brahim. There are patches where they have been dug up and left to dry for fuel. They look prehistoric and, even though there aren't many rocks, I redouble my efforts on the dinosaur front.

Addi and I are following a long channel of stone when I find an indentation that looks like it could be something. It is pressed into the rock and is filled with water. Addi and I compare it to the dinosaur prints I have saved from Google. 'Ighri,' says Addi, maybe. It does look exactly like them, but there is only one in isolation and it is not as big as it should be, so I reluctantly put it down as a probable puddle. I take pictures just in case.

We are now on an ancient trail named after a major Jewish family in Morocco, the Batboul trail. It leads us into a gorge. This is going to be a challenge for the camels. Sharp, striated rocks stick up in runnels from the hillside. We have to walk along them and they are narrow. The gorge is striped in various shades of brown and yellow and we wind in and out and up and down finding the best path. I worry about their feet on the sharp rocks. Towards the head of the gorge, the men have to build stone bridges so that the camels can step up over the big boulders and onto the next level. There are pools of perfectly clear, icy water and a rock of pure quartz the size of my head. Pink oleanders clump near the edges of the cliffs and wild rosemary grows out of the rocks.

At the neck of the gorge there is a shrine. It looks out onto the valley and, bizarrely, is piled up with about twenty teapots and some cooking equipment. Pilgrims must have left them as an offering. There are some graves to the side, with large headstones propped upright.

We have only done thirteen-and-a-half kilometres, but

271

the camels have stopped and one after the other they couch in the middle of the gorge. 'They're on strike,' I tell Brahim. 'They want better pay and working conditions. Hamish is the leader. They want more oats, less walking, a complete ban on gorges, a piscine of water every day and restitution of casse croute.' We have run out of oranges, so when we stop for our elevenses, they watch us with sad eyes, telegraphing the crucial question, 'Where is our orange peel, people?' I tried dividing my caramel wafer between them but no one was interested. They will accept dried figs but we have run out of those too. When we get to camp all is forgiven. Not only do they get oats, we have a watermelon and there is rind to eat. The melon is surprisingly cool and fresh. 'You put it in the sun,' Addi tells me, 'that keeps it cold.' 'Yes, don't ever put it in the fridge,' Ali chimes in.

We've entered the Midelt region, which is famous for its apples just in time for harvest. A bent old man with a cane sees us coming and yells for us to wait. He darts off into the trees and comes back with a bagful of apples wrapped up in a cloth. We thank him and all take one and start eating immediately. They are perfect: crisp, sweet and tangy. The camels get the cores. I tell the men that, when I first came to Morocco, I used to bring back Pink Lady apples from the UK, because I couldn't find good apples here, and they look at me with rightful disbelief.

The mountains start in earnest. Green maize and high pop-lars grow in the valleys and the peaks rise to our side. We are camped above Zawiya Sidi Hamza and will visit the shrine, but first we have to say goodbye to two of our team. It is time to retire Lachlan and Struan. They need to rest their feet and the difficult conditions of the High Atlas will be no good for them. Ychou arrives with two new camels, a sturdy blond, who I see instantly should be called Jock, and a languid brunette who I name Willie Willie Willie. I'm channelling Oor Wullie from Scotland, but this is also a phrase in Morocco which translates to something like 'eek' or 'look out' or 'what are you doing'. It makes the men laugh, especially as it turns out that Willie is a bit clumsy and not very strong.

The new boys are having an easy day to start with as we are spending the morning visiting the *zawiya*. The village is small, thirty to fifty houses, all traditionally built from the white clay of the riverbed. The fields surrounding it are rich and well tended, growing every type of daily vegetable – courgettes, potatoes, carrots – as well as apples and grain. Mohamed meets us at the *zawiya* which is reached through tunnels with house entrances on either side. He is a direct descendant of Ibn Hamza and is the current keeper of the shrine. The village has a very unusual feature: it has running water in all the houses, brought in by a network of underground canals. Each house has a 'well', basically a hole, down into the channel that runs under it and the householders can pull up water from that.

The *zawiya* is being restored and we are lucky enough to see it at an early stage with its old bones still visible. A magnificent wooden door, battered by time and covered in intricate, burnt–black spiral carvings, is at one of the entrances. The thick clay ceilings and walls are supported by timbers cut from the poplars that grow in the oued. We estimate that the central one is 14 metres long. There is a room for a *medersa* (a Quranic school) and rooms for the family.

The mosque has slim poplar trunks in place of stone pillars and the ceiling is wider logs interwoven with bamboo. Upstairs there are still some decorative cedar ceilings. They are intricate geometric patterns formed by inlaid wood in different shades from cream, through brown, to black. Some of the old wooden bookcases still remain, propped up in the different rooms, and I hope they will be reused when the renovation is complete.

To the side of the old buildings is a brand-new library, Al Ayachia Library, built by the government to house the treasury of over 5,000 books that the family has collected. Like the great libraries of Timbuktu and Tamegroute, these are religious, hand-written and illustrated books and texts. They are more evidence of that trail of learning that linked these religious centres through trade across the centuries. It is quite extraordinary to see the collection of immeasurably precious books kept safe here in a tiny village. I am allowed to hold one of them and leaf through the pages. It is 800 years old and is a life of the Prophet. It is written in the style of calligraphy called Maghrebi and is relatively easy to read. It is a total thrill to be able to read snatches of it and see the notes that students have made in the margins, as I did in Tamegroute and Timbuktu. I feel my heart lift at the thought of all those past pupils seeking knowledge and struggling through difficult Arabic phrases just like I do.

Even more intriguing, though, is the collection of artefacts that the family have kept. There is an old book press and Mohamed demonstrates how it would have been used to compress the pages of a volume that had been stitched or pasted together to stop them from warping. He shows us a travelling oil lamp that folds up handily, and a collection of antique hats and shoes that allegedly belonged to the saint. Mohamed explains all the different kinds to us: there are supple leather booties that were used as socks; high wooden clogs for the mud; indoor babouches and travelling shoes, which are made out of leather but which have a donkey's shoe nailed to the heel to make them durable. Leaving the *zawiya*, we pass women collecting in the corn, gathering it into stooks to dry and loading it onto donkeys. Time feels unchanged.

'This is the heart of Morocco,' Ali tells me. It is a series of fertile, agricultural valleys bordered by the mountains of the High Atlas. Tarmac roads are being built but have not yet reached everywhere and donkeys far outnumber cars, or even bikes, as a method of transport. The villages are cream or grey, as the clay here is a different type from the red I am used to in my home in Imlil, and they seem busy and prosperous.

As we are pulling up a hill I hear hooves tapping, and when I look back I see an older man, wearing a spotless white *chech* and striped jellaba, urging on a small donkey. He is our muqaddim for the day. In this region, we have been handed from one to the next as a precaution in the time of Covid. He is wearing his mask and is hanging back, presumably worried about us bringing in the virus, with his donkey equally worried about the camels. When we stop for our elevenses, Addi takes him some over and, when he finds out that Addi is a nomad from the Ait Atta tribe, some of his reservations disappear and he comes up closer as we continue on.

Every kilometre brings out his and his donkey's innate sense of camaraderie and when we reach a village in a dip and it is time for him to hand us on to someone new, he demands lots of selfies. 'Zahra, come here,' he commands, and when I approach, he opens his saddlebags and takes out a big round of bread and some apples. 'Thank you so much, Hajj, but we don't want to take your food, we honestly have enough,' I say, reluctant to deprive him of his packed lunch. 'Enough? Enough! Take this and enjoy it, Zahra.' He presses the goodies on to me and trots off, turning round to wave as he goes.

Entering the village, we cause a semi-riot. The kids are all out and when they see us they form an impromptu procession. The mothers all come out to the doors carrying their babies and we are preceded up the road by a cohort of young boys turning cartwheels and whooping. It is like Smara all over again but with more people. 'It is a different brand of Tashlaheet,' Brahim says. 'These are good people.' We are certainly back to the hospitality we enjoyed earlier in the trip, but I suggest to him this is simply because the people here have more and are able to share.

We come up against a new Covid-related problem. We want to take the old nomad path from where we are, Afraskou, across the mountains to Imilchil. Usually this path is very well trodden because Imilchil hosts an annual marriage festival for nomads from all over the Atlas. It takes place every year at harvest time and is a way for families to meet together and to arrange a courtship within the traditional constraints of society. There are fewer and fewer nomads remaining fully in their lifestyle and the festival has always been important to allow families to mix more widely outside their group.

The prospective grooms wear all white and the brides wear the brightly coloured, tasselled and sequinned Amazigh clothes of celebration. They may also put temporary tattoos on their faces – the older women have permanent tattoos but that custom is changing – and use natural make-up like kohl ground from black rock and crushed walnut shells which dye the cheeks and lips red. If a girl agrees to be married she says, 'You have captured my liver, *Tq massa n uchemt.*' Of course, the prospect of the wedding festival gives us all great fodder for teasing Addi, but he is having none of it. In any case, it's a moot point, because this year Covid has trumped true love and the festival is cancelled.

The reason this is a problem for us is to do with the route over the mountains. There has been a landslide a few kilometres in which has rendered it impassable. Normally, because there are people travelling to Imlil regularly, the path would be cleared or alternatives carved out, but Covid has cut off all that traffic and no one has an interest in doing the work to clear the route. It has remained blocked and we are told firmly that there is no way over. That means we have to walk the piste and go round the long way.

Othman is our muqaddim for the morning. He is a bear of a man with a personality to match his bulk. When he met us on the road he ran off to the side and came back with a big bag of apples and a motorbike to ride as we are on the piste. He has shaken all our hands vigorously and is not masked so we feel safe to push ours under our chins or into our pockets.

'Oh, Zahra. I hope you like our apples. I brought them for you but if I'd known you needed bread, I would have brought you oil and bread too. But don't worry, I have phoned ahead to the next village for some. God willing you will be well-provisioned by us.'

As always, we enquire about Corona in the area. 'Corona, what Corona? There is absolutely none here, thanks be to God. But if the government says there is Corona, then there is Corona. If it changes its mind and says there isn't Corona, there isn't. It is as simple as that. God is the Most High.' The men love him and chat away happily to someone so on their own wavelength.

We take lots of selfies and exchange numbers and he gets ready to leave us. 'Don't you worry, Zahra. We will be handing you on from one muqaddim to the next. You will never be alone. You will see the hospitality of the region. You will, if God wills it.'

His words make me think about perception. For me and the men, being handed from muqaddim to muqaddim is an intrusion, in a way, on our privacy. This region is the first that it has been so marked in and we don't resent the individuals, who are universally kind and helpful, but we do resent the system. It feels like a curb on freedom – even though it has no actual effect on where we go. Ali has to make sure he is in touch with the local authorities and Addi has taken on the job of muqaddim wrangler, but for a liberty-loving crew it is an irritation. However, from Othman's side it is an act of hospitality and welcome which is a much more positive way to look at it.

Every day we are going deeper and higher into the Atlas Mountains. There is water everywhere and the area is populated with lots of herdsman. Flocks of choughs and pigeons fly so low that I can hear the beating of their wings as they wheel past us. We are visited by a young man called Brahim who has been chatting to Addi and keeping him company. It is good for him to have someone his own age to talk to. Brahim eats with us and brings us two puffy rounds of bread, shaped like footballs, which rattle like a tambourine as I shake them. It is a new variation of bread: a loaf baked with a stone in it. You break it open, take out the stone, and it is soft inside and crispy outside.

Brahim leaves us for a bit to take the remainder of our soup down to his dad. Nothing is wasted here and people are always thinking of their family. When he comes back, he fills us in with the gossip from Izougaren, where we are camped. He tells us that several men are currently in prison for seven years for tribal fighting. They were caught battling the village we were in yesterday. The dispute was over grazing rights and between the two clans, the Ait Yehya and the Ait Haddido.

Ali explains that tribal fighting is still very common in the mountains. It is almost always centred on land disputes and the local government clamps down on it severely.

Our desert camels don't know what has hit them. Steep ascents, water, cool air, gorges and lines of poplar trees. One thing they do really like is the thistles that have started to appear and they gobble them up greedily. 'At last, thorns,' Brahim says approvingly. 'Much better for them than these oats we have been giving them.' After the blankness of the Sahara, the variety for the eyes feels almost obscene. We start our day in rolling, soft hills of gold, dotted with dark green juniper trees. Then we go down into a gorge with high banks flanking it. A stream runs all the way through it, washing the pebbles underfoot. Small fields are on each side and we stop to let a woman pass her baby under Farquhar's belly for luck and are rewarded with fresh peaches from her tree. We enter a tunnel of poplar trees, so tall they block out the sun overhead, and we have to pull back the branches to make way for the boys with their baggage. The first autumn leaves are lying in piles of yellow on the ground and the sheep are noticeably fatter. There is history too – shell fossils on the rocks.

The ascents are hard work, though. We are up over 2,500m now and, although we try to follow nomad paths where possible, here they are for goats and donkeys not for the wide-footed camels. Hector is our star in this terrain. He is from the Saghro so he is used to the mountains and is unfazed. Farquhar's sweet temper gets him through anything and Hamish ploughs up and over, but the others need coaxing.

We are heading for a pass to take us into the next valley. This is an area that could almost be Scotland. There is a heather–like shrub on the slopes and a rocky ravine with a path to one side. There is no way to avoid a very steep section of around 200 metres which will bring us out onto the top. Addi has given me his stick but, even with that, I slip backwards when I try to go up and need a couple of attempts. For the camels, the difficulty is multiplied. Addi and Ali stop them in a safe spot and Brahim gets out the pickaxe to dig a path. For about twenty minutes, the men dig and chip away at the hard ground to even it out a bit for the team. They cut rough steps in it and kick away all the loose scree so that at least when the camels get their pads onto a step they won't be sliding on the stones that lie like marbles on the surface. Then, they divide the camels to bring them up. Farquhar is at the front, led by Brahim and followed by Hector Saghro. Then Addi brings Jock, Hamish and Sausage in that order. Ali is at the back and in sole charge of Willie Willie Willie. Even with all the preparations, the camels' pads slip and the men have to urge them on, maintaining a steady stride and a calm demeanour.

We've navigated the steepest part and the path is now clear but there is another problem. It is only 10cm wide, with a cliff on one side and a drop straight down into the void on the other. The camels are basically walking along something that is just the width of their feet and if they falter and miss a step, they'll go over. I can't look. The trust that the animals feel in the men shows and they follow them steadily, placing their feet carefully, until we come out into a shallow glen right at the top beneath Tizi n Taghdwat, the pass of Taghdwat. The wind is so strong that we have to duck behind some rocks to hear each other and to eat our elevenses. Of course, there are snacks for the boys too. Ali tells me that if the going gets really steep for the camels, they can step up using the rough pads on their knees.

We are surrounded by colour. The wind has whipped the

sky into the brightest of blues and the earth on the hills is red. A new plant appears. It is called Anb n Ushun, 'the grape of the wolf', and is small and prickly like a bilberry with green seeds. We see a girl on her own with sheep in the distance and a boy with a donkey approaching each other and I ask Brahim whether young couples in the mountains get together before marriage. 'Of course they do sometimes. Human nature is strong,' he tells me. 'But if the girl gets pregnant, there is a big problem. Even if the boy wants to marry her, sometimes the family will not let him. They tell him that if she went with him then maybe she went with others. Sometimes they do get married and sometimes it can go to court and they get DNA tests but it is very difficult. Here, the wedding night is still very important. The man and the woman should be virgins.' Addi quizzes me closely about love and marriage in the UK and looks disbelieving when I explain our looser approach to pre-marital sex. 'You mean, in your country, everyone has sex before marriage?' he asks me several times in different ways just to make sure. 'And that is good for the women not just the men?'

We stop at the edge of an oued outside a village. There is a constant stream of women passing on donkeys piled high with brushwood. The women spend their days out on the steep slopes, cutting the shrubs. Then, they roll them down to the bottom of the hills where the donkeys are waiting and load them up. They store them at the side of their houses for heating and cooking in winter. 'Get those camels away from my mule or I will give you a good taste of my stick,' one doughty matron yells at Brahim as Hamish makes a beeline for her. Brahim grabs him and chases him and the others up the opposite side of the valley well away from the traffic. It is still too close for some of the donkeys, though, as they bridle and bray when they sniff eau de camel on the breeze. Brahim stays with them, out of reach of the matrons. We have to delay our leaving in the morning as we wait for seven different flocks of sheep and goats to pass through the oued from the village, moving into the mountains for their day's grazing and followed by the same women and donkeys we had seen coming down the night before.

17

FINDING DINOSAURS

Tabanast – Aguerzka

1 October 2020

We almost murder Addi. We are sitting after supper in the mess tent and return once again to his riddle, 'I am good when I go into something small, but not into something big.' It has been plaguing us for almost half the expedition. When we ask him for a couple of real clues, he starts laughing and can't stop. 'Addi, what is it? Why are you cackling?' asks Ali. 'Because I can't remember the riddle,' says Addi. 'I can't even remember the question.'

Our evenings have a rhythm to them now. Our idea of a big night in is to finish supper and have some light riddle-telling while we are drinking *luisa* (verbena tea) and then to break out the cards. I have taught the team the Memory Game. For this, you spread all the cards out face down and then you pick them up and reveal them in pairs. You have to place them back in exactly the same place if they don't match. If you get two of the same card value, i.e. two queens or two fives, you keep them. The aim is to remember where the cards are and to gather as many as you can.

Because I have played it before, I win the first few games easily but then I am overtaken by Brahim, who may have a small body but has an elephantine memory, coupled with a fiercely competitive nature. Ali also wins, he gets on a roll and then there is no stopping him. Addi is a late starter but once he has got the hang of it, he snatches up the pairs and flings them down with a flourish. We all try different distraction techniques on our opponents, including talking while they are concentrating and making eye contact with incorrect cards to try to sway their hands. I reckon I am heavily disadvantaged by coming after Brahim.

After two games, I am ready to stop but the men always beg for a third. Sometimes they let me go and do the dishes and they play on, but usually it is a case of the team having to stay together till the end. Once the final victory has been had, the victor has congratulated themselves hugely, and the rest of us have congratulated them grudgingly, it's dishes for me and a final camel check for the men. For this leg, Brahim has been doing double prayers before dinner rather than one prayer before and one after.

It has taken us much longer to get to Lake Isli than it should have. That is due to the fact we had to follow the piste round for the first part because of the landslide on the old nomad path. I have resented being on the piste for so long, but our final few days across the mountains have made me forget the tedium of the roads. The pass before Isli is 2,650m high and is covered in thick, prickly shrubs with shaved heads – azmoroy. The shepherds cut the sharp tops off so that the sheep can eat the tender underside without hurting their mouths. We meet a sociable shepherd at the top who joins us for casse croute. He is deaf and can only make sounds, not words, but it doesn't hinder him from talking to us. He makes me laugh when he tells me that he likes to drink a beer because it helps keep the cold out. Brahim looks very disapproving. From the pass we can see both Lake Isli and Lake Tislit, separated by about 9 kilometres, sapphires set in the muted browns of the mountains.

The twin lakes occupy a special place in Amazigh legend. Once upon a time, there was a beautiful girl who was sweet-tempered, kind and clever. She met and fell in love with a handsome young man who was pious and hard-working. A match made in heaven – but earthly matters interceded. The boy was from the tribe of Ait Brahim and the girl was from the tribe of Ait Ya'za. The father of the young man could not allow his son to take a wife from the Ait Ya'za, and the father of the girl would not let his daughter marry into the Ait Brahim. But the two lovers shared a passion so deep that they could not live apart. They decided to flee to the mountain of Isslan to be together. They ran off together but then they suffered tragically from buyer's remorse. When they arrived at Isslan, they cursed the fate that had forced them to leave their families and everything they knew for a desolate exile and began to cry. Their tears flowed and could not stop. They realised there was no way back for them and no way to be happy on this earth. Consumed with grief, they drowned themselves, each in the lake of their own tears. Legend has it that each night they come out of the lakes to meet one another, still in love. The lakes are named after them: Isli means 'bridegroom' and Tislit means 'bride', and the marriage festival at Imilchil is held in their honour.

We descend carefully, as it is steep, and set up camp beside a small ravine which is perfect for the camels, about 100m from Lake Isli. There is no one else there and the water is freezing but perfectly clean. I go in but don't linger long.

It is the deepest lake in Morocco and there are a couple of farms at the far edge. JP has brought raincoats for the camels. They are made from green tarpaulin and have been cut by his clever tailor so that they fit snugly round their necks and tails. There are canvas ties to go under their throats and around their bellies. They look extremely smart in them and I am sure Hamish has gone down to the lake edge purely to have a look at his reflection in the water.

The weather has turned cold and it is back to two sleeping bags for me at night. We have a day's rest and I go exploring with Brahim. We climb up a series of hills in the direction of Tislit and meet a muleteer coming down with his animals. He says there is an old fortress a bit further up and we go to investigate. It is situated in a strategic position on a flat-topped peak giving a full 360°-view of the plains beneath and the mountains behind. It was French-built during the time of the occupation. The French hold on the Atlas Mountains was always tenuous, and we are told by our shepherd that the Ait Haddidou fought the invaders in this area for a whole year, until finally the French brought in air power and beat them. But, full of pride, he tells us that his forebears managed to shoot down one of the planes and points to a far peak where it crashed. The old fort still has its battlements, although most of the inside is jumbled rock, destroyed by weather and goats.

We get back to camp to find Farquhar in a frolicking mood. When he spots us, he canters up from the ravine and then gallops around the bivouac kicking up his legs like a spring lamb and cavorting around Le Petit Fromage.

The walk to Lake Tislit only takes a couple of hours and Addi heads off to hitchhike to the suq. Lake Tislit is nearer town and is accessible by tarmac road. It is surrounded by rubbish: plastic bottles, dirty nappies, fruit juice cartons. I do a clear-up and get two big black plastic bags we can burn. This lake is much shallower – 'Ha, it is proof that women do not feel as deeply as men,' says Brahim triumphantly. 'The bride shed far fewer tears than the groom – poor thing.' When Addi gets back from the market he is very excited. 'It was full of women, Zahra,' his eyes brighten at the memory. 'Is that why you forgot to buy anything?' Ali asks him. 'Where's the bread? And the meat?' Addi has come back with just mint and coriander. 'But the tea, Zahra, taste the tea, it is delicious' is his defence.

We walk right past the site of the wedding festival, which is actually on the outskirts of Imilchil, at Ait Amaro. Covid has left it deserted and empty. It is set up for a livestock market, with an open space in the centre, which is currently being used as a football pitch, and pens for the animals around the periphery. Marriage and herds go hand in hand. The one sign that a big festival is held here are the men's and women's toilets carefully signposted.

In contrast, the fields are busy. It is time for the autumn sowing and we get to see all the stages. First they are ploughed using mules and wooden ploughs, then donkeys come in with big bags full of manure which the farmers dig into the soil by hand. After that, they do a second ploughing and finally the women take over carrying sacks of seeds which they scatter in the furrows. Women are also sitting harvesting grass for fodder. They sit on their haunches and scythe with blades that are curved and about as long as my forearm. They take the grass to the nearest water source, a stream or big irrigation channel, wash it, bundle it into sheaves and leave it to dry in the sun. 'Come and have a go,' one of them yells at me as I wave in passing, 'but I have to warn you the sun is hot on my head and my back is killing me.'

The fields are prettily filled with wild flowers, blue vetch and yellow dandelions in the free grass under the poplars, but the tarmac road through the villages is ugly. It has slashed across them, leaving them halved and strewn with road rubble and human rubbish. Crumbling old kasbahs with decorated, stepped walls stand at intervals and the little hotels and gites on the road all have their names written in the Tifinagh alphabet as well as Arabic and French/English.

Morning rush hour consists of women on donkeys going to work in the fields. The dress here is distinctive and pre-dominantly black with flashes of colour. They wear black scarves which cover their mouths and their foreheads and are kept in place with a headband, sometimes embroidered – I saw one in purple with tassels on the top. The base garments are leggings and a long-sleeved T-shirt with a dress over the top. Over the top of that is an apron. At their necks I see a glimpse of a necklace. Everyone wears a shawl knotted at the front or fixed with a traditional Amazigh triangular pin. I'm in my trousers and shirt and I think it puts a distance between me and the women. They approach me less than when I am wearing a jellaba over leggings and T-shirt.

To me the area feels vibrant. 'No,' says Ali. 'Look more closely. Almost all these women are old women. The last generation of their family. There are no young women. The old agriculture is dying. Mountain agriculture is not vital for the economy. It is just a leftover; now the people want to get to the towns. These places are going to die. That is the future.'

I'm glad to get off the tarmac and piste and back into the wilds. We are heading for Maghara Akhyam, which is a big cave system cut into the mountains. The area looks like a series of mini Grand Canyons, rose-red rock moulded by water concourses and seismological shifts. It feels like prime dinosaur-hunting country to me and I bring out all my pictures of tracks found elsewhere in Morocco to pore over with the men so that we have an idea of what to look for.

Addi and Brahim go on to set up camp and Ali and I left for the cave, following a sign up an oued. Ali walks far ahead of me, enjoying some rare alone time, and I stop to look at the tiny plants that are growing in slivers of crevasse in the big blocks of rock. After a few kilometres we turn up to our left. I see Ali disappearing up a slope of tumbled boulders and cliff face and I follow. The cave doesn't look anything like the picture on the sign. It is cool and has a kitchen area in the back where there are clear signs of fire. We decide to keep climbing and go different routes to maximise our coverage as we search for dinosaur prints. Nothing. We join up to come back down and meet a shepherd who we had seen in the distance earlier. He is called Lahcen and says, 'No, no, it's not the right cave. Come, I will show you.'

The gorge narrows and now we have a flock of sheep following us, or rather Lahcen, including a gaggle of lambs who play as they go. A fairy pool of water to our left is filled by a single stream of water.

Lahcen has gathered a big armful of brushwood and I am hopeful of tea as we clamber up. We are definitely on track for the correct cave, as steps have been formed in the rock. Around the corner, a massive archway of red-gold rock is silhouetted against the sky. There is a shallow grotto and in it are lots of plastic hairbrushes – the little round ones with a handle over the top that you put your hand through. Ali tells me that women come here to ask with help in conceiving and bring them as offerings. We walk along a narrow ledge and then down underneath the big arch and into the mouth of a cave. The arch above was just for show – this is the real deal. It is like a hobbit hole for giants.

We step through the rounded entrance and into darkness. It is pitch black. I put on my iPhone torch which is virtually useless. Lahcen lights up the brushwood and in the sudden flare of light I can see the cave stretching way back. I follow, trying to look up, down and around and not fall over anything underfoot. We go through two chambers. The inner one is an oval shape and there are myriad stalactites hanging down from the roof. There are lots of feathers from birds scattered underfoot. I can't see the top of the roof it is so high. At the end of the room, it narrows further and I see ladders going up and down. We don't have the right equipment to continue, but Lahcen tells us, 'It is really deep, so deep. It is many kilometres long. Some people have come to try to find the end at the other side of the mountain but no one ever has.' Lahcen accompanies us out and walks back a little way with us. He is happy to have company: his wife and children live in town and he is out in an encampment with the sheep and says he is lonely.

The next day we pass some small shops selling etchings on stone. There are quite a few dinosaurs pictured which gives me hope that I am on the right track. The country has changed again. When you are exploring and covering big distances slowly you get a chance to see the differences. These are bare, high lands. There are herds of camels in the mountains, which are rounded rather than peaked but still have steep slopes. The dominant colour is caramel and there are pools of water filled with plants and frogs. Dragonflies buzz overhead. The stones on the hillsides are sharp and we follow the piste which winds round the very edge of the hills, giving way to vertiginous drops. Stooks of grass, gathered by the women, are stored in shallow caves or under overhanging ledges to keep them dry and safe in the oncoming winter. The women wear different clothes: a dress with a bunched-up waist that looks more like a skirt and top, and not the black of Imilchil, but brightly coloured. I see one lady in a glorious purple and white chiffon on her donkey.

Brahim tells me that he was woken up at around 2.30 a.m. by voices and got up to see thirty women passing the bivouac on their donkeys. They were from the *douar*, group of houses, where we had seen the hay drying about one and a half hours behind us. Brahim thought they must have got up at about one and would get back home with their piles of brushwood at around noon, in time to carry out all the other household duties. He told me that there was a kind of rota in the villages and that women would gather the brushwood for the winter around three times per week over a period of four months so that they would have enough.

It is the day of the weekly suq in Tilmi and I want to visit. I haven't been shopping for ages and I feel the urge to buy. I'm hoping for some fluffy pyjamas now that the nights are so cold.

The suq is at the top of the hill. There are a couple of outdoor cafés open. It is mostly men and some are wearing masks, some not. The entrance is flanked by date stalls and chicken stalls with the victims waiting in their cages, including one skinny turkey. We dogleg past the mechanical and DIY shops and up to the clothes stalls. Ali gets some tracksuit bottoms, but there are no good fluffy pyjamas and my buying urge is unfulfilled. The vegetable stalls are not large but each one has a decent variety. There is a mound of yellow carrots: something I have never seen before but Ali tells me they are quite common. We shop for dates on the way out and buy a variety called Tahammout which are 12.50 MAD (95 pence) per kilo. Ali explains that these are preferred by the nomads. They are firm but not hard and have a deep, rich flavour. He says that many of the dates grown in California originated in Morocco when American farmers came over and then took back two varieties: Boufkous and Jihl. Lots of research is now being done into the health properties of dates and according to a recent study in the King Saud University, Jihl dates have the best anti-inflammatory properties.

As we are crossing a ridge, Addi points down to a big apple factory on the tarmac road beneath. 'I worked there, Zahra, I helped to build it. When I was seventeen I got a job. I drove down from Nqob on my Moto and stayed in a house with other men in Msimrir. They are great people here. Very kind. It was good money. I earned 70 MAD [£6] per day. I was paid by the metre. That was the best way because then I could work hard and finish. We got food too. We started at 8 a.m., then casse croute at 10 a.m. and then lunch at 1-2 p.m. After that I finished as fast as I could. It was a very good job. If you worked hard you could finish early and the pay was good.'

The walls of many of the houses in this area of Tinghir are decorated with Amazigh symbols and flags. 'It is really Amazigh; here, if you speak Arabic you will eat the stick,' Brahim tells me. 'In the 1970s, a man called Moura came from France. He needed workers for his factories. If you were healthy, he stamped your shoulder and off you went on the train. Hundreds went and sent back money and after that the region prospered. But then the people realised how much money you could make as a worker overseas and compared it to here.'

It is estimated that 10 per cent of Morocco's population is expatriate and working abroad, mainly in Europe, with

France, Spain, Italy and Belgium the main countries. In areas like Tinghir, up to half of the households have a family member working away and sending back money.

We keep up to date with the Covid news daily, comparing rates of spread and casualties between Britain and Morocco, and discussing what our respective governments are doing. The rates in Morocco have been much lower than the UK per head of population. One of the measures introduced to keep citizens safe has been to close the mosques, and this is something that has been very difficult for many people. One night we hear three different muezzins sing the call to prayer from around us. 'They are just howling in the wind,' I am told. 'Calling to prayer when the mosques are shut. The mosque is the House of God. It doesn't belong to the state or the people who built it. It belongs to God and no one has the right to shut it. Look at this one here on the mountain, with all the windows open with no glass. How can infection spread? We all wash before we pray. We can place our prayer mats far apart. Why should the mosques be shut?'

Every day brings new discoveries. We are back on a proper nomad path. 'When they are used, they live,' Brahim says. The area is full of fossils. One big rock is smothered in seashells, some imprinted and some raised up. I ask our muqaddim about dinosaurs and for once someone takes me seriously. He tells me that he has heard there are prints but that they are far away and he is not absolutely sure where. He says he once found an unusual track fossilised in the stone – like a cow print but with an extra-long toe. I whip out my pictures of dinosaur prints found in Morocco but he shakes his head, disappointed for me. 'No, they weren't anything like these.'

The gorge is a tirfist, which means it is blocked at one end and it is fortified. Almost camouflaged above us are stone walls and battlements. 'That was built by Dadda Atta, the founder of Ait Atta,' our muqaddim tells us. Ait Atta, Addi's tribe, is the largest in the southern region of Morocco and its heartland is not far off in Jebel Saghro. There are five sections of the tribe, all of whom are said to be descended from Dadda Atta's forty sons. They emerged in the 1500s and then fought a series of wars to capture more territory, spreading northwards and into the oases. They are famous for their valiant resistance to the French army during the colonisation of Morocco.

In the Sahara, it was water; in the Atlas, the weather has become our constant preoccupation. It is getting colder by the day and we don't want to get snowed in. The clouds are stormy above us, but the threatened rain and snow doesn't come. The path between Oussikiss and Mgoun is regularly used by the nomads and is in good condition. Nomad families and their herds are all heading down from the mountains for winter. Many of them have mountain camels with them and our boys scope them out when we are camped. The women are preparing by washing out all their rugs and blankets in the streams, scrubbing them hard with stones to clean them and dry them before the cold sets in. A travelling salesman turns up. He has a mule loaded with useful items like washing powder, plastic basins and cloths. He comes up and down this path to sell to the nomad families.

It's the men's home patch now and they know the ways well. Addi says, 'How many times have I walked this path, Zahra? Since I was this high [pointing to my knees]. This place is called Misslim Kissawin, the Tears of the Shepherd, because it is so easy to lose a goat here. Do you remember this oued, Zahra? Do you remember this rock? I had walked this part of the route with Addi and his family when I joined them for a section of the transhumance the previous year. That time we travelled in the opposite direction: going from their winter pasture in Saghro up to their summer pasture in Ait Bougemez. That is when I got to know his mother, Lalla Ito, and his sister and sister-in-law and the whole family. I saw first-hand how hard they worked, out from dawn till dusk with the flocks who grazed as they walked to the new pastures. It was Ramadan, and fasting and migrating was really tough but they didn't complain. They just got on with it and, after nearly eighteen hours every day of neither eating nor drinking and yet physically working extremely hard, celebrated breaking the fast together, welcoming me into their tent and sharing everything unstintingly with me.

Addi obviously loves being on his own turf, but Brahim has a different perspective. 'I prefer new paths because you always have something to find. What is behind that mountain? When you know the road, you can see it all outstretched from the beginning to the end. You just progress infinitesimally day by day.'

We are in a timridahl, a small, flat place in the middle of the mountains, and although we are at a trough where lots of nomads are bringing their flocks to drink, they aren't friendly to us. I go up to talk to some women who are washing their clothes but they cold-shoulder me. 'They're probably scared of you,' says Brahim. 'All we hear on the radio and on TV is how Corona was brought to us by foreigners, and how we have to be careful and we can't let the tourists return yet and you are a foreigner.' I realise I have to be more sensitive to this and not to take our previous hospitality for granted. 'They don't like us either,' Brahim goes on. 'They see us working with tourists and they think, *They don't need tea; they've got loads of money from the foreigners.* Tourism has lots of good things about it but there are also negatives.'

Farquhar is our most sociable camel. If a group of nomads come through and let their baggage camels graze near us, he is up and off to meet them. 'It is because he has no eggs,' says Brahim, and he certainly doesn't seem to attract any male aggression. Another factor is that, thank goodness, this part of the expedition is not taking place during mating time so we have been free of bubbling, frothing and passive-aggressive peeing. Farquhar dives straight into the new group and touches muzzles. He also sniffs under the camels' tails just like a dog and then raises his nose in the air for all the world like a perfume maker who has just smelt a delightful concoction. Once he has chatted enough, he scampers back to camp, kicking his legs out in glee.

There are lots of caves in the hills on this section. When I go in, they are warm and dry and show signs of habitation both human and animal. The nomads obviously still use them to shelter in. I desperately want to sleep in one when we park up at an enclosure nearby, but Brahim bans me: 'No, these ones are full of sheep poo; they are not healthy.'

The *azeeb*, enclosure, is terraced and LPF is pitched below the *giton*. A shepherd girl who looks around sixteen is herding goats and Addi gives her flour and asks her to make some bread for us. Her baby brother is with her. He can only just walk, but already he is learning how to herd, toddling after her and throwing stones to keep the group together. The goats are very friendly and come right into the tent while we are having lunch, hoping for snacks. When I look down to LPF, one little fellow is halfway in, with his bottom sticking out of the door, and another is luxuriating full length on the rug outside.

After lunch, Addi washes all over with my nice-smelling soap, puts on his blue robe and best *chech* and ropes up a load of containers for water. He has taken some small change to pay for the bread and heads off to the shepherdess's tent, whistling. Brahim, Ali and I exchange knowing looks. The muqaddim arrives and has tea, telling us that this *azeeb* belongs to his family but he doesn't have flocks any more. He lets the nomads use it so that he can collect the sheep and goat dung for his garden. I imagine the prospect of some camel poo would make him very happy, but I am wrong. 'No, camel dung is no good for the crops. Goat is the best, then sheep, lastly cows and donkeys.'

That morning, I wake up itching. Fleas from the dung. They have feasted on me overnight and I have big red lumps all over my belly and legs. Harsh experience has taught me that you mustn't scratch them or they will get infected. I down a couple of antihistamines and pull on my clothes, trying my best not to do what I want to, which is gouge them till they bleed.

As we are setting off, Jean-Pierre appears over the hill. It is totally unexpected and he is obviously fizzing with news. 'Alice, your dream is going to come true today,' he says with a smile. 'I have found a link to dinosaur footprints online, and Ychou and I came yesterday to do a recce. They are really near here. Finally, after all these days of expedition, you are going to find dinosaurs in Morocco!'

Back at headquarters, JP had been busy. He had scoured the internet to see if he could find anything for me and finally got a hit on Jacques Gandini's excellent website for prehistoric sites (https://www.prehistoire-du-maroc.com/) for a set of dinosaur tracks in a ravine near the village of Aguerzka. Gandini is a contemporary of JP and is a dedicated explorer of Morocco. He writes guidebooks (in French) for 4×4 travel across the country which are full of off-the-beaten-track information. It was here that JP had got the GPS area co-ordinates for the spaceships of the Draa. Now, there were co-ordinates for three sets of tracks which were discovered by Hassan Yamami, part of Gandini's team, who Ali's brother also works for. JP and Ychou had come up the day before and spent five and a half hours searching the ravine to find them – GPS co-ordinates only go so far in this kind of terrain – so that we could have a full day there.

We pack up the bivouac double fast and climb down an excruciatingly narrow path towards the village of Aguerzka. We get to the bottom and bivouac the camels in a ruined *kasbah* on the opposite side of the oued from the village. The oued is full and fast-flowing and surrounded by carefully tended fields of turnips, potatoes, carrots and hay with fig trees and bamboo groves flanking them. Immediately, a horde of kids descends on us. They are on a one-week-on, one-week-off system for school during Covid and are taking full advantage. The boys cluster worshipfully around Addi, who is clearly the coolest member of our group, and he gives them small tasks to do for the camels which they carry out with immense pride.

JP says that the set of prints is high up a cliff and in order to see them we are going to have to climb. He has brought climbing harnesses and ropes and the plan is that he, Ychou and Ali will go off first and set up the ropes and Brahim, Addi and I will come on after. The three of us are hopping with impatience, but we sort out lunch. I'm peeling the potatoes and talking to them. 'You lucky potatoes. Look, I am taking your dirty jellabas off, then I am going to wash you and you are going to be nice and clean and naked.' Brahim is in quick as a flash: 'No problem if the potatoes are naked, Zahra; they're men. It is these pretty tomato girls that we need to worry about.'

We eat and wash up and wait until, finally, Brahim can't bear it any longer. He packs up some lunch for the advance party and we go. The walk in is through the gardens flanking the river in the valley. It is cool and muddy and the birds are singing loudly. As we turn up the side of the ravine, pink oleanders choke the path on one side and thorn trees wait on the other, so I press hard into the oleanders to avoid getting ripped up. Suddenly, Brahim grabs my arm and points up, 'Zahra, look, can you see them? That line? I think it's dinosaur tracks.' I look up and there they are about five metres above us, a line of prints – fourteen in all – crossing the red brick of the cliff. Dinosaur footprints and absolutely crystal clear. What a moment, seeing these proofs of life from millions of years ago with my own eyes. I am ecstatic. They are in a straight line and are imprinted in what would have once been mud and has hardened into rock. As the plates under the Atlas shifted, they were squeezed up from their initial flat position to a vertical strip on the cliffs. Later we see that this line is the one marked 'A' on Gandini's site.

Brahim, Addi and I are all buzzing as we press on up the mountain and round the corner to where JP, Ali and Ychou have established a base camp to get up to a different set which are heading up the rock face in a double vertical line directly behind them and also to the right of them (marked 'B' on Gandini's site). These look bigger and you can see where the animals slipped slightly in the prehistoric mud.

JP is waiting for me with a harness and a lilac My Little Pony riding helmet. The cliff is about 30 metres high I estimate and the surface is fragile. The climb doesn't appear too bad from down below. Ali is already up there on a rope beside the first juniper tree. The plan is to get up to him, then to traverse across the cliff to a second tree and then go on to a third carabinier and hook myself in. The best prints are in between trees one and two. Ychou has hold of my rope end and is securely squeezed into a crevasse on my left. 'Shiddi mizayn, Ychou' – hold tight! JP with his GoPro is opposite us across the gorge. Brahim is roped up below me, and Addi is on roving duty and desperate to get a rope of his own.

The drop below is enough to kill you if you fall off the cliff, but I have Ychou holding my rope. We don't want to destroy anything and the rock is crumbly under my hands and feet so I step carefully. I climb up to Ali who is nonchalantly hanging off his rope over the drop at the first tree. He has done lots of climbing and is completely at ease. Then I look down. This is a big mistake. My stomach plummets. I put one foot and one hand out to start the traverse of the cliff and immediately bring them both back to the juniper tree and cling on to it like a baby koala clinging on to its mother. The men confer and send Brahim up to the second juniper tree to spot me. This is the first time he has ever used a harness or a rope but he is a natural. He scampers up to a ledge ahead of me with no fuss. I am still clinging and wishing that I couldn't hear the pebbles that are slipping out from under Brahim's feet echoing down into the chasm below. With much coaxing, I edge along the cliff towards him.

He gives me confidence and I stand on the ledge. The absolute magic of putting my hand carefully into an actual dinosaur footprint chases all fear out of my head. I measure two of the prints (53cm x 60cm and 90cm x 60cm), take lots of photographs and videos and can't stop grinning. 'I've got my hand in a footprint that was made by a giant sauropod millions of years ago.' They look like very enlarged camel prints and the best ones are beside the juniper tree. What makes it very convincing is that the prints are in a trail; you can see the actual route that this enormous beast walked.

Finally, though, I have to go back, and this is the moment when my body takes over and decides that moving is the worst idea I have ever had. It sends urgent messages to my brain telling me to stay exactly where I am. 'Look at me, look at me,' yells JP, trying to give me courage from across the drop. The only issue is that when I look at him, I also have to look across the deadly plunge into the gorge, and that makes me even more determined not to budge an inch but to keep safe here. I know logically that I am safe, because Ychou has me on a rope, so the most I could fall would be about 5 metres swinging out from the first juniper tree, but emotions win and I am stuck against the wall. My heart is absolutely racing. I can barely hear the men over the thumping of my blood in my ears. I can't look down or across and I keep my eyes on the rock. My skin pumps out sweat. I am 100 per cent frightened animal.

Ali looks at me from his perch. 'Zahra, do you think we have looked after you and cared for you for sixty days to let you drop now? Come along, come to the tree.' His common sense and stern tone cut through the fear. Of course he is right and I start to edge back along the cliff face. I grab the tree under Ali's feet and Ychou eases the rope slowly as I climb down. I silently promise myself never to do that again and then immediately change that to 'at least not before I get some climbing confidence'.

Ychou is all smiles when I crumple beside him on the shelf. 'You see, I held you tight, Zahra.' Addi is all sniggers at my cowardice: 'All right, Zahra?' But he gets his comeuppance

quickly. It is his turn now and he climbs up – I can tell he is
a bit nervous too – only to be held there dangling by Ychou
and Ali, who hoot callously at his pleas to come down.

We all descend safely after everyone has had time to have
a good look at the prints. 'Thanks be to God,' we chorus at
each other sporadically as we head back towards the camp.
We are high as kites with all the excitement. On the way
out, we stop to look at the first site again and when we go
up closer, these prints are enormous too. JP says that he can
see that they are pads surrounded by 'toes' with one longer
at the front. I can't really see that, but what is absolutely clear
to me is the trajectory – the path walked.

'Are you happy now, Zahra?' Addi asks me. 'We succeeded.
Thanks be to God. We found dinosaurs.'

'We did. I am so happy,' I reply. 'We are the Number One
Team. Today is one of the best days of my life.'

18

A Triumphant Finish

Aguerzka – Ouarzazate

15 October 2020

And it was one of the happiest days of my life, but now, two days on, I have a niggle. I want to find my own dinosaur prints, not be guided to them by someone else's GPS co-ordinates. When I say this to the team, I am met with puzzlement. 'But why? You have already seen them,' says Addi. 'Yes, it is true, but they were found by Hassan Yamami. I want to discover new ones so that we can add to the information about dinosaurs in Morocco,' I say. 'It's different.'

Ali is angry. 'You should have done your own research, then,' he says. 'You are a journalist. If this whole expedition was about dinosaurs then you should have focused on that.' That stings, but he does have a fair point. I put out the idea both to the team and to JP that I want to go back to Aguerzka and search for prints in the vicinity that have not been marked on any site. The idea is pooh-poohed – we are on schedule to finish the expedition on time and are very near the end. There is no appetite for delay or going back.

Brahim is, as always, my counsellor. 'You have to be

patient, Zahra. There are two things. The first is now that we know what they look like, these prints, now we have seen them, we must look very carefully along the rest of the road and perhaps we will find them. If you want to return to Aguerzka then wait until Toundout. It has good transport there and we can spend one day of rest for the camels and then go back to Aguerzka or maybe JP will give us the truck.' He is right and, although I want to push the issue and get everyone on board, I take his advice and just wait.

The village of Assaka lies in a valley which is one of the most beautiful I have ever seen in Morocco. The mountains surrounding it are a cornucopia of colours: rich red stripes contrasting with the lightest of lemon yellows. The oued is fertile and broad as we walk through the groves of pink oleander and it is flanked by traditional hamlets built of the dark red clay of the mountains that support them. Most are still free of the modern concrete homes that are now the norm. Concrete is much cheaper and quicker to build with than the old compressed clay and brick and it doesn't need nearly as much maintenance. If there is rain, it doesn't mean you are going to have to fix your concrete house, as is the case with the clay. However, apart from the aesthetics of it, there are some functional disadvantages. I live in a concrete home in Imlil and it is freezing in winter and boiling in summer. The clay and stone-built houses of my neighbours are much more adapted to the weather. They keep you cool in the heat and retain their warmth in the sub-zero winter temperatures.

There is wild thyme everywhere and Ali tells me that in Morocco there are thirty-six different types as opposed to twenty-eight in the whole of Europe. We collect some to add to our tea. It is very good for the stomach and I also like the aromatic taste.

We are just at the end of the valley, about to cross towards Toundout, when Brahim grabs my arm. 'Look up there, can you see them? That line?' I follow his gaze and see what he has spotted. It is a line of what looks like dinosaur prints. We stop the camels and climb up the shallow cliff wall – no ropes needed here. The prints are even bigger than the ones we had seen at Aguerzka but less deeply imprinted. Again, there is a visible trajectory, three at one end and three at the other, but these prints are less rounded, like a camel's paw, and are narrower at the bottom, fanning out near the top. I register a GPS point for future reference and we take pictures and videos. I send these off to Dr Susannah Maidment at the Natural History Museum in London, who has discovered dinosaur remains in Morocco.

She emails back: 'It's pretty hard to tell from the photos. The spacing between the indentations is reminiscent of tracks, but the morphology of the indentations could have been made by wind and water erosion. We often see hollows like this forming in sandstones where the grains are cemented with carbonate minerals. It's possible that these started off as dinosaur tracks and the wind and rain have enlarged them and eroded the edges. Bit difficult to say, but I'm glad you have your eyes peeled for dino fossils!'

I take that as a definite maybe.

Kasbahs are now a part of every settlement we pass, show-ing that this area was on the old caravan routes. The earth is a dark, chestnut brown and so are the buildings. With dino-saurs still on my mind, we park our camels in Toundout, in the car park of the dinosaur house. This is a spectacular new building. It was built by a private foreign donor to contain the bones of a very large dinosaur that was dug up on the site. I visit the crater where it was found, which is 20 metres away down the hill away from our tents, but the building is empty and closed. The dinosaur skeleton was taken away, initially to France for research, but we couldn't find out where it is now. Some of the townspeople said they thought it was still in France, while others said it had been brought back to Rabat. Where it wasn't was in its brand-new house.

My patience has paid off and JP has agreed that we can rest the animals while I go back up to Aguerzka to hunt for new dinosaur prints. It took us six days to walk here, but it only takes a few hours to drive back. Hussein takes me, Brahim and Ali in the 4x4 and we leave Addi to look after the boys. We have set up camp on top of a hill because rain is threatening. There is an enclosure for the camels at night and a stream nearby, so Addi should have all he needs. He also has company; Hussein brought one of the lads from Dar Daif to stay with him so that he wouldn't be alone. The drive is exhilarating. We pass the caves, now occupied by nomads for the night. We can see their campfires burning. As the sun sets, we have to navigate the rocks and treacherous holes in the darkness. Hussein drives fast and I swap from the front seat to give it up to Ali. His eyes are so much better than mine and he can see hazards and help Hussein avoid them. We arrive at Aguerzka late and exhausted but are given a very warm welcome in the gite, Chez Mouha Oulatmane, and fed a kind of thick doughy grain, before we go up and collapse into bed.

I am awake very early and hurry the men, grumbling, outside. We don't aim for the third Hassan Yamami discovery, marked on Gandini's site, but go further round the corner of the hills, deeper into the oued. Then, we split up. We only have this one day and I want to maximise our expedition's chances of finds. I am not nearly as nimble up the hills, but that isn't going to stop me, and soon we are all separated and I am alone.

It is the most glorious day for exploring. The sky is completely clear and the sun is out but it is still quite cool. I can hear the sound of the river flowing in the oued and the sheep and goats bleating in the valley. I revel in the feeling of being alone for a whole day with only one thing to do – hunt dinosaurs.

The mountain is stratified into sharp-edged strips of rock, and I clamber up, using those edges to grip on to. At 8.57 I make my first find. There are two indentations that look like prints but, bearing in mind Dr Maidment's thoughts on erosion, I don't proclaim a victory. I keep going higher. Just half an hour later, I come across a set of four. These are a completely different shape – a heel with four sharp toes. They look reptilian and are deeply carved into the rock. I think it would be hard for mere erosion to make four shapes like this, so take a GPS point and stop for a water break.

The drop below me is sheer and there are buzzards overhead. The world is a perfect place. I am here on this mountain, searching for these messages from the past, etched into nature, and I take time to just enjoy the excitement and wonder that I feel. The tiredness and discomforts fade away and I don't worry about not being fast on my feet or good at climbing or perfect at Tashlaheet. None of it matters; what matters is to do what you can where you are and to fully live the great moments, like these ones, that come along in every life.

But philosophy will find me no prints.

I am about halfway through my allotted time and so I head down to the river slowly, with the loose pebbles cascading noisily below me, using my hands and my bottom to steady myself. About a kilometre in, I hit a really good line of prints embedded in the vertical of the wall not too far above the water. They aren't big, about the size of my spread-out hand, but there are lots of them and they patter along. I count fifteen before they disappear into oleanders so thick I can no longer push through.

Brahim shouts down to me from the top of the cliff and I wait where I am for him to join me. He has hit paydirt too and takes me back along the oued to show me his finds. A series going upwards, hidden in a corner cave, and two sets on a smooth expanse, high up on a flat piece of rock on the opposite side of the river.

Our time has run out and we are also starving, so we set off back to the gite. As we get closer, the noise of hundreds of goats and sheep reaches us. The nomads are driving them down from the mountains and they are converging on the river like a swarm of bees. Winter is getting very close.

Ali catches up with us as we are nearly at Chez Mouha. He has also found some prints, but nothing spectacular, he says. 'Are you finally happy, Zahra?' he asks. And, yes. I finally am.

For the entirety of the trip, we have been running a competition in the team. Every day, after we have eaten lunch, each of us guesses how many kilometres we have walked that day. I am using the inbuilt steps and distance app on my iPhone to measure because it is the one thing I always have on me. Once everyone has decided on their distance, and sometimes that takes a while – Addi always changes his mind at least three times – I open the app and reveal the answer. The closest person wins – we use 100-metre increments – and then crows loudly and at length while everyone else moans that they were robbed. Tactics have come into play and suddenly the team is very polite; 'After you, O Professor Zahra.' 'No, no, after you, O Brahim, O Learned One.' We are all playing the margins, as 0.1 of a kilometre could make the difference between winning and losing. It is a big advantage to guess last and we form a rule that the winner of the last round goes first, then we follow in order.

For the first two months, I am in the lead. It kills Brahim. He is so competitive that he can't bear it, which of course makes my victory all the sweeter. He is in second place, nipping at my heels, Ali is in third place and Addi is trailing, but hopeful of a comeback. I love winning but sometimes I am delighted when it is someone else. There have been times when one of us has been having a really down day and then they win the competition and it totally lifts them. I am not nice enough to try to lose, though.

We have only a few days left of the expedition and Brahim has overtaken me for the lead, but is only one ahead so I still have a chance. The other two are way behind and the competition has taken on a new intensity. If I win at lunchtime, Brahim says it is the Will of God, but that, God willing, he, the Amazigh Nation and Morocco will win next time. If I win, I flap my crow wings around the tent, shake hands with everyone and say Better Luck Next Time, May God grant you Success, and then fly my little Scottish flag outside LPF.

The village of Tagghraghra is relatively close to Ouarzazate but is completely unmodernised. It is like the secret garden and we walk down past a rare mulberry tree. There is a tall, slim red kasbah and store (*agadir*) in the centre of the orchards and Ali explains it is a typical style for these mountains as opposed to the wider, shorter *kasbahs* of the desert. The buildings mimic their environment.

The people here are very friendly, but I wonder why some of them don't return my *salaam alaykum*. 'You are saying it too early,' says Ali. 'If you say it when people are far away like that, it is a greeting which actually means "keep away from me; I don't want to speak to you".' I think this is the opposite of the UK, where you say 'hello' quite far away. Brahim makes me practise it by saying it at the right time to electricity posts as we pass.

Agadirs are not just limited to the *kasbahs*; we detour off the path so that Ali can show me some that are carved out of caves high up a sheer cliff. I can see the holes but I can't see anything that would get a human and their goods up there. We get out the binoculars, and with them I can just make out the edge of the path. Ali tells me that each house in the village would have an *agadir* and that they would put everything from grain to treasures in it. The path had to be narrow so that marauders couldn't get up easily.

It snowed in the night. We wake up to see Mgoun in the distance topped with white. We are in a desert area with scattered green patches near the oued and the contrast is spectacular. Our timing has been perfect and we have been lucky. If it had snowed while we were still in the mountains, we would have been in trouble. Now, we are on the plain approaching Ouarzazate. There has been rain here recently too. We can see green shoots sprouting under the dried-up shrubs. We have become dinosaur experts (self-styled) and agree that the chestnut ridges opposite us look like a prime spot for remains and more footprints.

In two days, we will be walking into Ouarzazate and the official end of the Atlas Expedition, but today is a very special day for Addi, Brahim and me. We set off as usual, marvelling at the snow on the peaks and the chill in the air and trying to remember the heat when we started in Nador. The terrain is very familiar: sandy plains, ruined *kasbahs*, flocks of goats and sheep grazing at the sprouts of green popping up after the rain. At casse croute time, we get there.

Addi and Brahim and I stand on the exact spot where we first met in January 2019 and started the Draa Expedition. 'I remember the first time I saw you, Addi, you were right here and you came up and said hello and then started unloading the pickup. Brahim, you were over in the plain with the camels. I could only see you in the distance, walking in with them. I think you were wearing your grey jellaba, the one that got all Hamish's blood on it.' Brahim replies, 'And we remember the first time we saw you, Zahra. We were waiting on the side of the road to bring you to the camp and we had the tea ready on a carpet and everything was perfect. The pickup approached . . . and then you drove straight past us without even stopping, without a *salaam alaykum*, without even a glance or a wave.' I am horrified. 'Really? I know we went on to look at the water channels and then doubled back, but I had no idea you were here waiting.' Brahim just laughs. I suppose after seven and a half months together he can forgive me that first missed meeting.

We don't retrace our original route but nudge close to the barrage, the Al Mansour Eddahbi dam. The water is very low and the mudflats extend far from the edge. The water shines silver in the early light and we greet a fisherman who is having a morning glass of tea beside his rowing boat. A heron the size of two swans circles, waiting for the fisherman to set off and supply some fresh food. There are occasional palm trees and lots of tamarisk for the camels who grab sneaky mouthfuls as we walk through them. It would be wonderful to bivouac right on the edge of the dam but this side is too muddy and we perch a few hundred metres away in a small copse of trees.

A weird lunar landscape surprises us. The earth is so dark it is almost black and there is a forest of electricity pylons. There are so many that I can feel the electricity jangle through my body. It is all connected to the Nur solar power plant, which we catch glimpses of, needling into the sky. It is supplied with water by the barrage – Ali says it uses a whopping 8 per cent of all the water of the dam. Brahim joins in that when he first came to Ouarzazate in 1994 the barrage was much fuller; it has shrunk greatly. He puts it down to lack of rain and snow. At that time, the mountains were absolutely covered in snow from November straight through to March, which translated into water. Now, only the peaks stay snowed under for the whole season. It is more evidence of climate change. Brahim is sad all day and when I ask him why he just says, 'The separation.'

At lunch, it is our final round of 'guess the distance'. It is still neck and neck and Brahim and I stare at each other long and hard trying to second-guess the other. I go with 18.4km; Brahim goes with 18km. Ali won yesterday and Brahim is one ahead, so I still have the chance to draw. Addi changes allegiance about twenty times as to who should win, but Ali keeps his stance that the victory belongs to Morocco. The distance is revealed and . . . it's 18. Brahim has won. His face transforms with utter delight and Addi and Ali jump up and clap him on the back and hug him. 'Morocco won! Morocco won! Go Amazigh!' and similar chants resound. I am both devastated and overjoyed. 'We better have a party tonight,' says Addi.

Tomorrow is our big celebration day and we have been told that the British ambassador, Simon Martin, and his wife, Sophie, are driving all the way from Rabat to walk us ceremoniously in. We are all very excited at this badge of approval. It means a lot to me but also to the men that *almakhzan*, the authorities, are recognising our efforts. Equally as exciting is that our two other team members, Brahim Boutkhoum and Ychou, are coming too and will spend the last day with us.

In preparation, and thanks to the preponderance of water, all of us do some serious personal grooming. Hamish may like how I smell but I very much doubt that the ambassador will. The gas is on constantly as water is boiled and we dodge off to different parts of the copse to scrub and scour ourselves and our clothes. I have actually kept a brand-new shirt and trousers specially for the occasion but I still have to wash out my *chech* and cap. The men launder their clothes and shave and trim their beards.

Once I am clean, and have had a power nap in LPF, I turn my mind to the party. I have a few cashew nuts left, so our feasting is taken care of. Next is the issue of prizegiving for the distance competition. I search through all my belongings and try to find things for the doughty competitors and come up with the requisite three. I also fashion Brahim a medal out of a sardine carton and a piece of pink twine.

It is time for our party. I wind my battery-powered fairy lights up the pole of the *giton* and light the scented candle. I put the cashew nuts in a bowl and the prizes in a pile under the fairy lights. The prizegiving commences. Brahim loves his medal and wears it all night, frequently drawing our attention to it or just quietly admiring it. It is macaroni for our final supper in camp, with *luisa* and pomegranates afterwards and the obligatory game of cards.

And then it is the last day. I wake up with butterflies. We have a fire in the morning and tidy up the camp so it looks nice for our guests who are arriving a little later. We spread the rugs and cushions outside, build another fire and prepare the tea tray.

Over the horizon our guests start to appear. Brahim Boutkhoum is looking very dapper in a red top and matching *chech* and Lhou is in a striped jellaba. Lhou has brought me a kilo of cumin from his farm and it smells wonderful. The whole team is reunited and our greetings go on for a considerable time. Once we have ascertained that everyone is in good health and everyone in everyone's family is in good health, we have tea. Next, Martin and Sophie arrive. We are all very respectful and the men hover at a distance. I am very proud of my country when Martin and Sophie both win instant friends by coming forward and shaking hands with all of us straight away, in spite of Covid. Also, they have brought homemade shortbread for us, which is both thoughtful and very delicious. I explain to the men that this is one of the traditional foods of Scotland and we snaffle the buttery biscuits down.

All the mixed feelings of ending an expedition wash over me as we pack up the camp, but it is a blessing that we have so many guests. This day is not just for the four of us; it is for everyone, and I resolve to enjoy it to the maximum and worry about post-expedition blues when they come.

'*Bismillah*,' and we are off. It is another perfect day, cool with the sun shining. The boys know that something is up and have a spring in their step, especially Hector Saghro. While we were waiting for our guests, he found the vegetable box and managed to open it with his nose. Since it is the last day, Ali let him off and he scoffed the lot. The rhythm takes over and everyone slots into it. I barely notice the scenery because I am so involved with all the stimulation of new people.

We leave the side of the lake as we see the desert walls of Ouarzazate approaching. Ouarzazate is one of the gateways to the Sahara and it has been intertwined with my Moroccan story. This is where the Marathon des Sables ends and all those memories come back as we approach. At least my feet are intact this time, and not destroyed by the six marathons in six days across the sands that make up the race.

The plan is to walk through the city, cross into the palmeraie and end up at JP's beautiful guest house, Dar Daif. The camels are then going one door down to stay in JP's uncle's back garden and be fed vast amounts of hay and oats until they can be taken back to their grazing with the rest of the herd further south. JP is such an integral part of the expedition that I want him to walk the whole day with us, but he has to organise things and so is still at Dar Daif and will arrive later.

We stop for a picnic lunch under a shady palm tree on the outskirts of the city. Every treat imaginable has been included, from duck paté to marinaded roast chicken. We tell Martin the superstition about passing under the camel's belly and he selects Farquhar as his target – he has the longest legs – and does it to our wild applause. Sophie has been learning Arabic and practises it with everyone. Again I feel proud that my country is making such a good impression on my team. 'They are very good people,' Addi whispers to me. '*Darif*, nice.' 'Not snobbish,' adds Brahim.

We are on to the final part. JP joins us and the team is complete. He is buzzing with excitement and whispers, 'I have a surprise for you.' JP is a glutton for surprises. Now we have to have the masks on as we enter the city proper and a TV crew tracks us from Channel 2, Morocco's national station. We wind through the streets between the high clay buildings and along the main boulevard past the Kasbah. People stop and wave and take pictures and videos, but the streets are thankfully rather empty because of Covid. Ouarzazate has been very strict about enforcing the regulations and everyone is wearing a mask. It is a foretaste of reality after our wilderness freedom.

We duck down into the palmeraie and the temperature drops in the shade. There are crunchy palm fronds underfoot and we have to retrace our steps a couple of times as we reach waterways that the camels can't cross because they are too wide and deep.

Dar Daif is on the very outskirts of the palm grove, looking out onto the now snow-tipped mountains and is at the edge of a village along a dirt road. It is about 5 o'clock and we are nearly there. In the days of the great caravans, whenever a caravan arrived home the whole village would turn out to meet it. Everyone would celebrate: dates and fresh camel milk for the homecoming and musicians to sing in the travellers.

JP is waiting for us and, with tears in his eyes, he turns and embraces me. 'You have done it, Zahra. I am so proud of you and the team and the camels. This has been a magnificent journey. Bravo.' As his last words sound, the music begins. This is his surprise – he has given us a hero's welcome.

A troupe of traditional Saharan musicians is waiting for us as we pop up out of the palms and onto the road. They are wearing different coloured jellabas, blue and green, with embroidery at the neck. They have celebratory yellow slippers and embroidered skull caps. The music is the rhythmic beat of the desert played on drums, flutes and horns. The leader, in green, has a round drum like a very large tambourine which sets the pace. Behind him is the head of the wind section with a long, slim horn – it must be at least a metre – which calls high and loud.

The drummers all sing and dance as they beat out the tempo. They advance and retreat, bowing and swaying, and

we walk behind them. Attracted by the music, the doors of
the village open and everyone runs out to see what is happening. The women and children dash down the banks at
the side of the road and fall in dancing behind the musicians,
joining in the songs and clapping in time. A voice rises in
ululation and the dancing intensifies. A girl grabs my hand
and I am pulled into the middle. I look up and a young boy
on top of the bank is laughing with pure joy, his arms raised,
silhouetted against the sun.

I fall back to walk the last part of our journey with the
camels and the men. I think the camels recognise the honour
that is being paid to them; their heads are up and they are
walking in time to the music. I am beside Brahim and Addi,
as I have been for so long.

And that is how it ends. My heart is full of pride, gratitude
and love. The golden light of dusk haloes us. Dust motes
dance in the gentle evening sunlight. Laughter and music fill
the air. We are home.

CONCLUSION

When I set off on this adventure I was hopeful that I would enjoy it, that it would challenge me and that I would find interesting things to share with others. I had no idea, though, of how incredible it would be. Of how joyous I would find the process of walking across the land and simply being at one with the wilderness. I did not realise just how much there was to discover and that I would be clambering over ancient cities or exploring the tombs of the giants. I could never have imagined the relationship I would build up with the men or that I would come to truly love camels.

The three stages were all so different. The Draa was all about exploration and excitement coloured at the end by the spectre of climate change. The Sahara was hard, relentless, stripping us all back to the core, a 'real adventure'. The Atlas was beautiful and varied and additionally fascinating because we did it at the time of Covid.

There were huge highs, like stumbling across the 'lost' city and finding dinosaur footprints, and there were grinding lows, like having an ear infection and a snot river in a sandstorm. But everything happened as it should have and in its proper time and place.

Every journey changes us. This one has certainly changed me. I have learnt more patience (although Brahim might harrumph at that) and acceptance and that we humans are nothing in the face of nature. I've seen our planet drying out and the fading of the nomad way of life but I have also held those Stone Age tools in my hands and felt our common history and resilience sounding across the centuries.

I believe in exploration. Every time you step outside your door and see or hear something different, you are exploring and learning more about the world. Exploring is for everyone and it doesn't matter where you do it or what you find. The thing is just to get out there and appreciate the place and time we exist in.

I hope you liked walking with me and the men and the camels. I hope you now love this place as much as I do and have felt the warmth and kindness of the people through the pages. You will certainly win the pub quiz if there is a round on the sex lives of camels. The last words of a book are like finishing the journey. This is a transcript of a piece to camera I did when we got to the spot where we started the whole thing. I'm standing with my back to the plain squinting into the sun. It's not polished but it's heartfelt and it is in the moment.

Thank you for your company.

'I am standing on the spot where I started my cross-Morocco exploration on 9 January 2019. I'm with Addi and Brahim from the very initial expedition and Ali who joined us for this one and also for a week of the Draa. Of the camels we think we only have two [originals] with us, Sausage and Hamish. The others have all changed, although I think maybe Hector Saghro was with us from the very beginning, Saghro. Anyway, I never dreamed when I started that I would walk the whole of Morocco and it's strange because I should feel elated or woo-hoo at the moment and I don't. We still have two days of the expedition left and I think for me the end of the expedition is when I will have those feelings because we still have to get there safely.

'It's been quite a ride: lost cities, stone spaceships, quick-sands, landmines and finally dinosaur prints! In terms of exploration it has been amazing, but more than that it's been an incredible journey for me. I feel I've changed a lot in all this walking. I think I've become more patient, more open. I've certainly become more informed about Morocco and I hope I will always be friends with my team of men – particularly with Brahim and Addi who have been with me from the beginning. But also with Ali, Brahim Boutkhoum and Lhou, who have been with us for stages.

'I also know an awful lot more than I did before about camels. When I started, I didn't really like camels and now I really, really do. I think they are one of the wonders of the world, one of the wonders of creation. It's been incredible. We walked three stages. We walked all the way down to Oued Chbika on the Atlantic coast, we picked up the expedition there and went all the way to Guerguerat, right through the Sahara Desert. This stage we started in the very north at the Mediterranean Sea and we walked across the mountains; through all the richness that that brought, through uphills and downhills. The snow is on the mountains behind us which is incredible because when we started it was 48-50°C.

'That's the thing about walking. It's very slow but if you just keep going you get there, and what a metaphor for life.'